NONE OF THE ABOVE

SECULAR STUDIES
General Editor: Phil Zuckerman

Losing Our Religion: How Unaffiliated Parents Are Raising Their Children
Christel J. Manning

The Varieties of Nonreligious Experience: Atheism in American Culture
Jerome P. Baggett

None of the Above: Nonreligious Identity in the US and Canada
Joel Thiessen and Sarah Wilkins-Laflamme

None of the Above

Nonreligious Identity in the US and Canada

Joel Thiessen

Sarah Wilkins-Laflamme

NEW YORK UNIVERSITY PRESS
New York

NEW YORK UNIVERSITY PRESS
New York
www.nyupress.org

© 2020 by New York University
All rights reserved

References to Internet websites (URLs) were accurate at the time of writing. Neither the author nor New York University Press is responsible for URLs that may have expired or changed since the manuscript was prepared.

Library of Congress Cataloging-in-Publication Data
Names: Thiessen, Joel, 1981– author. | Wilkins-Laflamme, Sarah, 1987– author.
Title: None of the above : nonreligious identity in the US and Canada /
Joel Thiessen, Sarah Wilkins-Laflamme.
Description: New York : New York University Press, [2020]. | Series: Secular studies | Includes bibliographical references and index.
Identifiers: LCCN 2019029129 | ISBN 9781479817399 (cloth) | ISBN 9781479860807 (paperback) | ISBN 9781479864225 (ebook) | ISBN 9781479813421 (ebook)
Subjects: LCSH: Atheism—United States. | Atheism—Canada. | Irreligion—United States. | Irreligion—Canada.
Classification: LCC BL2760 .T45 2020 | DDC 200.973—dc23
LC record available at https://lccn.loc.gov/2019029129

New York University Press books are printed on acid-free paper, and their binding materials are chosen for strength and durability. We strive to use environmentally responsible suppliers and materials to the greatest extent possible in publishing our books.

Manufactured in the United States of America

10 9 8 7 6 5 4 3 2 1

Also available as an ebook

CONTENTS

Introduction: Nonreligious Identity in the US and Canada   1

1. I'm Done . . . and I'm Not Going Back!   27

2. Nones of All Shapes and Sizes   58

3. We Are Just as Moral . . . If Not More!   92

4. I Want Everybody to Have the Same Chance to Find Happiness   119

5. It's Too Bad Your Parents Aren't Christian . . .   141

Conclusion: Darlene, Patrick, Corrine, and Sandra   171

Acknowledgments   197

Appendix A: Interview Guide Used in Semistructured Interviews with Religious Nones   199

Appendix B: Further Statistical Results from Chapter 2   205

Appendix C: Further Statistical Results from Chapter 3   207

Appendix D: Further Statistical Results from Chapter 4   215

Notes   227

Bibliography   229

Index   249

About the Authors   259

Introduction

Nonreligious Identity in the US and Canada

Darlene, a former Evangelical and now a self-identified "religious none" in her sixties, agreed to meet in a nearby coffee shop. Reminiscing about her upbringing, she reflected, religion influenced "every spare minute you had." This all-encompassing religious life troubled Darlene from an early age. She especially became critical of the perceived closed-mindedness of Evangelicals, saying, "They kept very much to themselves . . . could not see the good in something else. They couldn't see past what was in front of them." Later in the same interview with Darlene, she compared her current beliefs about God with those of her former Christian group: "Mine's not judgmental. Mine does not put huge demands on you. He allows you to experience . . . other people, and love other people for what they are, not what they believe." She built on this idea of personal freedom, autonomy, and individualism throughout the interview, later celebrating the benefits of leaving her religious affiliation and involvement behind: "I gain more freedom . . . to think what I want, to work it out rather than being told, 'This is how you should think.'" When asked how confident she was in her status and worldview as a religious none, Darlene replied, "How confident does a person have to be? . . . I don't think I could be more confident."

Darlene's experience has become an increasingly common one in recent decades in both the United States and Canada. Religious nones—those who say they do not belong to any religion—are the fastest growing "religious" tradition in the United States and Canada, and much of the modern Western world. Nearly one-quarter of Canadian and one-fifth of American adults report that they have no religion in recent General Social Surveys, with an even larger one-third of teens and young adults in these countries claiming the same. Best estimates suggest that religious nones will continue to grow for the foreseeable future.

Canada and the United States are very similar in some respects, but as we will see, the proportion of religious nones grew earlier and more rapidly in Canada versus the United States (only recently have religious nones grown sharply in the United States). Some believe that currents in Canada may foreshadow what will happen in the United States. While as sociologists we avoid making predictions about the future, our comparative study in this book explores how a nonreligious identity intersects with several aspects of daily life in sometimes similar and sometimes differing ways in these two nations, offering insights that may help us to understand societal and political trends. This volume offers a look at the paths to becoming a religious none, including how the (non)religiosity of the surrounding region and society affects these biographic pathways; the diverse religious and secular attitudes and behaviors present among religious nones; the sociopolitical beliefs and practices of religious nones in areas such as gender, sexuality, the environment, poverty, and immigration; and the relationships between those who profess to have no religion and religious people and organizations. The knowledge base we provide in this book may help to explain social divides in both moral and political values, and how we can explain these divisions along religious/nonreligious lines.

As with all ways of identifying and understanding aspects of our social world and our daily lives, this concept of the religious "none" as someone who has no religion is a social construct in itself. It is a way of imbuing meaning to a reality that has become taken for granted by many in our society, a product of this time (the last half century or so) and this place (notably European and North American societies) because of a series of historical, cultural, and physical factors shaping the social environments in which we live. For the "none" phenomenon to become possible, there needs to be a context where religion is understood as distinct from other aspects of life (e.g., the economic, the political, the domestic), with distinct memberships, beliefs, and practices—a context where individuals can thus conceive of being without a religion. These conditions are now present for many in the United States and Canada, and in many traditionally Judeo-Christian societies across the Western world. Other scholars have explored some of the roots of this evolution in how religion and nonreligion have been understood throughout Judeo-Christian social history (see, for example, Berger 1967; Taylor

2007). In this book, however, we focus more on how individuals who say they have no religion define and use this aspect of their identity, and how it influences other aspects of current social life. Although the religious "none" is at its core a social construction, as with all such constructs it has become real in its consequences for many individuals and for our societies.

Some aspects of Darlene's life changed when she left her religion behind. Notably, she stopped taking part regularly in religious group activities. Yet, though she was now identifying as a religious none, Darlene acknowledged attending the occasional Christmas service when she visited her mother. However, she was quick to note, "I don't enjoy it." She also watched the Gaither Vocal Band on television on occasion, for the "harmony," not the lyrics, which she noted she had a "hard time believing a lot of times." Darlene's reflections remind us of the Christian reference point that many religious nones have in the United States and Canada. Yet, it is also important to understand that, although some of the same "religious" behaviors may exist among the religiously affiliated and unaffiliated, individuals in these two groups attach different personal and social meanings and functions to those behaviors—meanings and functions that we will explore in this book based on firsthand accounts from religious nones. Additionally, we argue in this book that, as individuals become further removed from organized religion and with many members of younger generations having little to no religious upbringing, not only do differences in personal and social meanings grow between the unaffiliated and affiliated, but so do differences in some behaviors as well.

Alongside the rise in recent decades of individuals saying they have no religion, studies of this topic have also begun to appear, fulfilling calls in the late 1960s and early 1970s for rigorous social scientific research into this phenomenon (Bahr 1970; Campbell 1971; Vernon 1968). Three key observations stand out from the research to date. First, these studies have stressed that the proportion of religious nones is growing. And we know a lot about their sociodemographic characteristics. Although religious nones come in all shapes and sizes, in most settings they are more likely to be male, younger, higher educated, not married, without children, and more liberal in their opinions and values (Clarke and Macdonald 2017; Gee and Veevers 1989; Hayes 2000; Hout and Fischer 2002;

Hunsberger and Altemeyer 2006; Kosmin and Keysar 2008; Lewis, Currie, and Oman-Reagan 2016; Putnam and Campbell 2010). Second, we are gradually learning more about what contributes to the growth of the religious none category: social acceptance toward irreligion, negative reactions against religious fundamentalism, rejection of the fusion between religion and politics, irreligious socialization, and intellectual disagreement with religious beliefs and practices (Bengtson, Putney, and Harris 2013; Bruce 2011; Bullivant 2008a; Clarke and Macdonald 2017; Hout and Fischer 2002; Putnam and Campbell 2010; Schwadel 2010; Thiessen 2015; Thiessen and Wilkins-Laflamme 2017; Zuckerman, Galen, and Pasquale 2016). Third, recent research sheds light on the heterogeneous religious, spiritual, and secular beliefs and practices among religious nones (Baker and Smith 2015; Lim, MacGregor, and Putnam 2010; Manning 2015; Storm 2009; Voas and Day 2010; Wilkins-Laflamme 2015). Although many nones are nonbelievers or agnostics, as we just saw with Darlene's story, there are also those who hold beliefs in a higher power.

Yet amid these existing research findings in the field, much of which comes from the United States, we are surprised at how few regional and international comparisons have been made between religious nones from different social contexts, and in particular across the United States and Canada. Little has been written on religious nones in Canada at all (recent exceptions, as we wrote this manuscript, include Beaman 2017; Beaman and Steele 2018; Bibby 2017; and Clarke and Macdonald 2017)—a nation that is significantly less religious on a range of indicators compared with the United States and, until recently, has had a much larger proportion of religious nones. This dearth of research particularly struck us as we were independently working on qualitative interview and quantitative survey projects respectively on Canadian religious nones (Thiessen 2015; Wilkins-Laflamme 2015), only to discover each other's work in the process. This point of contact laid the groundwork to pursue collaborative work (see Thiessen and Wilkins-Laflamme 2017), of which this book is one aspect.

Of course, the gaps in the existing literature go well beyond the absence of comparative studies on religious nones in the United States and Canada. Several other research opportunities stand out to us: (a) While we know that different types of disaffiliation as well as irreligious socialization play a role in the rise of those who say they have no religion, we know little about the biographic pathways into becoming a religious none and how these are influenced by the surrounding social environment. Here we have an opportunity to develop a comprehensive model of factors that lead people to say they have no religion. (b) There is a need for a thorough model of macro-demographic trends affecting the size of the religious none population. In this regard, while many authors assume that the religious none population will continue to grow, will countervailing forces such as non-Western immigration and lower birth rates among religious nones slow or reverse this growth in certain areas? (c) Works on spiritual and secular meaning systems among nones in the United States are increasing, but few similar works exist in Canada. (d) Data in the United States reveal distinct sociopolitical attitudes and behaviors among religious nones, but how does this compare in Canada, and might beliefs and practices shift as the religious none group grows? (e) What attitudes exist among religious nones, religious majorities, and religious minorities, and how do these attitudes affect group interaction?

Our central aim in this book is to fill these gaps by exploring the dynamics of being a religious none in contemporary America and Canada and how this willful distance from organized religion affects other aspects of daily and social life. Our main argument is that there is a decline of organized religion happening in both countries: a gradual decline happening in stages across time and generations and at different rates in various social, cultural, and regional contexts, leading to the rise of religious "nones." Yet, this form of decline does not imply the disappearance of all things religious and spiritual, as a diversity of spiritual beliefs and practices along with nonbelief and secular attitudes coexist and are constantly evolving. The decline of organized religion among large segments of the US and Canadian populations also does not mean that religion is necessarily less relevant for everyday interactions and social life. If anything, that there are now large groups of religious and nonreligious individuals coexisting in both countries could mean there is a greater social divide and distance in moral and political values and behaviors along religious/nonreligious lines, as well as in interactions and attitudes between the religious and nonreligious.

We arrive at these conclusions upon carefully examining several data sources. Sarah analyzed quantitative data from a number of high-quality national censuses, surveys, and opinion polls, including the 1985–2016 American and Canadian General Social Surveys (National Opinion Research Center 2017; Statistics Canada 2016), the 1971–2001 Canadian Census (Statistics Canada 2015a), the 2011 National Household Survey (Statistics Canada 2015b), Pew's 2014 Religious Landscape Study (Pew Research Center 2014a), the Project Canada Survey (2005), a CROP (2006) survey on religious beliefs, the Pacific Northwest Social Survey (2017), the 2011 and 2015 Canadian Election Studies (Fournier et al. 2017), the American National Election Study (2016), and the 2017 Pew American Trends Panel (Pew Research Center 2017).

We also draw upon thirty face-to-face interviews that Joel conducted with religious nones in Alberta, Canada. These interviews occurred between June 2012 and August 2013, as part of a larger study that compared active religious affiliates (those who identify with a Christian tradition and attend religious services nearly every week), marginal religious affiliates (those who identify with a Christian tradition and attend religious services mainly for religious holidays and rites of passage), and religious nones (see Thiessen 2015). A snowball sample resulted in semi-structured interviews with seventeen females and thirteen males, spread fairly evenly across three age groups (18–34, 35–54, and 55+). Interviews lasted from 24 to 100 minutes long, with most taking around one hour. Questions centered on a wide range of past, present, and possible future (ir)religious perspectives and experiences, as well as views on the role of religion in society (see appendix A). In this book we focus on material from these interviews not fully analyzed or developed in our previous writing. As we develop our ideas, we additionally turn to excellent qualitative research with religious nones in the United States, sometimes to reinforce insights from our Canadian-based interviews and other times to show how religious nones might be different between the two nations.

In building our main argument throughout this book, we give special attention to similarities and differences between religious nones in the United States and Canada, accounting for the distinct historical, cultural, and religious landscapes in each nation and its regions. We begin this task in this introductory chapter by examining current-day rates of nones in American and Canadian regions, how these numbers have evolved since the 1970s, their demographic composition, and the major frameworks used in sociology of religion and religious studies that attempt to understand and explain the religious none phenomenon.

Past and Present Nones in the United States and Canada

In some respects, religious nones in the United States and Canada have followed similar trajectories, from once constituting relatively small proportions in each country to more sizeable figures in recent decades. Figures in 2016 among adults in the United States show that an estimated 22% say they have no religion (based on our analyses of the 2016 US General Social Survey (GSS); see also Pew Research Center 2015). This figure is up from 5% in 1972, with slow and gradual growth up to 7% in 1980 and 8% in 1990, and then the more recent and sudden jumps to 14% in 2000 and 22% in 2016 (US GSS 1972–2016; see also Pew Research Center 2015; Sherkat 2014, 37). Similar trends are noted among American teens and young adults. In 1972, 10% of eighteen- to twenty-nine-year-olds reported that they had no religion, a figure that rose to 32% by 2016 among this younger age group (US GSS 1972–2016; see also Lipka 2015; Putnam and Campbell 2010, 122–23). In Canada, 2016 General Social Survey data revealed that an estimated 23% of residents declared they have no religion (based on our analyses of this data). This figure is an increase from below 1% in the 1950s and 4% in the 1971 census. Since then, Canada overall has witnessed progressive growth to 12% in the 1991 census and 17% in the 2001 census (based on our analyses of these censuses; see also Bibby, Russell, and Rolheiser 2009, 176; Clarke and Macdonald 2017). Once again, similar trends are noted among Canadian teens and young adults: in the 1971 census, 6% of eighteen- to twenty-nine-year-olds disclosed they had no religion, a figure that has risen to 34% by 2016 among this younger age group.

It is important to note that the growth of religious nones in Canada started earlier than in the United States, though in the last decade this growth has plateaued somewhat in Canada, and growth in the United States has accelerated to catch up (see figure I.1; see also Brown 2013 for a comparison with other Western countries). A stages of decline framework is a helpful way to understand the varied developments in both countries. Part of our task in this book is to address several historical, social, and cultural explanations that assist us in understanding both

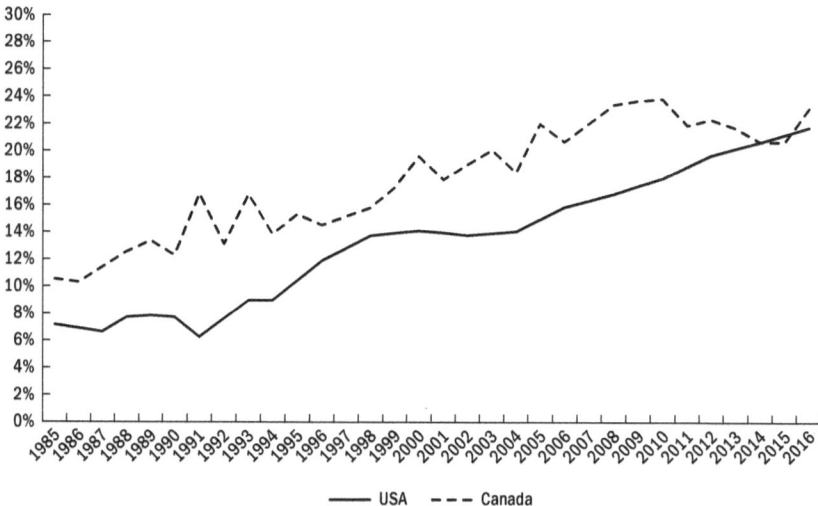

Figure I.1. Rates of religious nones, 1985–2016, USA and Canada. *Source:* (1) 1985–2016 USA GSSs. N = 38,992. Data points missing for 1992 and then every odd year after 1994; replaced with mean from year before and after. (2) 1985–2016 CND GSSs. N = 425,681. Data points for 1987, 1997, 2002, and 2007 missing and replaced with mean from year before and after. All estimates weighted to be representative of general populations.

why the growth of religious nones started earlier in Canada and why this growth did not start until later in the United States. But to begin, it is valuable to examine four key reasons that help to explain the extensive rise of religious nones during this period of time across the United States and Canada, reasons that in some cases are distinctly situated in American or Canadian social contexts and narratives.

Greater Social Acceptability toward the Nonreligious

First, it has become socially acceptable to say that one has no religion. With both nations emerging from strong Christian roots, until relatively recently for someone to say they had no religion was to risk social stigma in the eyes of their family, friends, coworkers, and society. In Canada, where more people attended religious services regularly compared with Americans during the mid-twentieth century (Bibby 1987,

17; Bowen 2004, 13; Noll 1992, 548), the onset of diminished religiosity from the 1960s forward opened the space for religious none identification to gradually become normalized (see Clarke and Macdonald 2017). This normalization process would be delayed in the United States and, as will be seen, is a process still very much underway. What partially sets Canada and the United States apart in this regard is their historical narratives surrounding the place of religion, notably Christianity, in social life. As is well documented, Evangelicalism is the single largest faith group in America, and it along with a civil religion discourse that sacralizes historical symbols, figures, and narratives around a Christian ethos has had and continues to have a strong influence in American social and political life (Bean 2014; Reimer 2003; Smith 1998). Whether it is the narrative that America is (or was) a Christian nation, beliefs that tie America with Israel as God's chosen people, or expectations that laws conform to conservative Christian values, there is a strong undercurrent of American Evangelicalism that dominates much of American social life. This sizeable Evangelical subculture, history, and memory in the United States, not present in Canada, has served as a buffer against the earlier growth of religious nones in the United States versus Canada. For example, a fervent stigma still exists in some regions toward those in the religious none community in the United States (see Schmidt 2016). Research likens "coming out" as a religious none, especially for atheists, in some areas within the United States to processes and experiences of those who "come out" as gay, lesbian, or transgender (Cragun et al. 2012; Linneman and Clendenen 2010; Niose 2012; Williamson and Yancey 2013; Zimmerman et al. 2015).

This social and historical context does not exist in Canada. While Canadians are generally aware of and even sympathetic to Christianity's influence in Canada's formative years, and in some laws that remain today, Canadians have become far more progressive and liberal over time on a range of social and moral issues. These social changes are related to a combination of changed and weakened ethnic-religious ties (English-Protestant and French-Catholic) following World War II, the growing centrality of multiculturalism to Canadian identity since the 1970s, and the relative absence of a strong conservative religious subculture as that found in the United States to fight against and delay liberal-leaning changes on social and moral issues (Adams 2006; Reimer 2003).

As just one example when comparing Americans and Canadians, 32% of Americans maintain that an atheist is unfit for political office versus 18% of Canadians, and fewer than half of Americans would vote for an atheist president (Bibby 2011, 92–94). Within a more permissive Canadian cultural milieu, rather than stigmatizing religious none identification, there is a sense among some that the stigma is reserved in part for those who are overly religious (see Haskell 2010; Thiessen 2015). In many ways, Canadian skepticism toward those who are too religious can be linked to illustrations and connotations of American Evangelicalism that Canadians are exposed to in the media, the subject of our second substantive observation.

A Reaction to the Religious Right

In 2018, Joel attended a gathering of Evangelical leaders in the United States. One of the church leaders recalled a debate in their church over whether to have the American flag on the platform under the cross on the wall, or off the platform. Neither of us can imagine such a debate taking place in a Canadian church, or even to have a Canadian flag present at all in a church (or if so, this would be extremely rare). The presence or absence of a national flag in a religious building is reflective, in part, of the ties between religion and politics in these two nations.

The robust political and media presence of the Christian Right and religious fundamentalism in the United States initially helped to delay the rise of religious nones in this country versus Canada yet has been, paradoxically, influential to the rapid rise of religious nones over the last three decades (Baker and Smith 2009; Clydesdale 2007, 196–97; Hout and Fischer 2002, 168; Hunsberger and Altemeyer 2006, 15; Kinnaman and Hawkins 2011; Niose 2012; Putnam and Campbell 2010, 499–501; Zuckerman 2012). In short, many see what in their minds is the problematic fusion between religion and politics, namely, between Evangelical Christianity and the Republican Party. For instance, 81% of white Evangelicals voted for Donald Trump in the 2016 American election (Smith and Martinez 2016). A growing segment of the American population believes that Evangelicals have too much power and influence in the political arena—imposing their values and expected behaviors onto others who think or act differently—with broad sweeping influences over family, education, the healthcare system, the legal realm, and foreign policy. Moreover, there is a sense that Evangelicals are too political, judgmental, insincere, exclusive, homophobic, hypocritical, and sheltered (Kinnaman and Hawkins 2011)—traits unbecoming of a modern, democratic, liberal, and diverse society. American political scientists Robert Putnam and David Campbell (2010), and sociologists Michael Hout and Claude Fischer (2002), argue that the Christian Right emerged politically in the 1980s as a reaction to the flourishing liberal sexual morals of the 1960s and 1970s. In turn the sudden rise of religious nones in the United States since the 1990s has been a counterreaction to the Christian Right and religious fundamentalism there.

While Canada has not experienced the overarching presence of Evangelicalism in public life to the extent felt in the United States, ordinary Canadians are not immune from such effects. Canadians consume American media, and many are well aware of the role that Evangelicalism plays in American society, and indications of religion playing a central role in Canadian life are viewed with a certain degree of suspicion (Bean 2014; Reimer 2003; Reimer and Wilkinson 2015). A 2015 Angus Reid survey reveals that religious nones in Canada have the strongest negative perceptions toward Evangelicals, and not coincidentally, Evangelicals have the strongest disdain for atheists. Suffice it to say, as it relates to religious nones in Canada, some, following their American counterparts, attribute their decision to identify as a religious none to their disdain toward the public presence of religion in the world (not just Evangelicalism but religious extremism in general).

Apostasy

Third, to this point in American and Canadian history, apostasy has been the driving source and background for most of those who say they have no religion. A large majority of Canadians and Americans through the 1950s identified with a Christian tradition or denomination. Although there are religious nones from a variety of Christian and non-Christian faith backgrounds, the rise of nones is attributable in large part to those who set aside their Christian identification, especially among mainline or liberal Protestant groups (Bibby 2011; Clarke and Macdonald 2017; Sherkat 2014). Some members from other traditions have also left their religious identification behind, though far fewer than from Christianity (Drescher 2016, 16–17; Pew Research Center 2015; Sherkat 2014). Some recent qualitative research studies give us a glimpse into the reasons for apostasy. These range, among other factors, from Christianity being too exclusive to scandals and hypocrisy, negative experiences with others in their religious group, and intellectual disagreements (see Drescher 2016; Manning 2015; Thiessen 2015; Zuckerman 2012). Regardless of the reasons, the current religious none population across the United States and Canada is predominantly comprised of individuals raised in some kind of faith tradition but who left their religious involvement and identification behind. According to the 2008 US GSS, 56% of religious none Americans had two parents (or in the case of a single parent household, had only the one parent) with a religious affiliation when the respondent was growing up. In Canada in 2005, 55% of religious none respondents expressed their parents were religiously affiliated at the time of the survey (based on our analyses of the 2005 Project Canada Survey). A majority of religious nones in both countries then seem to emerge from homes where parents identify with a religion.

Growing Irreligious Socialization

Last, a trend that we are seeing and anticipate will become more common is those who are raised without any religion. As the religious none population has grown in recent decades, it is more common for children to be born into families with parents who say they have no religion. In contrast to previous generations where parents may be nominally or actively religious and provide their children with some exposure to religious beliefs and rituals, religious nones today who may have little or no religious background themselves are raising their children without any formal exposure to religious beliefs or behaviors in the home, at school, and in the community (Bengtson, Putney, and Harris 2013; Clarke and Macdonald 2017; Manning 2015; Thiessen 2016; Thiessen and Wilkins-Laflamme 2017). If we return to the figures at the end of the previous section, 44% of religious nones in the United States come from homes where one or both parents similarly identify as religious nones versus 45% in Canada. Irreligious socialization should thus not be lost as one of the contributing factors to the rise of nones across the United States and Canada.

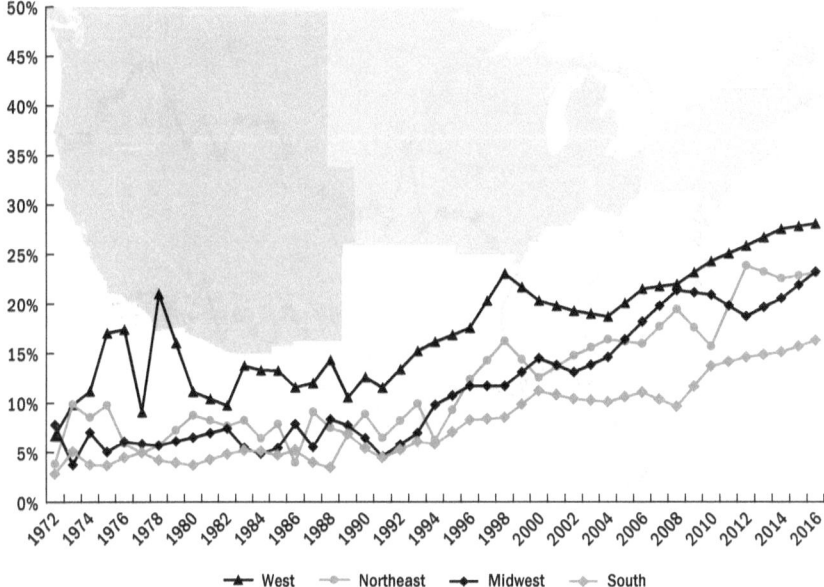

Figure I.2. Evolution of rates of religious nones, by census region, USA, 1972–2016. *Source:* 1972–2016 US GSSs. N West = 9,917; N Northeast = 10,571; N Midwest = 14,202; N South = 20,118. Missing data for 1979, 1981, 1992, and odd years from 1995 onward replaced by averages from preceding and posterior years. All estimates weighted to be representative of general populations.

Regional Variations in Nones

Although there is a similar process of decline of organized religion and rise of religious nones underway in both Canada and the United States, the timing, rate, and sometimes nature of this change does vary between the two national contexts. These variables can also differ between regional cultures within and between both countries. In figures I.2 and I.3, we first show the regional variations of proportional none increases since the 1970s. In the United States, religious none figures are highest along the entire West Coast moving eastward into the mountain states, and to a lesser degree in the Northeast. In Canada, religious none populations follow a similar pattern and are also highest on the West Coast, in the northern territories, and in Alberta. In comparison, the nones form the smallest proportions of the overall

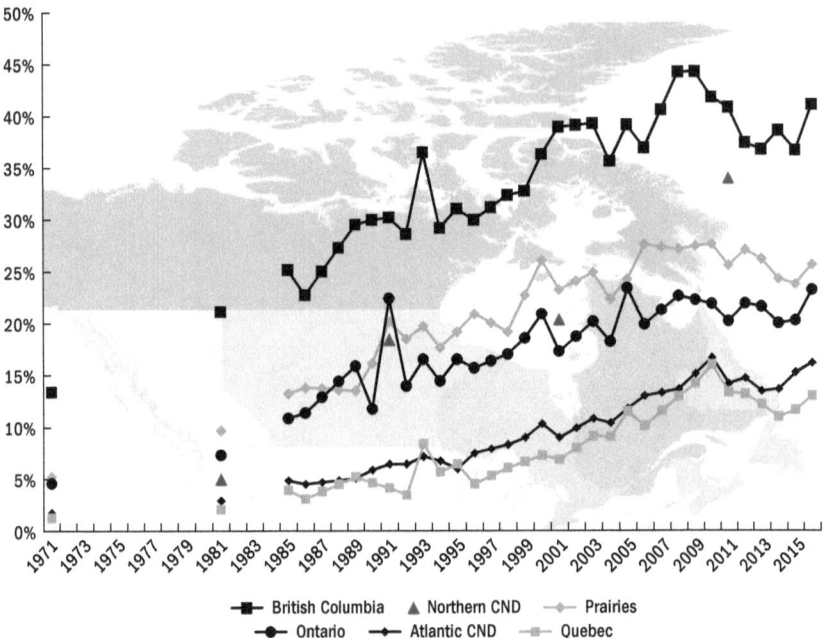

Figure I.3. Evolution of rates of religious nones, by census region, Canada, 1971–2016. *Source:* 1971 census, 1981 census, 1985–2016 CND GSSs (N British Columbia = 35,497; N Prairies = 78,242; N Ontario = 99,591; N Quebec = 83,299; N Atlantic Canada = 83,093). Missing data for 1987–1988, 1997, 2002, and 2007 replaced by averages from preceding and posterior years. Northern Canada: 1991 census, 2001 census, and 2011 NHS. All estimates weighted to be representative of general populations.

populations in the midwestern and southern US states as well as in Quebec and the Atlantic Canadian provinces.

Regarding the evolution of rates of religious nones across the four US Census regions and the six Canadian Census regions, two patterns stand out. First, in every region the rates of nones have steadily increased over time. In the United States, the religious none figures have grown from their lowest points, between 3% in the South and 7% in the West in 1972, up to 17% and 28% respectively in 2016. In Canada, statistics range from 2% in Quebec and 13% in British Columbia in 1971, up to 13% and 41% respectively in 2016.

Second, the most and least religious regions across the United States and Canada (measured here strictly by affiliation status) remain stable over time, with some fluctuation among regions in the middle. The West Coast states in America have long had the highest rates of religious nones along with British Columbia in Canada, while the southern states in America along with Quebec and the Atlantic provinces in Canada have consistently had the lowest rates of religious nones. Historical and cultural factors play a large role in these distinctions (Block 2017; Martin 2005; Meunier and Wilkins-Laflamme 2011).

Demographics among the Nones

Shifting our focus to figure I.4 and the demographic composition among religious nones in the United States and Canada, several clear patterns arise that extend a growing consensus among scholars who study religious nones (many of the following findings are even more pronounced among atheists—see Cragun, Hammer, and Smith 2013; Zuckerman, Galen, and Pasquale 2016). First, religious nones are disproportionately younger than those who affiliate with a religion, a finding that is slightly more pronounced in Canada than in the United States. In the United States, 44% of religious nones are under the age of thirty-five versus 49% in Canada. Second, religious nones are more likely to be male when compared to those affiliated with a religion, representing 54% of nones in the United States and 57% in Canada. Third, in comparison with those affiliated with a religion, religious nones are less likely to be foreign born. When contrasting the United States and Canada, Canadian nones are more likely to be born outside the country (18%), compared with American nones (12%).

It would seem then that, although there are religious nones of all stripes, the processes leading to their growth are more prevalent among certain subpopulations, notably younger generations, men, and those born in the United States and Canada (and Northern and Western Europe). If we narrow our focus only to religious nones between the ages of twenty-five and forty-four years in order to control for the age effect to a certain extent, several additional observations emerge. Religious nones are less likely to be married when compared with those who identify with a religion. This fact is most pronounced in the United States (45% of nones have never married) versus Canada (31%). Relatedly, religious nones are less likely than affiliated individuals to have children, reflective

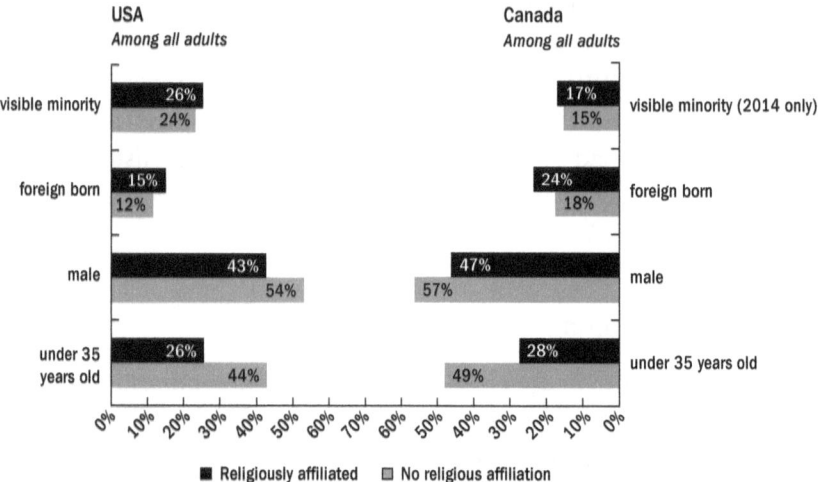

Figure I.4.A. Demographic composition of religious nones, USA and Canada, 2010–2014 averages. *Source:* 2010–2014 USA and CND GSSs. Estimates weighted to be representative of the general populations. N USA 18 year + respondents = 6,556; N CND 15 year + respondents = 118,763.

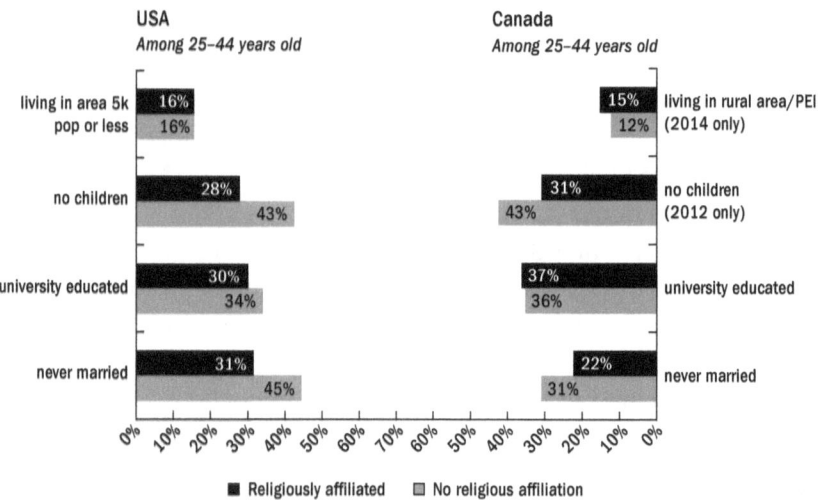

Figure I.4.B. Demographic composition of religious nones, USA and Canada, 2010–2014 averages. *Source:* 2010–2014 USA and CND GSSs. Estimates weighted to be representative of the general populations. N USA 25–44-year-old respondents = 2,400; N CND 25–44-year-old respondents = 31,856.

of 43% of both American and Canadian nones. Traditional family structures, taught and valued by most organized religious groups, thus seem to be less present among religious nones.

Somewhat surprisingly though, when it comes to university education, rural contexts, or visible minority status, no discernable differences emerge between the affiliated and the unaffiliated. In both Canada and the United States, almost as many religious nones are university educated, live in rural settings, or are visible minorities as those who affiliate with a religion. Small exceptions to this include education in the United States, with a slight edge among religious nones with a university education (34% versus 30% among the affiliated) and rural populations in Canada where 15% of the affiliated live versus 12% of religious nones.

Frameworks for Understanding Nones

Those scholars studying religion have framed their analyses and interpretations of these realities of the religious nones in several ways. There are three notable and commonly used conceptual and theoretical frameworks for studying religious nones: stages of decline, individualization, and polarization. While we favor a stages of decline interpretive framework, we see merit in each for helping to describe and explain different aspects of what is to be known about religious nones in the United States and Canada. Thus, each of the chapters in this book draws on aspects of these three frameworks in turn.

Stages of Decline

Beginning with the stages of decline framework, the relatively recent surge of religious nones is understood here to be a consequence of long-standing, progressive, and generational religious decline over time. As prominent Scottish sociologist Steve Bruce (2002, xii) puts it, "Liberal industrial democracies of the Western world are considerably less religious now than they were in the days of my father, my grandfather, and my great-grandfather." Against this backdrop, the growing presence of religious nones is not a sudden or surprising social development. The late sociologists Peter Berger (1967) and David Martin (1978) initially articulated this narrative best, alerting researchers to the powerful relationship between modernity and religious decline. Instead of suggesting that secularization is inevitable or irreversible in modern society, they suggest rather that it unfolds at different speeds and in different ways due to historical and cultural factors. Berger and Martin draw attention to social changes that link religious decline at the societal, organizational, and individual levels (see Dobbelaere 1981, 2002), changes such as rationalization, improved material conditions, pluralism, individualism, and declining religious authority in the public sphere. In the last decade, scholars like Bruce (2011), Clarke and Macdonald (2017), Norris and Inglehart (2011), Voas (2006, 2009), and Voas and Chaves (2016) have extended this stages of decline framework, drawing on extensive survey and institutional data across the modern Western world. Bruce (2002, 3) aptly notes "the declining importance of religion for the operation of nonreligious roles and institutions such as those of the state and the economy; a decline in the social standing of religious roles and institutions; and a decline in the extent to which people engage in religious practices, display beliefs of a religious kind, and conduct other aspects of their lives in a manner informed by such beliefs."

The Enlightenment era, characterized by rationalization, science, and empiricism, is a helpful starting point for considering the stages of decline process because of the supposed inherent conflict between modernity and religious belief in the unmeasurable. As a rationalistic and scientific worldview gains legitimacy in society, religiosity tends to diminish, given its fundamentally different ontology and epistemology; people no longer believe they need the gods to keep them safe or heal them or grow their crops when they can turn to science and medicine instead. Similarly, in the area of material security, people's perceived need for the supernatural diminishes the greater their economic standing; people do not need compensators, in this life or the next, from the gods to deal with their current economic deprivity. A related variable in the stages of decline framework is social and religious pluralism (see Berger 1967; Bruce 2011; Woodhead 2016). Where pluralism exists, it is rare and difficult for any one religion to receive a privileged or taken-for-granted status in society, to shape politics, healthcare, or education, for instance. Religion is but one of many social institutions with specialized roles and functions in a differentiated society. The result is that religion lacks social relevance to reinforce certain religious plausibility structures and beliefs and practices. In this context, political leaders, teachers, and healthcare professionals do not advance ideologies or act on behalf of a religious group. Further, in a religiously and culturally plural society, individuals become aware of perspectives that are different from their own. This awareness can create the conditions for weakening the legitimacy of one's religious beliefs, sometimes resulting in doubt over one's religious worldview. The combined effect of these realities where pluralism exists is subjectivized faith. Here individuals turn inward as the arbiter and authority over their religious beliefs and practices, somewhat devoid of a shared religious framework. Canadian researcher Alastair Hay (2014) recently offered a compelling case that Berger's theory of secularization, notably pluralism, individualism, and science and rationalization, helps to explain secularizing trends in Canada.

At a very practical level, the stages of decline framework reveals that individuals initially diminish their religiosity by gradually dropping their church attendance and religious group activities. Their religious identification and occasional involvement with a religious group may persist (e.g., for religious holidays or rites of passage), as people maintain social and cultural ties to their faith tradition (Bibby and Grenville 2013; Clarke and Macdonald 2017; Day 2011; Demerath 2000; Inglis 2007; Lamoureux Scholes 2003; Meunier and Wilkins-Laflamme 2011; Thiessen 2015; Voas 2009; Walliss 2002; Zuckerman 2008). Yet these ties to one's religion also progressively lessen given that one has fewer social reinforcements in society or their religious group to sustain ongoing affiliation, belief, or involvement. Simply put, as religion loses its influence in society, the social pressures to uphold religiosity at a private level, with involvement in institutional religion or otherwise, also weaken. And this dynamic is circular. As fewer people say they identify or are involved with a religious group, the social acceptance toward such a declaration increases, which in turn normalizes the "no religion" option for others in society. This process is aided when those with little religiosity have children of their own and raise their children without explicit religious socialization. It is unlikely in these circumstances for people to suddenly "take up" religious affiliation or belief, if for no other reason than they lack the social environments (e.g., family, education, politics, and media) to expose or teach them about such options (Bengtson, Putney, and Harris 2013; Clarke and Macdonald 2017; Dillon and Wink 2007; Manning 2013; Merino 2012; Zuckerman 2012).

As this process unfolds, researchers in secular and nonreligion studies have begun to focus not just on the decline of traditional forms of religion but more specifically on what is replacing them among cohorts of nonbelievers. Burgeoning research is just now beginning to provide a more substantive understanding of how nonbelievers construct and make sense of their world as well as their various attitudes and behaviors in societies where they must coexist with believers (Ammerman 2014; Beaman and Tomlins 2015; Bullivant and Lee 2012; LeDrew 2015; Lee 2015; Taylor 2007; Zuckerman, Galen, and Pasquale 2016). Since many religious nones also do not hold to traditional religious or spiritual beliefs, we will explore these emerging findings on unbelief in more detail with our own results in the chapters to come.

Individualization and Spiritualization

In contrast to the stages of decline framework, where researchers focus on declining institutional expressions of religious affiliation, belief, and practice, some say that religion and spirituality are not necessarily declining but rather changing (e.g., Bowen 2004; Davie 1994; Drescher 2016; Heelas and Woodhead 2005; Houtman and Aupers 2007; Miller 1997; Wuthnow 2007). Rather than narrowly defining and measuring religion against conventional institutional markers, such as church attendance or communal-oriented religious activities, the individualization framework stresses ongoing private spirituality among individuals. For example, this can include belief in a god, supernatural being, or higher power; belief in an interconnected natural world and universe; and belief in some form of afterlife, prayer, meditation, or mindfulness activities. Individuals draw on a number of beliefs, rituals, and practices from a variety of sources, some of them linked to religious groups and some of them not, to build and maintain their own personalized faith systems (Hervieu-Léger 1999).

And yet a parallel case to this narrative is a sense among some scholars that expressions of spirituality apart from institutionalized religion do not necessarily entail wholly private spiritual quests. In *Sacred Stories, Spiritual*

Tribes, American sociologist Nancy Ammerman (2014) draws attention to the nuanced ways in which individuals, particularly those with weak or no ties to institutional religion, invoke the sacred in the ordinary, from life at home to work, relationships, and health. For such individuals, spirituality is not strictly an individualized endeavor. Ammerman contends that spiritual practices are "neither utterly individual or strictly defined by collective tradition . . . people draw on practices that they learn about from others, both inside and outside traditional religious communities; and occasionally they come up with something genuinely new" (290). In turn, Ammerman urges sociologists to think about the Durkheimian sacred-profane distinction along a continuum rather than in dichotomous terms; the boundaries between the two are much fuzzier than many assume (see also Day, Vincett, and Cotter 2013; Lee 2015).

Although not explicitly stated among proponents of the individualization framework, an argument could be made that individualization is a manifestation of individualism within the stages of decline framework. That is, religious, social, and cultural pluralism help to set in motion the movement away from institutionalized religion toward more subjective expressions of spirituality. This social transformation specifically occurs as societies gradually embrace individualism, personal autonomy, and choice as prized cultural values. British scholar of religion Linda Woodhead (2016), writing in the context of Britain, captures this shift well when she speaks of the "liberalization" of society. By this she means "the conviction that each and every individual has the right if not the duty to make choices about how she or he should live her or his own life" (255). As it relates to religion, this turn happens from authority that was once widely located externally in a deity or a religious leader to one now resting largely with the individual. This means that people can and do embrace the cultural freedom to believe or belong on their own terms, including the freedom to say that one has no religion. This narrative is increasingly accepted across the United States and Canada, though as hinted at earlier, the social costs for doing so remain higher for Americans versus Canadians.

Polarization

The polarization framework is another way of making sense of religious nones in contemporary social life. In its broadest sense, polarization refers to the widening gap between those who are actively religious (i.e., identify with a religion and attend religious services on a regular basis) and those who do not identify with any religion and score low on all or most religiosity scales. Implicit in this account is the shrinking middle category of individuals who may, for example, identify with a religion and attend religious services for religious holidays and rites of passage but do not position themselves at either extreme of the religious-irreligious continuum (see Bibby 2011; Olson and Beckworth 2011; Putnam and Campbell 2010; Wilkins-Laflamme 2014).

Emerging research is showing that, in areas where religious decline has been underway for a longer period of time, a bottoming out has occurred where there is a small but stable core of religiously active individuals that remains (Kaufmann, Goujon, and Skirbekk 2012; Voas 2009; Wilkins-Laflamme 2014; 2016a). Despite finding themselves in a landscape where secular values and behaviors are normalized, this demographic still values the rewards attached to their faithful religious adherence and involvement. Religion thus becomes more of a niche market of sorts in society, with the actively faithful being able to reproduce their numbers at these now lower levels due to their sometimes higher fertility rates and most notably due to gains from non-Western immigration. Some faith groups, notably Evangelicals, are also adept at creating and maintaining their own alternative social activities and institutions for their members. Meanwhile, the rest of society moves more and more in a secular direction. In this sense, the polarization framework can be understood within the stages of decline narrative, only that religious decline does not necessarily touch everyone in society.

There is, however, another element to polarization that scholars deal with in their research on religious nones: an antagonistic and hostile relationship between the actively religious and irreligious in society. Recent research (Wilkins-Laflamme 2016b) highlights sharpened attitudinal and behavioral differences between the actively religious and irreligious, prominent especially in areas with a larger concentration of religious nones. Namely, religious nones tend to be more liberal (e.g., on issues of family life and sexuality) and less personally religious where advanced secularization is present. In their 2015 report on religion and faith in Canada, opinion pollsters at Angus Reid found that 63% of respondents inclined to reject religion felt uncomfortable around people who are religiously devout, and 41% of respondents inclined to embrace religion felt uncomfortable around people who had no use for religion (Angus Reid Institute 2015). There is also some credence to sociologist José Casanova's (1994) deprivatization thesis in such contexts, where the highly devout who reside in overwhelmingly secular settings may feel a need to hold on to or reassert their religious presence in the public realm (Achterberg et al. 2009; Wilkins-Laflamme 2016a). At the same time, religious nones may also push for greater cultural legitimacy, particularly at the expense of religion playing any substantive public role. Returning to Woodhead's observations about liberalization and people's belief that they have the right and duty to live, believe, and behave as they see fit, for religious nones this can mean the freedom *from* religion in society. Some religious nones maintain that in a plural and secular society, religion should have no role in public life, where religious groups and individuals cease imposing their attitudes and behaviors onto others. As one would imagine in a context like the United States, where there is a strong contingent of devout theologically conservative religious adherents alongside a growing religious none segment who are evermore committed to a secular orientation to society, a battle for cultural authority and legitimacy over and against the "other" is very much present.

Taken together, the stages of decline, individualization, and polarization frameworks, though distinct, are in some ways extensions of one another. The stages of decline framework sets in motion individualization taking place, and may in turn be reinforced by processes of individualization. As people become less religious and declines among the actively religious bottom out, it is not surprising that polarization between the highly devout and the irreligious emerge. Moreover, as once religious societies experience progressive secularization, religiously conservative individuals and groups will no doubt take issue with how society is changing. Similarly, as religious nones grow in proportion and social legitimacy, we also see them vie for a stronger cultural space, potentially to the exclusion of more religious folk. Yet even these realities of polarization are evidence of later stages of secularization at work.

Mapping the Journey

To summarize, religious nones have "come out" and grown rapidly in a relatively short period of time across the United States and Canada. We are gradually learning more about this group's demographic composition and how religious nones are similar or dissimilar from the rest of the population in both the United States and Canada. As already demonstrated in a preliminary way in this chapter, when studying religious nones in a comparative fashion, our understanding sharpens because we can identify and isolate social, cultural, and historical variations surrounding the rise and experience of religious nones. The remainder of our journey in this book is straightforward: we seek to better understand religious nones in contemporary America and Canada, and how nonreligious identification shapes other aspects of daily and social life.

In chapter 1 we turn to both qualitative and quantitative empirical data to explore the individual and demographic factors affecting rates of religious nones. Subjects include the prevalence of religious disaffiliation and the reasons individuals give for disaffiliation, irreligious socialization, more secular social environments, potential for reaffiliation, and birth rates and migration among religious and nonreligious populations.

Chapter 2 entails an investigation into the dynamics of believing, religious and spiritual behavior, indifference, and active atheism and secularism among the nonaffiliated, and how these dimensions among the nones compare between American and Canadian regions. We explore in this chapter the diversity of spiritual beliefs and practices along with nonbelief and secular attitudes that coexist in society. More specifically, we explore five subtypes of religious nones in the United States and Canada: involved seculars, inactive nonbelievers, inactive believers, the spiritual but not religious, and religiously involved believers.

Equipped with a better understanding of the diversity present among American and Canadian religious nones, we turn our attention in chapters 3 and 4 to the broader social and civic impact of religious nones in American and Canadian social life. We explore the extent to which a gulf exists regarding many moral and political values and behaviors between the religious and nonreligious. In chapter 3 with both survey and in-depth interview data, we highlight how being a specific subtype of religious none in both the United States and Canada can be linked with certain values and positions on issues of sexuality, reproductive rights, gender roles, governmental aid, environmentalism, and immigration. Then in chapter 4 we study the levels of political and civic engagement that are present among religious none populations and how these compare with those who are affiliated and more actively involved with a religion.

In chapter 5 we turn our attention to American and Canadian public opinion data as well as data from qualitative interviews with nones to determine to what extent there is dislike, indifference, apprehension, or respect among nones toward individuals affiliated with various religious traditions. Further, we examine attitudes and perceptions among affiliates from different religious groups toward religious nones. In other words, this chapter looks at the levels of social distance that exist between nones and members of religious groups in the United States and Canada, and what impact this is having on interactions between both types of individuals.

We then end this book by offering some central conclusions from our research in the context of our main argument laid out earlier in this introduction. We discuss the features of late modernity as a way to help make sense of our central observations regarding religious nones in the United States and Canada. We then distill some of the similarities and differences between religious nones in the United States and Canada, before exploring the possible future, quantitatively and qualitatively, for religious nones in both countries, including potential challenges and opportunities for coexistence among the affiliated and unaffiliated. In doing so, we give careful attention to national and regional variations in play, as well as theoretical and methodological considerations. Last, we raise a number of possibilities for future research on religious nones in the United States, Canada, and further afield.

1

I'm Done . . . and I'm Not Going Back!

Patrick grew up in a small bilingual French-English village in Eastern Canada. Raised in the Catholic tradition where he was "forced" to attend mass most weeks, Patrick described his first communion as "an obligation to the grandparents." He, his parents, and his siblings ceased attending weekly mass once the youngest in the family had their first communion, and he noted that many in the community gossiped about his family's decision to stop attending regularly. Unlike Darlene's experience described earlier, Patrick did not describe his family as particularly religious growing up. They did not pray or read scripture or talk about their faith in the home. Now in his early thirties, Patrick listed his grievances against the Catholic Church and religion overall. He cited the heavy emphasis on Jesus rather than God, religion's negativity toward scientific advances, religious diversity and uncertainty of which religion is right, the oppression of women, and attempts by religious groups to control people's attitudes and behaviors. Patrick still believes in God, though not as an active force in the world. He is unsure about the afterlife, saying, "I view our time on this world as a short-term thing . . . just enjoy yourself, rather than [worry] about what's after . . . there's joy in life so why not try to achieve as much joy as you can while you're alive." Regarding attending church, he adamantly claimed, "I don't attend, and I never plan on attending again." He carried on to reflect that religion can be both positive and negative in society. As for his level of confidence in his perspectives on religion and life? Patrick declared, "I might not believe that I'm right, but I know that if you came and tried to push religion on me, I would believe you are wrong." Patrick's confidence, like others we will encounter, alerts us to the stable "none" identity that many who say they have no religion seem to possess.

When looking at statistics that show that a growing segment of Americans and Canadians have done away with a religious identity, one of the first questions that often come to mind is why. How do individuals such as Patrick describe their own journey that led them not only to stop any regular religious practice or contact with a religious group but also to go one step further and break all identity ties from their family's, potentially their region's or their culture's, and their own predominant religious tradition? This chapter explores some of these biographic pathways leading someone to say they have no religion—a group that sociologist Stephen Bullivant (2017) winsomely identifies as "nonverts"—and what such individuals often share in common.

As we will show, and confirming existing literature, a majority of religious nones in the United States and Canada fall into this nonvert category, meaning they were raised with a religion and later set it aside. Yet, not everyone who says they have no religion grew up in a religious tradition. Some are, again to borrow from Bullivant (2017), "cradle nones." When they were children, these individuals had little to no contact with religion, experiencing irreligious socialization. For both "nonverts" and "cradle nones," we show how their individual narratives must be understood in relation to their wider social environments, within a broader, notably generational, stages of decline process, and that there are also a series of macrolevel historical, cultural, political, and demographic factors affecting the overall size of the religious none population in a given area.

Reasons for Becoming a Religious None

As we saw in the introduction with the stages of decline framework, as organized religion plays a smaller and smaller role in other aspects of social life, such as in education, health and cultural identity, disaffiliation, or leaving one's religion becomes a viable option for some individuals in society. In turn, this initial exit from one's religion can generate a snowball effect: as irreligion grows, the stigma that was once attached to it gradually fades and it becomes increasingly socially acceptable to be unaffiliated. More individuals become willing to adopt this detached stance toward religion.

Then, when these individuals are ready to start families, their children are born into homes that are either indifferent toward religion or even sometimes actively against it. Fewer children receive any religious socialization during their formative years: fewer step foot in a place of worship, even for special occasions, and fewer receive any form of religious education at home, at school, or elsewhere. These individuals then have a good chance of remaining nonaffiliated as adults, for example, not even considering religion as a possible place to turn to for comfort in times of hardship later in life. And when they are ready to have children of their own, the pattern of raising nonaffiliates continues (Baker and Smith 2015; Bengtson, Putney, and Harris 2013; Clarke and Macdonald 2017; Dillon and Wink 2007; Manning 2013; Merino 2012; Zuckerman 2012). Although present among those of many different religious backgrounds, these processes leading to nonaffiliation have been most common in the United States and Canada among individuals and families from Christian backgrounds (Bibby 2011; Clarke and Macdonald 2017; Reimer and Hiemstra 2018; Sherkat 2014). In the United States, mainline Protestants have historically been the main feeders to the religious none category, followed by Catholics and Evangelical Protestants of late (Bengtson, Putney, and Harris 2013, 152; Drescher 2016, 16–17; Sherkat 2014, 71). In Canada, the same trends are present, along with those raised Buddhist who are disproportionately prone to identify as nones in their adult years (Clarke and Macdonald 2017; Reimer and Hiemstra 2018, 12).

While all people have their own unique biographic story of how their relationship, or lack thereof, with religion has developed over the course of their lifetime, among religious nones we often group their pathways into two broad categories: those who were exposed to religion during their childhood but who chose to leave it behind at some point later on in their lives (disaffiliation, which characterized twenty-four of our thirty interviewees) and those who grew up with no religion (irreligious socialization, found among six of our thirty interviewees; Baker and Smith 2015; Bullivant 2017; Merino 2012; Thiessen and Wilkins-Laflamme 2017; Zuckerman, Galen, and Pasquale 2016). We observe these two main pathways of disaffiliation and irreligious socialization when asking questions in surveys, and also when interviewing the unaffiliated in depth about how they became a religious none.

Nonverts and Religious Disaffiliation

As shown in figure 1.1, in the United States in 2008 56% of religious nones reported that their parents had a religious affiliation, and half

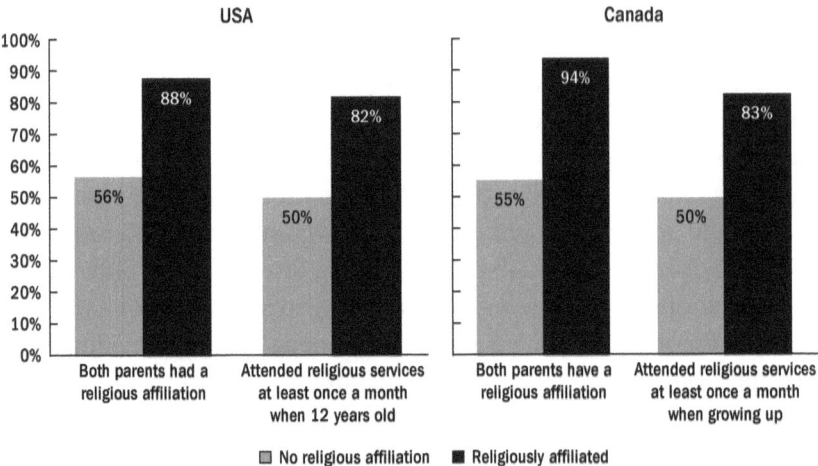

Figure 1.1. Disaffiliation indicators, USA (2008) and Canada (2005). *Source:* (1) US GSS 2008. N = 1,344. (2) Project Canada Survey 2005. N = 1,933. All estimates weighted to be representative of general populations.

conveyed they attended religious services at least once a month when growing up. In Canada, these percentages in 2005 are very similar at 55% and 50% respectively. Consequently, a (slim) majority of religious nones in the United States and Canada appear to be coming from religious backgrounds.

Among the twenty-four religious nones interviewed who fall into the category of disaffiliates, what is first apparent is that twenty-three of them left their childhood religion during their teen or young adult years. In other words, we are not dealing with religious nones who maintained religious affiliation well into their adult years and then turned away from it. This is in line with what many researchers studying the nonreligious have found: late adolescence and young adulthood is a crucial time for becoming a religious none (Bruce 2011; LeDrew 2013; Pasquale 2010; Roozen 1980; Zuckerman, Galen, and Pasquale 2016). Moreover, in line with other excellent qualitative research in the United States (Drescher 2016; Zuckerman 2012), the disaffiliation process among interviewees is typically a gradual rather than a sudden development. Religious nones often do not leave their religion behind overnight (see also Bullivant 2008a; Jamieson 2002).

Sixteen of the interviewed unaffiliated experienced what researcher Phil Zuckerman (2012) calls a mild form of disaffiliation, meaning that these disaffiliates were not overly religious to begin with. American scholar Elizabeth Drescher (2016) indicates that this type of less or untroubled passage into disaffiliation seems to occur most often among those from liberal Protestant backgrounds in the United States, a finding that resonates with our Canadian interviewees too. The remaining eight unaffiliated individuals interviewed underwent a more transformative disaffiliation experience where they broke away from a stronger and typically more conservative (e.g., Catholic or Evangelical) religious background (also see Bengtson, Putney, and Harris 2013; Roof 1999).

So what contributed to these different trajectories for disaffiliation, and how are these processes at work in people's lived experiences? Although we cannot identify with our data if any one factor plays a key role over others, here we do turn to four central reasons that help to account for the disaffiliation process among the twenty-four nonverts interviewed, as well as mentioning, when relevant, other important catalysts identified in the existing literature. For some interviewees, only one of the following variables was necessary for their religious exit; for others, a combination of these factors facilitated their disaffiliation.

Parents Give Choice to Children

The first factor is that parents gave their children in their preteen or teen years the choice of continued religious involvement, and many took this opportunity to step away from their religious group. Barbara is in her early fifties and has worked in retail her entire career. She stated, "Mom was Catholic. We were dragged to church every Sunday. Dad was Anglican. Didn't go to church until later in his life when we moved back to Calgary. . . . Mother took us up until age sixteen. We had to go every Sunday. We did the midnight mass. We did Easter. We did it all. And then at sixteen, we were given the choice if we wanted to keep going. And of course, we're all, 'No! That's it. I'm done!'"

Along with parents giving religious choice to their children, it was clear in the interviews that religion was not that salient for parents either. Many discuss that, aside from their family attending religious services, sometimes more to see friends and gossip than for explicit religious reasons, religion was rarely spoken of in the home and religious practices such as prayer or scripture reading were absent in the home so far as they could recall. Samantha, in her midtwenties and a recent university graduate with a bachelor of science degree, recalled, for example, that her family attended a conservative Protestant congregation when she grew up: "We did go to church sometimes, but it was never, like, a solid part of who we were as a family." Identifying with a religion was often equated simply with being a good moral person.

Consequently, there is a fine and often fuzzy line between disaffiliation and irreligious socialization. On the one hand, parents valued religion enough to provide some religious exposure to their children. Their children had sufficient association with religion in order to make a conscious decision to disaffiliate. On the other hand, parents who gave children choice over religious affiliation and involvement, especially in homes where religion was not that important to parents to begin with, could be interpreted as evidence of irreligious socialization (or at the very least, the absence of intentional religious socialization). We lean toward the former interpretation because even weak religious socialization is still religious socialization; however, we think that weak religious socialization is indicative of the gradual secularization processes discussed in the previous chapter. It seems that parents do not value and pass on religious belief and practice in the same ways today than in previous generations where choice was rarely an option (see Crockett and Voas 2006; Manning 2015; Thiessen 2016). As such, we see a logical connection from disaffiliation due to choice during one's teen years to weak religious socialization and irreligious socialization. Additionally, without a solid and long-standing religious base themselves, it is unlikely that religious nones would in turn attempt to pass on religious affiliation, belief, or involvement to their children—at least in any substantive way where religion would play an important role in their life or their children's lives.

Intellectual Disagreements

Second, intellectual disagreements contributed to some interviewees setting their religious affiliation aside. These ranged from tensions between evidence-based science versus faith (see also Baker 2012) to personal experiences not aligning with religious or church teachings (e.g., God is loving yet pain and suffering exist in the world) and the many faith groups in existence that make it difficult for individuals to settle with any one religion in particular. The strong ties between political and Christian rhetoric in the United States, especially at the right end of the political spectrum, which researchers such as Hout and Fischer (2002) and Putnam and Campbell (2010) argue may drive some individuals to say they have no religion, would also fall into this category.

For interviewees in Alberta who disaffiliated, theirs was a gradual process as time, experience, and heightened awareness of different viewpoints culminated in officially adopting a religious none status. Many of these same realities come to the surface in an American context too, such as with Phil Zuckerman's (2012, 33–39) interviews with apostates, and with a Pew Research Center survey (2016) of just under nine hundred disaffiliated Americans that shows 49% identifying disagreement with or lack of belief in religious teachings as a reason they disaffiliated, along with 20% saying they left because they disliked organized religion. We return to Patrick, whom we introduced at the beginning of this chapter. He identified science as a significant reason for his gradual disbelief:

> All the wonderful things that we're doing with science, kind of put in question . . . you need to believe in what I say and you can't question the approach of the church, and then the big bang theory . . . what's the science behind it? And then religion tells you, don't worry about the science, just believe blindly . . . but explain to me the science, and it's like, don't believe in the science. . . . Focus on just believing and . . . do what I say . . . don't follow your heart . . . just go with blind faith . . . and then you know your question goes unanswered . . . then . . . every time the community gets a dumbfounded question, it's like, have faith, and then that's the answer . . . give me a little bit more. . . . And then we've seen evolution, and especially in the 1900s, if you don't believe in evolution then look around you . . . the evolution that we've gone through in the last hundred years . . . and I think that's where . . . the church has a hard time . . . science versus the religion. . . . I saw the science . . . it's more mathematical, science, than religion where . . . you don't have proof other than the Bible, which was written how many years ago by people you don't even trust.

Tracie is a manager in a marketing department, now in her late thirties. She attended Anglican services with her mom and siblings growing up. Her dad was not religious. After she was confirmed at around ten years old, Tracie recalled that her mom gave her the option of continued religious involvement. Tracie stopped attending almost immediately, mainly because her personal experiences did not align with church teachings:

> I didn't really believe in it . . . I believe in lots about it and I believed those people were really good people . . . so I would go for my mom. But . . . I didn't have that faith gene. I'm just missing it. . . . I just lack faith. . . . I remember when I was getting confirmed and all the other kids just bought in and I was asking like, "But you can't actually see God so how do you know he's there?" The priest was really patient, but I didn't feel like he made it make sense to me. I thought it was a great story, but I couldn't actually believe it.

Later in her university years, Tracie took various courses on world religions, and there too her previous doubts were reinforced. Norman's reflections on different religions build on Tracie's conclusions. Norman, in his midfifties, works in mortgage financing and lending. He was raised in an Anglican home and described his disaffiliation as a process:

> The older you get, the more experience you have. The more people you meet, the more experiences you see. And it was just through that whole process that I really started to not see the point of identifying with any one religious group because . . . there's so many of them. . . . I did say to myself, "Why . . . what's so different about this one?" . . . So I started to say, "Well . . . there's so many . . . they can all be right. They can all be wrong." But you don't have to identify with anything to believe in things. . . . I don't have that need to identify with . . . a certain group anymore.

As demonstrated with several of those quoted to this point, some interviewees come from mixed-marriage contexts. Recent research in Canada reveals that religious intermarriage is on the rise, led by marriages between one affiliated and one unaffiliated spouse (even though rates of religious nones who are in mixed marriages are on the decline, as they progressively have more unaffiliated spousal options; Lee et al.

2017). Interviewees did not single out their parents' different faith backgrounds as a contributor to their disaffiliation, yet in line with other research (Arweck and Nesbitt 2010; Crockett and Voas 2006; Zuckerman 2012), these contexts do not appear to help interviewees to remain part of a religious group. In total the net result of these intellectual barriers, including exposure to different faith traditions, was for interviewees to reject formal religious affiliation, typically manifested in what Zuckerman (2012) calls "deep apostasy"—disaffiliates set aside all traditional religious beliefs and practices as they embraced their new unaffiliated identity.

Social Influences

Third, religious nones turned from their religious affiliation due to close social influences that pulled them away from their religious group. This reality played itself out in two ways among the interviewees. For some it was their parents who stopped attending, and by default as teenagers, those interviewed also ceased their involvement. Other interviewees diminished their involvement because they started hanging out with others in high school or university who did not share an affinity for religious affiliation or involvement. Gradually their friends' influence, particularly to party and hang out late on weekends, contributed to interviewees turning from their religious groups and eventually identifying as religious nones. Although none of the interviewees had undergone this particular experience, we could imagine that entering into a serious relationship with a nonreligious partner could also be a contributing factor toward disaffiliation for similar reasons.

Earlier, we introduced Norman, who struggled intellectually with the many religions in existence. In addition, Norman shared that his social ties played a role in his disaffiliation:

> When it started to change . . . was in high school . . . we would go for Christmas service all the time . . . traditionally, I would always go to my best friend's place. His mom was there. His sister was there, and all my friends were there . . . none of them went to church, and they were all having beers and staying up late. And I always was . . . in a suit, and I was the guy who had to leave at ten-thirty . . . to go to church. And so it's

one of the first times I was sort of like, "What's all this about? . . . Why am I doing this?" . . . As I got a little bit older, I'd say probably seventeen, eighteen years old . . . it's just really more about having too many beers on Saturday night, and not wanting to get out of bed on Sunday.

Norman went on to express that he resisted being told what to do or how to think, whether from his church or from his parents. As he went to university, he appreciated not having this "thumb" at his back, and his religious involvement "fell to the wayside" along with his religious affiliation.

The experience for Norman, like others in Phil Zuckerman's (2012, 94–100) interviews with American apostates, for example, is very much in line with the stages of decline process that we detailed earlier. In religiously and socially plural contexts where individualism is highly esteemed and where no single religion is endorsed or reinforced in political or educational or legal environments, it becomes socially acceptable for religious belief or adherence to be seen as one choice among many that individuals make. Such a process progressively opens the door to normalize an unaffiliated status, most keenly expressed and felt via one's association with close friends and family. That is, either our closest associations do not pressure us to necessarily "believe and belong" as they do or we become emboldened to deviate from the beliefs and practices cherished by those around us as society at large becomes more diverse.

Life Transition

Fourth, as with some of Phil Zuckerman's (2012, 40–55) apostate interviewees in the United States, our interviewees disaffiliated because of a significant life transition. These ranged from moving due to a job change or to attend university, to a divorce, to losing a parent or grandparent who was the strongest influence in the family to encourage active religious belief and involvement. Previous research shows that the death of a family member can help those considering disaffiliation to remain part of a religious group (Vargas 2012). This was not the case for some of our interviewees. Louis is in his midforties and works in the insurance industry. He was actively involved in the Roman Catholic Church until his father passed away: "When my dad was alive, we attended a lot more. It was kind of mandatory in our family to go to church. After he passed away, by that time it was really up to us if we went or not. I would only go maybe Christmas and Easter sort of thing with friends, not really with family or anything."

Louis recalled that his mom stopped attending thereafter, mainly because she was busy caring for her children as a single parent. Louis also noted that his mom "didn't grow up as a religious family either. She only actually started going to church when she met my dad. His family was really strong onto the Roman Catholic side." When asked if religion was important to his family growing up, Louis summarized, "Maybe more so when dad was alive." It is important to note the convergence of factors that extend back two generations, from his mother's parents who were not religious to his mom marrying a fairly religious person, to religion no longer holding much importance after his dad died, and the eventual impact that this had on Louis.

Beyond these driving explanations for disaffiliation, we would be remiss if we did not highlight two additional variables that were not key catalysts for the initial disaffiliation process but that interviewees noted as barriers for greater involvement if they were to consider reaffiliation. These include being too busy and opposition to exclusivity in religious groups. In terms of being too busy, religious nones did not disaffiliate because they were too busy, but eventually being too busy with sports or school or work or their own families became an additional reason that cemented their decision to no longer affiliate or attend religious services. Additionally, some mentioned that religious groups who hold exclusive beliefs about salvation, sexuality, or women in leadership, for example, were problematic for them. Unlike several apostate interviewees in Phil Zuckerman's (2012) study in the United States, exclusivity of this kind did not drive our interviewees away from their religious group as such. Yet, the further they stepped away from their religious group and the more they thought about whether they would eventually return to their religious group (e.g., if they had children), they cited exclusivity as a reason for not seriously entertaining this possibility.

Cradle Nones and Irreligious Socialization

As we saw earlier, not all religious none interviewees are disaffiliates as such. Six describe their childhood as devoid of any conventional religious beliefs or practices. Consistent with other qualitative studies in the United States on cradle nones and irreligious socialization (Bengtson, Putney, and Harris 2013; Manning 2015), most of our interviewees who were raised without any religion shared how their grandparents were actively religious; how their parents were raised with a religion of some kind only to set aside active religious affiliation, belief, and involvement; and how in turn their parents chose not to actively raise their children with any explicit religious instruction. Corrine is a teacher in her midthirties. She recalled, "My dad . . . was Catholic growing up, and my mom . . . she was Lutheran. . . . She just was not practicing at all, and nor was my dad." Corrine was not sure what contributed to her parents no longer participating in their childhood religion, but she was clear that religion was never discussed in the home, nor did Corrine attend religious services with her parents growing up. She referenced in passing that she attended for a few holidays with her aunt on occasion, but this was the extent of her exposure to religion as a child.

Jay is in his late thirties and works for an engineering firm. He mentioned that his mother was raised Catholic and his father was raised Lutheran, though neither parent was actively religious as Jay grew up. When asked if his family ever talked about religion, Jay said, "All the time. . . . Generally pretty negative . . . talking all the time about how . . . organized religion, came from one place and really went to another place, a very negative place, in their opinion and I think in my opinion now." He went on to mention that he was baptized because of his grandmother: "My grandmother certainly started off very, very religious. And went away from it later. And she was . . . very adamant that myself and all my cousins be baptized . . . she believed in God and damnation and her grandchildren would go to hell . . . if we weren't baptized." Jay is similar to other interviewees who may have observed a few religious services or rites of passage in their early years out of respect for a grandparent or extended family member, but religious belief and practice were certainly not embraced or passed on within their immediate family.

Others, like Dustin, a software developer in his early thirties, epitomize what we anticipate will increasingly be the case for irreligious transmission across the generations as the proportion of religious nones becomes larger in society. Neither of Dustin's parents is religious, and his dad identifies as an atheist. Dustin's family was not religious, they never attended religious services, but his dad talked about his atheist views from time to time: "Not necessarily directed at us. More directed at maybe something we heard on the news that spurred kind of a thought. And then he would just kind of give his opinion about something . . . he wasn't . . . forcing anything upon us." When asked to expand on the nature of his dad's views, Dustin could only muster out that "he's very scientific . . . he thinks of things very logically." In response to whether he ever thought about religion growing up, Dustin responded: "No . . . I never really had a moment where I was . . . thinking of whether I should join a religion or not. That never really crossed my mind, I guess." Dustin's experience is akin to what more researchers are referring to as secular, nonreligious, or irreligious socialization (Baker and Smith 2015; LeDrew 2013; Manning 2015; Merino 2012; Zuckerman, Galen, and Pasquale 2016). Importantly, and characteristic of the stages of decline framework, Dustin's dad's aversion to forcing his beliefs onto Dustin is key in an irreligious socialization context (see Manning 2015; Thiessen 2016). As Zuckerman, Galen, and Pasquale (2016, 127) note, "Secular people tend toward nonconformity, independence, and antiauthoritarianism . . . to base their maturational goals on personal independence, and their childrearing philosophy emphasizes autonomy rather than obedience to authority." Still, we would stress that modeling a "hands-off" approach to religion in the home does, in fact, pass on a particular individualist and secular orientation to religion and the world more generally. Such an approach strengthens the likelihood that someone who identifies as a religious none will raise children who also say they do not identify with a religion.

What limited survey data exists on the topic shows that religious nones are much more likely to have experienced aspects of an irreligious socialization than individuals who say they belong to a religious tradition. As we can see in figure 1.2, in the United States in 2008 44% of respondents with no religion identified having at least one parent also with no religion, and 28% never attended religious services while growing up; this compared with only 13% and 5% respectively among the religiously affiliated. In Canada in 2005, the rate of religious nones saying they had at least one parent who was also a none is about the same as in the United States at 45%, and compared with only 6% among the religiously affiliated in Canada; and, similar to the rate in the United States,

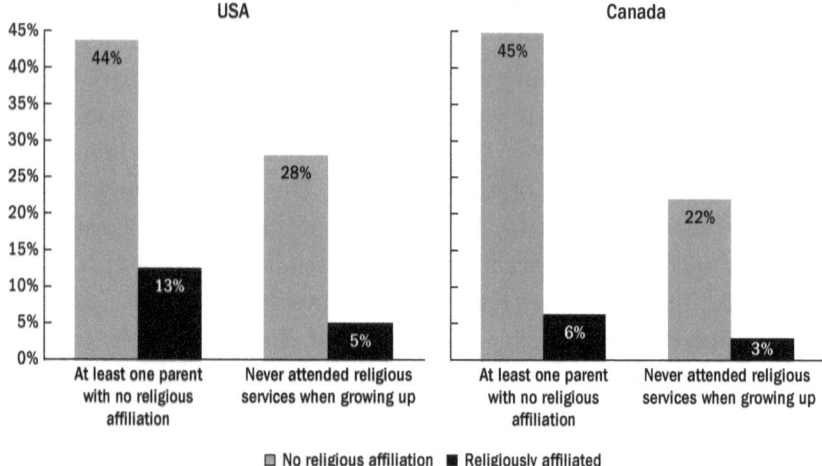

Figure 1.2. Irreligious socialization indicators, USA (2008) and Canada (2005). *Source:* (1) US GSS 2008. N = 1,344. (2) Project Canada Survey 2005. N = 1,933. All estimates weighted to be representative of general populations.

22% of Canadian nones revealed they never attended religious services when growing up, compared with only 3% among the religiously affiliated in Canada.

So although not all those who have an irreligious background go on to be nonaffiliated as adults, a very high proportion do: 61% of American respondents in the 2008 GSS who revealed they grew up with no religion remain religious nones as adults (see also Bengtson, Putney, and Harris 2013). Additionally, in both the United States and Canada, religious nones among younger post-Boomer generations have higher rates of irreligious socialization than their pre-Boomer and Boomer counterparts: 39% of religious nones in Canada born after 1964 had at least one religious none parent and attended religious services less than once a month when growing up, compared with 19% among Boomer nones (born between 1945 and 1964) and 25% among pre-Boomer nones (born before 1945); in the United States, 34% of post-Boomer nones come from a similar irreligious background, compared with only 20% among Boomer nones and 11% among pre-Boomer nones (in line with findings from Schwadel 2010). Consequently, among younger nones irreligious socialization seems to be becoming a more prevalent pathway into nonaffiliation.

The Important Role of Time and Place

So far, we have explored the reasons individuals offer for having no religion as adults. However, we cannot isolate these individual- or microlevel explanations from their surrounding macrolevel social context, or in other words, from the peculiar nature and influence of where and when individuals find themselves. Figure 1.3, originally produced for our *JSSR* article (Thiessen and Wilkins-Laflamme 2017, 77), brings together the explanations of irreligious or weak religious socialization as well as the reasons for disaffiliation and highlights that these would not be possible, or at least would not be as prevalent as they currently are, without the influence of the larger social context currently found in the United States, Canada, and Europe. The broad realities of this context, as seen in the introduction, are that religion has lost much of its social authority and relevance, there is greater religious diversity than in the past, there is what is often seen as a competing scientific worldview, and individualism is rampant. When exploring the testimonies of religious none interviewees in the previous sections of this chapter, we see these realities interwoven in their life choices regarding religion and nonreligion.

In turn, a larger number of religious nones than in the past, or when compared with other societies, not only is the product of a given social context but also can have an important reciprocal impact on the social environment. A larger population of nones can contribute to further reinforcing many aspects of the secular nature of some societies: making it more socially acceptable to identify as a religious none and being irreligious, potentially providing public support to advocates of church-state separation and the removal of religion from public spaces, and so forth.

Regional Social Environments

Figure 1.3 illustrates the more general process of some of the broad social factors found in Western societies that facilitate weak or irreligious socialization as well as disaffiliation. This being said, we saw in the previous chapter that rates of religious nones are not all the same across American and Canadian regions, which means there are also more specific regional and cultural influences at play.

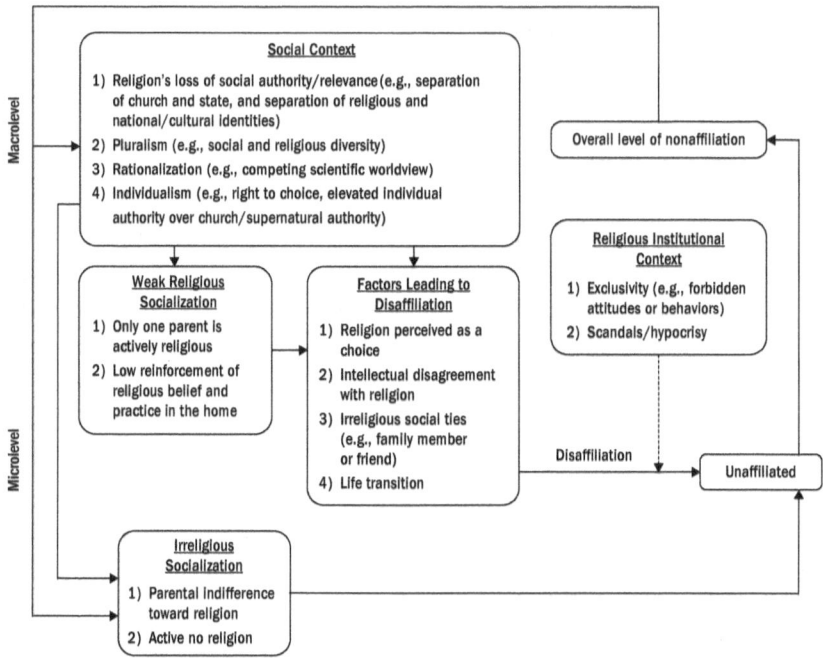

Figure 1.3. Explanatory model for declaring no religious affiliation.

Take the example of the Pacific Northwest, referring to the region west of the Rocky Mountains encompassing notably large swaths of British Columbia in Canada, and the states of Washington and Oregon in the United States. As seen in the introduction, on both sides of the national border here we find the highest rates of religious nones in the United States and Canada (see also Killen and Silk 2004; Pasquale 2007; Wilkins-Laflamme 2017). In the 2011 National Household Survey, the rate of nones in British Columbia rose to 44%; in the 2014 Pew Religious Landscape Study, religious nones made up an estimated 32% of Washington's and Oregon's population. Looking specifically at one city within the region, Victoria, British Columbia, had 51% of its population identifying as religious nones in the 2011 NHS. These high rates of nonaffiliation are not only found among the many Chinese and Japanese immigrants and their families in the region, East Asian groups characterized by high rates of no religion due to Western indicators of religion and religiosity not applying well to them, but also transcend the demographics of race, gender, income, and education levels in the Northwest.

As well as larger processes of secularization, pluralization, rationalization, and individualization being at play, processes found in most areas of the United States, Canada, and Europe to varying degrees, other more local historical, political, social, and cultural influences are also present in the northwestern religious and nonreligious landscape. Historically, one or a few churches had difficulty in establishing a monopoly or oligarchy in matters of religion in western Canada and the western United States. Protestantism could be found among a majority of residents from roughly the mid-nineteenth to mid-twentieth centuries, but it was fractured in nature: there being not only Anglican, Methodist, and other liberal Protestant denominations present but also many Evangelical groups that still make up substantial proportions today (Grant 1998; Hayes 2004; Reimer and Wilkinson 2015; Stackhouse 1998). A frontier mentality focused on mobility and resource extraction, political contestation between indigenous, British, and American groups, a physical and psychological distance from the rest of the continent, and a desire to be free of the Establishment in all its forms ensured that organized religion did not get as strong a foothold in the region in the nineteenth century as elsewhere in the United States and Canada (Barman 2008; Block 2017; Bunting 1997; Marks 2017; O'Connell 2003; Robbins 2001; Todd 2008).

In fact, some argue that what defined northwestern exceptionalism in matters of religion was most notably the "irreligious experience" of many of its residents (Block 2005; 2010; Marks 2007). The Pacific Northwest was to a certain extent "born secular" (Marks 2007), characterized by lower rates of regular church attendance among its population long before the 1960s. Religion never became as institutionalized during the mid-nineteenth to mid-twentieth centuries among a majority of its population as it did in more eastern and southern parts of the continent. Additionally, the large waves of Asian immigration to the region, among whom saying one had no religion was much more common, contributed to making nonreligion even more socially acceptable on the whole.

Consequently, with no one church or religious tradition having established deep roots with overall regional culture, and with individual and family ties to religious groups often being more precarious, religious affiliation was not as resistant to decline in western regions of the United States and Canada from the 1960s onward when the more general processes of secularization, pluralization, rationalization, and individualization became heightened in Western societies. Regional factors in the area appear to have led to earlier generational decline of organized religion in the Pacific Northwest, the cycle illustrated in figure 1.3 having unfolded earlier than elsewhere. The American context does seem to act as a bit of a buffer against this though, even in the Pacific Northwest: the strong ties between Christian and American identity and the stigma attached to nonreligion that persisted throughout the second half of the twentieth century and still exist today to a certain extent, much more so than in the Canadian context for the same period, may be one of the reasons rates of no religion in the American Pacific Northwest are still lower than those in British Columbia.

The high rates of no religion in the Pacific Northwest, more so in Canada but also in the United States, do not mean, however, that individuals there are devoid of beliefs in the supernatural as well as various forms of spirituality and religion altogether. We will see in the next chapter that saying one has no religion does not necessarily imply nonbelief and nonspirituality for a significant portion of religious nones. Indeed, some scholars argue that the extraordinary natural beauty of the Pacific Northwest, with its rugged mountains, Pacific Coast, and wild boreal and temperate rainforests, has inspired a peculiar form of "reverential naturalism" and openness to nontraditional spiritualities among many of its residents (Albanese 1990; Bramadat 2016; Dunlap 2004; Ferguson and Tamburello 2015; Goodenough 1998; McGrath 2002; Shibley 2011; Todd 2008). But organized forms of religion, including identifying with a religious tradition, are much less prevalent among the general population there than in the rest of the United States and Canada.

To summarize, although there is a general process of decline of traditional forms of organized religion across generations in most areas in the United States and Canada, including a decline of religious affiliation, the timing, depth, and specific nature of such changes can and do vary between different regional contexts. One size does not fit all in this sense.

Factors Influencing the Proportional Size of the Religious None Population

Once underway, the cycle illustrated in figure 1.3 and the stages of decline process could be seen to continue indefinitely, until all in society are irreligious. In fact, most researchers studying the growth of the religious none populations in the United States and Canada over the last few decades often explicitly say that we should expect this demographic to continue to grow for the foreseeable future. However, these accounts as well as the sections of this chapter so far have only focused on the gains that religious none populations make from birth rates among the nonreligious or those indifferent toward religion (leading to irreligious or weak religious socialization among their children) as well as from disaffiliation. There are also other countervailing demographic and social forces that can mean losses for the religious none populations, affecting their size in various regions and societies over time. The last section of this chapter explores these in- and outflows of the religious none populations in the United States and Canada.

Age

As we saw in the introduction, the religious none population has youth on its side when compared with those who say they belong to a religion. In both the United States and Canada, religious nones are on average younger than their religiously affiliated counterparts. As we saw in the previous sections of this chapter, younger birth cohorts are much more likely to have grown up with minimal or no exposure to religion as children and find themselves in more secular social environments than in the past. The age pyramids in figure 1.4 illustrate the extent of this age gap between the nones and the rest of the (religiously affiliated) population in both countries.

With figure 1.4, we can see that individuals belonging to a religion are much more middle and top heavy in terms of age, with the largest age groups here being found among those aged forty to sixty-five years in both the United States and Canada. By contrast, the none population is more bottom heavy, with its largest age groups being found among fifteen- to thirty-five-year-olds. The size of the religious none group among

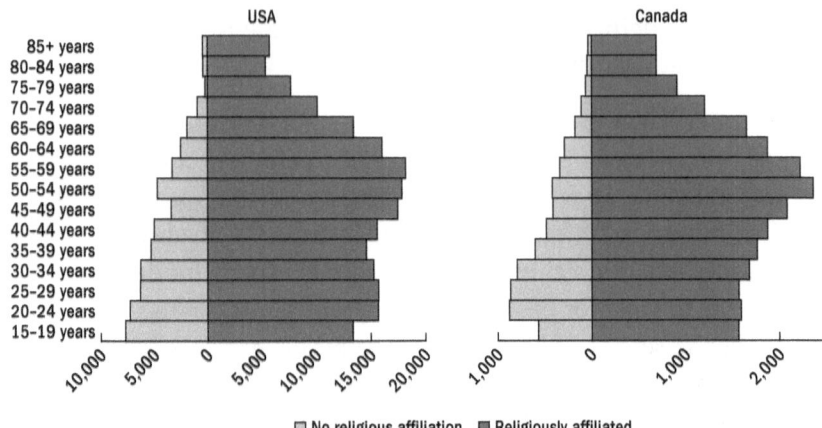

Figure 1.4. Age pyramids for religious nones and the religiously affiliated (number estimates in 1000s), USA and Canada, 2014. *Source:* Weighted estimates for religious affiliation and nonaffiliation for each age group generated from 2014 USA (N = 2,513) and CND (N = 32,299) GSSs. Estimates for population size of each age group in 2014 based on US Census Bureau data (https://factfinder.census.gov) and Statistics Canada estimates (www5.statcan.gc.ca).

fifteen- to nineteen-year-olds in Canada seems to be a bit of an exception here in 2014 with smaller numbers than the twenty- to thirty-five-year-old groups (but still relatively high with 27% of this younger cohort saying they have no religion in 2014; see also Bibby 2011). This could be due to the fact that estimates for the size of the none population among this age group in Canada are based on data from respondents aged fifteen to nineteen years old. Those aged fifteen to seventeen have not yet gone through that crucial late adolescent/early adulthood phase when disaffiliation is more likely to take place, compared with estimates in the United States based on respondents aged eighteen to nineteen years only.

If we were to take the age pyramids as they stood in 2014 and move them through time, this would mean that, as more religious individuals of older birth cohorts at the top of the age pyramid pass away, the proportion of religious nones overall would grow to match those higher proportions currently found among younger birth cohorts. Nevertheless, age is not the only factor at play when considering the proportional size of none populations.

Religious Immigration

Immigration is an important demographic variable to keep in mind in the United States and Canada. Only an estimated 17% of those born in a foreign country disclosed they had no religion in the 2014 General Social Surveys (GSSs) in both the United States and Canada, compared with 21% among the American-born population and 22% among the Canadian-born population. Looking specifically at American and Canadian immigration trends, the results in figure 1.5 indicate first of all that where immigrants come from has a big impact on their likelihood of being religious nones. Interestingly, American-born immigrants to Canada have a higher rate of no religion overall at an estimated 28% than the general American population in 2014 at 21%. This may indicate that religious nones in the United States are either more likely to immigrate to Canada in the first place (possibly to escape a prevailing dominant Christian subculture in the United States for a more favorable secular Canadian climate) or that American immigrants are more likely to disaffiliate once they arrive in Canada (perhaps reflective of the broadly secular Canadian environment they now find themselves in). Asian immigration, notably from China and Japan, is also another important source of religious nones to both Canada and the United States, mainly because as we saw earlier in this chapter, individuals from these countries often do not adopt Western religious affiliation labels to describe practices such as ancestral worship (see Bramadat and Seljak 2005).[1]

In turn, immigrants to Canada from Europe (including from the more religious eastern and southern regions as well as from less religious Western and Northern Europe) have lower rates of religious nones on average than the general Canadian population, whereas in the United States European immigrants have a much higher rate of religious nones. This may be due to the different national composition of European immigration to each of the two countries. In Canada, immigrants from Africa and Central and Southern America also have lower rates of religious nones on average than the general Canadian population. In the United States, it is immigrants from the Americas, the Middle East, and Africa who show lower rates of nonaffiliation.

With Eastern European, Southern European, African, Latin American, Middle Eastern, and South Asian groups representing an estimated

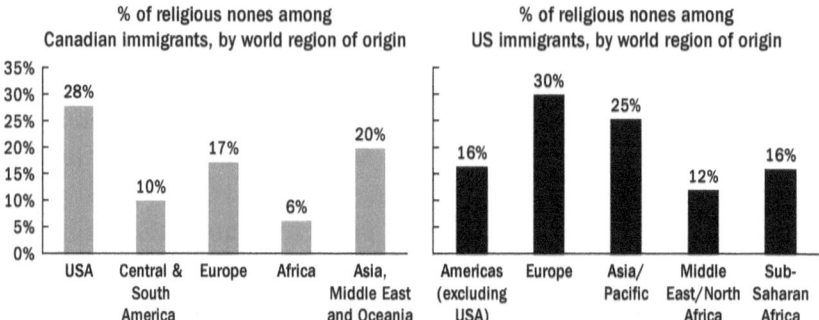

Figure 1.5.A. Rates of religious nones among immigrants, by world region of origin, USA and Canada, 2014. *Source:* (1) 2014 CND GSS. N world region of origin among immigrants = 6,965. (2) 2014 Pew Religious Landscape Study, USA. N world region of origin among immigrants = 3,932. All estimates weighted to be representative of general immigrant populations.

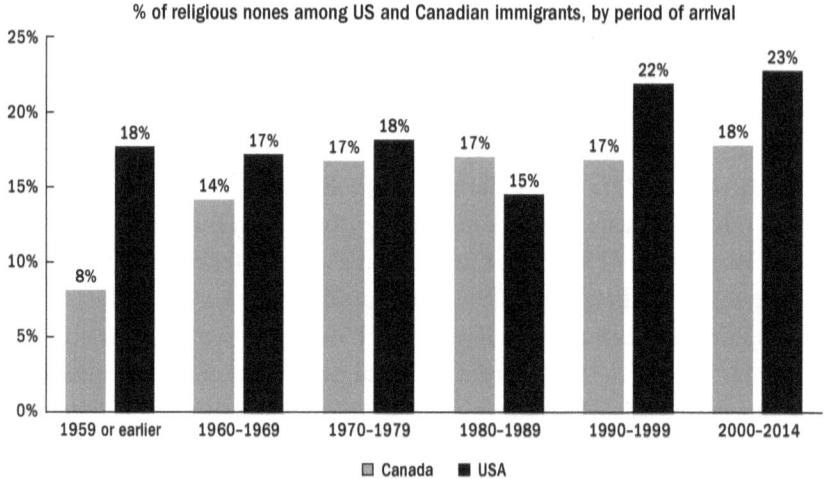

Figure 1.5.B. Rates of religious nones among immigrants, by period of arrival, USA and Canada, 2014. *Source:* (1) 2014 CND GSS. N period of arrival among immigrants = 5,942. (2) 2014 Pew Religious Landscape Study, USA. N period of arrival among immigrants = 3,748. All estimates weighted to be representative of general immigrant populations.

63% of the nearly 2,800,000 immigrants who arrived in Canada between 1991 and 2006,[2] it is especially the religiously affiliated in Canada who are making gains from this immigration originating in countries where being a religious none is a much rarer phenomenon (see also Connor 2014; Reimer and Hiemstra 2018).[3] Period of arrival does not seem to play as large of a role in Canada in this regard: immigrants arriving in the decades from the 1970s onward all show similar average rates of non-affiliation (around 17%).

This does not mean, however, that the more secular Canadian context does not have an impact on these immigrants once they arrive and on their children who grow up in the country. Indeed, rates of declaring no religion among second-generation Canadians (born in Canada but who have at least one parent born outside the country) are very similar to those among third-generation or older Canadians: 23% compared with 21% in 2014 respectively (also see Reimer and Hiemstra 2018). As immigrants assimilate over time, they may also become less religious due to more secular social environments (see Beyer and Ramji 2013; Cadge and Ecklund 2006; Collins-Mayo and Dandelion 2010; Connor 2008, 2009; Madge, Hemming, and Stenson 2014; van Tubergen 2006, 2007; van Tubergen and Sindradottir 2011; Wuthnow and Christiano 1979). But since non-Western immigration has become such an important force in Canada, overall the religious none population is losing out from immigration there.

In the United States, the story is a bit different. Immigrants who have arrived in the United States since the 1990s count a higher rate of religious nones among their ranks. Rates of nonaffiliation among second-generation Americans are an estimated 28% according to the 2014 Pew Religious Landscape Study, compared with only 23% among third generation or earlier Americans. So, although overall the United States' immigrant population still has below average rates of no religion, in recent years the United States' religious none population seems to have begun making modest gains from immigration.

Religious None Emigration

Religious none populations can also lose out from emigration if higher proportions of religious nones are leaving either Canada or the United

States, but here there is very limited good-quality information on such trends. In figure 1.5, the finding that the rate of religious nones among American-born immigrants to Canada is higher than the US average in 2014 is the only indication we currently have that American religious nones may be more likely to permanently leave the United States, negatively affecting in turn the size of the religious none population in that country (but not enough to affect overall trends of religious none growth there since the 1990s). Since religious nonaffiliation is currently so strongly tied to youth and younger generations, a time of life when individuals are often more mobile, it could be that religious nones are more likely to leave their country of origin than the religiously affiliated.

Lower Fertility Rates among Religious Nones

Fertility rates are another area where the religious none population loses out to a certain extent compared with the religiously affiliated. Although individuals do not necessarily have to be born to a nonreligious mother to receive an irreligious upbringing, children born to nonreligious mothers are nevertheless probably the most likely to receive such an upbringing. Yet, religious none female respondents aged eighteen to forty-four in the 2012 American GSS had a much lower mean number of children (1.035) than religiously affiliated women of the same age range (1.826). The same goes for Canada: in the 2012 GSS, religious none female respondents aged eighteen to forty-four had on average 0.909 children, compared with 1.226 among religiously affiliated women of the same age range. Zuckerman, Galen, and Pasquale (2016) attribute these differences in fertility rates to the nonreligious often delaying family formation by a number of years, either to complete higher education or to dedicate themselves to their careers, thus narrowing the amount of time available for childbearing. Nonreligious individuals may also differ at times in their fertility intentions, desiring a smaller number of children to make up their ideal families. A further consideration is that immigrants from many of the aforementioned regions of the world, who tend to be religiously affiliated, also tend to have more children than Canadian- or American-born citizens, at least in the first generation before eventually returning to the mean with subsequent generations.

Reaffiliation

Individuals who affiliate or reaffiliate with a religion after identifying as religious nones earlier in their lifetime also negatively affect the size of the religious none population at a given time and in a given region. Some have found evidence for an age effect regarding reaffiliation (Schwadel 2010; Uecker, Mayrl, and Stroope 2016), meaning that some individuals may return to religion in their later adult years once they have formed families of their own and life meaning questions become more pressing with children to raise and with personal experiences of death. However, other studies have not found much evidence for this age effect (Crockett and Voas 2006; Dillon and Wink 2007; Smith and Snell 2009; Wilkins-Laflamme 2014). According to the few studies on the topic, the phenomenon of reaffiliation does not appear to be all that common (Altemeyer and Hunsberger 1997; Bruce and Glendinning 2003; Uecker, Mayrl, and Stroope 2016; Voas 2006).

During our interviews with religious nones, we inquired about any potential desire for greater involvement in a religious group if they found it worthwhile for them or their family. Nineteen of thirty indicated that they do not desire greater levels of involvement; they are content with their current inactivity. Of the remaining eleven religious none interviewees, six believed they desire greater involvement while five pronounced they "perhaps" desire more involvement in a religious group. Not surprisingly, most of these eleven individuals had some degree of religious exposure and involvement as children. What might contribute to greater involvement? Responses ranged from finding community with others in a religious group to getting married or having children, finding a religious group that is less exclusive and dogmatic in its beliefs and practices, or finding religious folk who practiced what they believed (e.g., helping the poor). Janice is in her early thirties and works in retail. She said she would consider greater involvement for the "right reasons," including "the sense of community, belonging, without pressure, and understanding." Robert is in his late thirties, he works in the information technology sector, and is a self-described atheist. He would consider attending if it was "good for my kids. . . . I wouldn't do it for me, but if my wife said she really wanted me to do this thing, I'd do it. . . . It wouldn't be for me to enhance my spirituality. It would be purely for other people." Reinforcing the influence that family can have, Jocelyn, in her late twenties and single, intimated, "At this point, probably if I was in a relationship with someone that it's very important to them that I would give it a chance anyways." Tracie, whom we were introduced to earlier in this chapter, would entertain greater involvement "if I actually believed that a church could exist without being corrupt. If I thought my kids could think on their own. . . . I don't want them to not be able to think on their own. And if I thought it would change something or make the world better for doing it, I would."

At first glance, these testimonies seem to indicate that some religious nones may well pursue greater involvement with a religious group in the future. But in probing interviewees further, it became clear that first, no religious none interviewees had ever attempted to find a religious group that met their supposed "wish list." Second, when asked on a scale of one to ten how likely it is that they will pursue greater involvement in the future, most answered with a score of three or lower, with the highest response of six emerging for a couple of interviewees. Janice, whom we just met, offered a hesitant six in response, adding, "It's funny, because I don't know how interested I am in going to a church every Sunday morning . . . and sitting through a service. I don't know how much I really want to do that." Without tracking these individuals over time, it is difficult to say for certain whether religious nones will affiliate or reaffiliate in the future. But as Patrick clearly stated in our opening vignette, "I don't attend and I never plan on attending again." We think the insights gleaned from interviews indicate that we should not hold our breath for many religious nones to go back to regular church involvement. Unfortunately, to the best of our knowledge, no qualitative work exists in the United States with religious nones on this "greater involvement" question. But we suspect that our findings with nones in Canada would generally hold true for nones in the United States too.

This being said, Lim, MacGregor, and Putnam (2010) as well as Hout (2017) show that a certain portion of Americans can be defined as liminal nones, meaning they move back and forth between affiliation and nonaffiliation when asked about their religion across different surveys. Hout (2017) estimates these liminals represent roughly one in five adults in the United States between 2008 and 2014. However, these studies also indicate that more and more liminals, after an initial back-and-forth period, are sticking with the "no religion" option. For some then, liminality seems to be a transitional phase to a more permanent state of having no religious preference. Yet for others, this more fluid back-and-forth grey zone that occupies the space between affiliation and nonaffiliation, and which may depend on the context these individuals find themselves in, may also be an ongoing identity negotiation that lasts a lifetime.

Additionally, in the 2008 American GSS, an estimated 19% of respondents who said they were raised with no religion also stated they belonged to a religion and attended religious services at least once a month at the time of the survey in 2008; another 18% of those with no religious background also communicated they belonged to a religion but attended religious services less frequently at the time of the survey. These reaffiliated respondents represent 4% of the religiously affiliated overall. Alongside interviewing religious nones, we interviewed those who identify with a religion and attend religious services nearly every week. Some of these individuals grew up as religious nones, experiencing irreligious socialization during their childhood before converting to Christianity. What stands out for most of these converts is that they eventually took up religious affiliation and involvement upon the invitation of a trusted friend, some of whom were converts themselves (see Stark and Bainbridge 1985, 308–9). In fact, most followed the path of first *belonging* to a religious group because of their trusted social ties, then gradually *behaving* in the expected ways of the religious group, followed by progressive *belief* in the teachings of that religious group. These interviewees did not suddenly turn to religion in response to life cycle effects (i.e., marriage or children), nor did a major life crisis initially turn them to religion (though for some a crisis would help to eventually cement their ongoing involvement in their religious group). Caleb is in his late twenties and is currently actively involved in the Catholic Church. Recalling his gradual conversion experience, Caleb pointed to a close friend of his:

> He had a pretty big influence on me . . . first of all, an example of somebody who was believing it but not living it and then changed, and, secondly, he was an influence in that he reinforced the challenge by calling me out. . . . Like, "If you believe this, then do something about it." And then the third way is just by, sort of, introducing me to the idea of going

on in these schools ... an active self-catechesis, and that's how I learned about the faith ... was going into a private Christian university college with the purpose of integrating myself into it because I knew, with all of my friends and family who weren't religious, it wasn't going to happen. And, at the same time, starting to go to ... church. ... So I was basically self-converted that way.

Catherine has recently turned thirty and works in marketing and advertising. She was first exposed to Christianity through her older sister, who attended church with her neighbors. Catherine reflected, "It was weird. Very, very accepting ... people were eager to just know about me ... they were just happy to get to know me ... versus what do I do or what can I do for them. ... I liked the singing. I liked that people were doing things, like, all together. Like, the service was all together." Now Catherine is actively involved in a conservative Protestant congregation. Fred, like Caleb and Catherine, was not raised in a religious tradition, though he was exposed to Christianity through a "girl I was chasing at a youth group." He attended for a period of time in his teen years until they broke up, and he was not involved in a religious group until later in his life when he experienced significant life upheaval associated with a divorce and substance addictions. During this period, a coworker and friend "invited me to the church for an Alpha course. ... And I went with him to that course, made a really good connection with ... my table leaders, and we're still really good friends. ... And they answered all of my questions to the best of their ability, and ... it was through that process ... that I received the Lord. ... And from then until now I have not left that church. I've remained at it."

In sharing the various narratives regarding affiliation, reaffiliation, or possible future levels of religious involvement among religious nones, we want to reiterate that such connections to and involvement with a religion may persist throughout the individual's lifetime, or may be temporary before their return to no religion; the verdict is still out and much more research is needed in this area before any answers are definitive. Still, the cumulative knowledge of survey and interview data provides us with some helpful clues.

To summarize, although disaffiliation and irreligious socialization can be powerful forces driving the growth of religious none populations

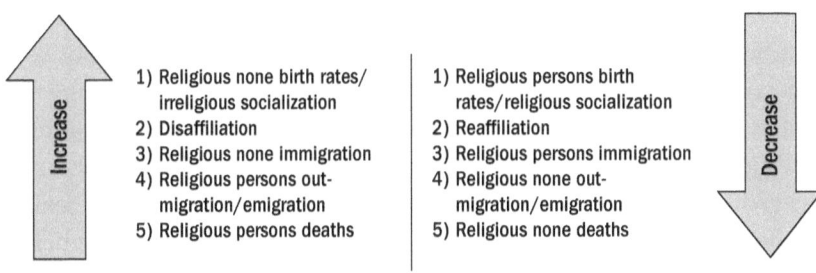

Figure 1.6. Factors influencing the proportional size of the religious none population.

in the United States and Canada, especially between the early 1970s and the late 2000s in Canada and since the early 1990s in the United States, there are also other factors at play in determining the proportional size of this group. Figure 1.6 lists the factors that contribute to either an increase or a decrease in this proportional size.

Recent Canadian Trends of Stalled None Growth

Regrettably, there is not enough existing quality data on some of the factors listed in figure 1.6 in our opinion to make solid predictions for the exact size of none populations over the next few decades in the United States and Canada: these include notably missing data on religious and nonreligious migratory patterns as well as patterns of disaffiliation and reaffiliation throughout the life cycles of individuals. This being said, we can look at some current trends in the none population as an example of these forces at play.

As we saw in figure I.1 in the introduction, the religious none population in Canada has been growing numerically and in its proportional size of the general population since at least 1985 when the GSSs began, and the beginning of this growth is usually dated to the early 1970s in Canada with the 1971 census. However, since 2010 these religious none numbers and proportions have stopped increasing, even decreasing in some recent years, and this across all Canadian regions (see figure I.3 in the introduction). According to the 2010 GSS, the overall religious none population represented an estimated 24% of Canadians; in 2016, an estimated 23%.

Why this plateauing of the none population since 2010 in Canada? A number of factors are most likely at play. As we saw in the previous sections of this chapter, these could include lower fertility rates among the nones, some reaffiliation, and arriving non-Western immigrant adults. Additionally, after four decades of disaffiliation being a strong factor in the growth of religious none populations in Canada, we may be seeing the beginnings of a slowdown in this respect. In a context where being a religious none has been socially acceptable for many decades, those individuals and families who were going to disaffiliate may have already done so, and those who are left affiliated are more willing to hold on to their religious identities—reflective of one type of polarization summarized in our introduction.

Finally, specific rates of religious nones are also somewhat sensitive to how the religious affiliation question is asked in a given survey. Prior to 1999, the Canadian GSSs asked about respondents' religion using the following question: "What is your religion?" Between 1999 and 2011, however, the question was asked, "What, if any, is your religion?"[4] Adding that small change of "if any" to the question has been shown to slightly increase the proportion of respondents who indicate they have no religion because more perceive it as a possible answer (Baker, Hill, and Porter 2016). The more recent 2012–2016 GSSs went back to the earlier "What is your religion?" format, which may be a contributing factor in why we are seeing slightly lower rates of religious none estimates in the Canadian GSS over the last few cycles. This being said, this is probably not the only reason, since with this question format between 1985 and 1998 we still saw an important increase in rates of religious nones in Canada, and these rates did decrease slightly between 2010 (24%) and 2011 (22%) when the question format was the same (including "if any" in the question).

Unfortunately, this is about as much information as can be offered at this time with these cross-sectional survey data: it is not possible with these data to pinpoint exactly which factors are having the most impact in trends and by how much. We will also have to wait for future Canadian GSS surveys to see if this plateauing trend in religious nones since 2010 will continue, much like the plateauing none proportions experienced in the US between 1998 and 2004 (see figure I.1 in the introduction), if growth will return or if the population will even begin to decline. In Canada, the religious affiliation question is also asked every ten years in the long-form census questionnaire. The last time it was asked in the 2011 National Household Survey (which replaced the 2011 long-form census) was roughly at the peak of the religious none population according to GSS estimates. We will have to wait for the 2021 long-form census to see what trends may come for the nones in Canada, and also to what extent recent GSS estimates are on the ball or may have a wider margin of error than in previous cycles in this regard.

Conclusion

There are a variety of childhood and life experiences as well as social, historical, and regional factors affecting why some people begin or continue to say they have no religion in their adult years. This chapter explored some of the main variables in this stages of decline process and how irreligious and weak religious socialization as well as the many reasons for disaffiliating are affected by wider social environments. Although these are important processes at play in the current American and Canadian contexts, which means that the religious none population will probably continue to grow over the coming years, especially in the United States, there are also countervailing demographic forces at play, which means that the whole population will probably not be engulfed by the none phenomenon. Rather, the United States and Canada are currently and will continue to be societies where both religious and nonreligious individuals, along with all the internal diversities found within these two broad categories, coexist. Stages of decline is a process present in Canada and the United States, but also does not affect everyone in the same way.

In the next chapter, we will turn to the internal diversity among religious nones. So far, the focus has been on how some individuals do away with religious labels and say they have no religion, what groups these religious nones together into one broad demographic. Nevertheless, these individuals are also characterized by a large range of their own meaning systems and in some cases spiritual beliefs and practices. Religion for the most part does not play a large role in their lives, but other things do, and we explore these next.

2

Nones of All Shapes and Sizes

As we worked on this book, we received several invitations by church groups to share some of our insights on religious nones. They wanted to first understand who the religious nones are and how they think about the world. Implicit in these questions was a desire for some to explore if there was an openness or way to turn religious nones into religious affiliates within their faith tradition. Following one of our presentations, we met a kind and pleasant church leader (whom we will call Wayne) who was very receptive to our work. During our conversation Wayne conveyed his understanding that religious nones might claim to have meaning and purpose in life apart from religion, and that they may be content not attending religious services. However, he could not shake his conviction that all people, including religious nones, have a God-shaped hole inside them—religious nones just did not label or perceive it as such. We probed Wayne further, and he shared that surely religious nones must attempt to fill this vacuum in their life with all kinds of things (e.g., exercise and healthy living, friendships, materialism, or nature) that provide them with a level of spirituality, transcendence, and meaning in life. We could tell that challenging Wayne's conviction might shake him to his core, but Wayne's theological beliefs alongside what he heard in our data reminded us of the many ways we think about what is or is not "religion" or "spirituality."

If there is one question that has caused the most exacerbation, arguments, and spillage of ink in the social scientific study of religion, it is how we define the concept of religion itself. Some, such as the nineteenth-century scholar Émile Durkheim (2008), argued that religion should be defined primarily by what it does, by its function in society: religion is what brings people together in a moral community to worship the sacred, creating and reinforcing social ties between individuals in the process. From a psychological and religious economies viewpoint, religion is the means to cope with the hardships and stresses of life; it provides comfort in the face of death and potentially offers some level of certainty and meaning in the search for answers to life's big questions (George, Ellison, and Larson 2002; Stark and Finke 2000).

Yet, many define religion instead by what it is and how it manifests itself. We adopt this more substantive understanding of religion throughout this book, with a special focus on how individuals live and experience nonreligion. Even with a more substantive definition though, religion can mean many things. When talking about religion, and nonreligion, some refer to (not)belonging to a religious group or tradition; others, to (not) believing certain things related to the supernatural and the transcendent; others still, to rituals and practices that symbolize and reinforce this faith. Religion is a multidimensional concept in this sense, defined notably by belonging, believing, and behavior (Leege and Kellstedt 1993; Smidt, Kellstedt, and Guth 2009; Voas 2007; Wald and Wilcox 2006).

When we use the term "religious nones" in sociology, we are often grouping individuals together according to their nonbelonging in terms of religion. In this sense, religious nones are similar on the dimension of religious belonging, in that they have none. There is some diversity among the nones in exactly how they define themselves: some are atheists, humanists, secularists, freethinkers, agnostics, spiritual but not religious (SBNR), or nothing in particular. However, they do all say they have no religion. As we saw in the previous chapter, some are steadfast in this nonbelonging, saying they have no religion whenever the question is put to them; others are liminal nones who may change their answer depending on the context and where they are in their life cycle.

Nevertheless, even though they do not see themselves as belonging to a religion, some nones do hold beliefs about the supernatural world and will even at times take part in religious or spiritual activities. The three dimensions of religious belonging, believing and behavior, are at times intertwined, but not always. Not all those who belong to a religion and believe in God or a higher power take part in regular religious practice, for example. Similarly, some nones may believe without belonging (BWB), as sociologist Grace Davie has shown in her work (1994, 2000), or may be more spiritual than religious (Ammerman 2014; Chandler 2008; Drescher 2016; Fuller 2001; Heelas and Woodhead 2005; Houtman and Aupers 2007; Roof 1999; Stark, Hamburg, and Miller 2004; Watts 2018). Nones come in all shapes and sizes.

The goal of this chapter is to explore this internal diversity among the nones when it comes to their beliefs, their meaning systems, and their religious or spiritual behavior: (1) to establish different types of nones according to their believing and behavior, or lack thereof, and to estimate how large these different types of nones are in Canada and the United States; (2) to measure how the composition of these subgroups among the nones vary across age groups and regions in the United States and Canada; and (3) to grasp what this all actually looks like when interviewees describe their own experiences. Religious nones may be on the rise in the United States and Canada, but that does not necessarily mean all forms of religiosity and spirituality are disappearing entirely from the landscape.

Before examining these matters, we want to highlight the challenges associated with terminology here. Terms such as religious "nones," "irreligion," or "(non)religion" tend to implicitly or explicitly normalize religious belonging, belief, or behavior. Ryan Cragun and Joseph Hammer (2011) helpfully document various language constraints among scholars who have studied these phenomena over the years. In the end, we agree with Cragun and Hammer that "religious none" is the most appropriate and expansive term to capture the concept in mind—those who do not identify with a religion—without any intent to normalize religion or pejoratively characterize religious nones as deviant in any way. We agree with sociologist Lois Lee (2015) who argues that rather than looking at nonreligion as a deficit and subtraction-based narrative, we should look at this subject through a positive and addition-based lens. Research is clear that saying one has no religion is a positive descriptor for many. For example, scholars document individuals who joyfully convert *toward* the religious none identifier, rather than speaking of de-converting or dis-affiliating (Altemeyer and Hunsberger 1997; Bullivant 2008b; LeDrew 2013; Wright et al. 2011; Zuckerman 2012, 133–38). Our task in this chapter, therefore, is to understand better the range of spiritual and secular beliefs and practices that religious nones adopt, and the degree to which these are salient in their lives.

Believing without Belonging

Figure 2.1 contains the percentages of religious nones and the religiously affiliated in the United States who hold various beliefs, as measured by the 2014 Pew Religious Landscape Study (Pew Research Center 2014b) and the 2014 General Social Survey (National Opinion Research Center 2017). Belief in God or a universal spirit is virtually a universal phenomenon among the religiously affiliated in the United States and is also held by a majority (64%) of religious nones. Although 36% of nones in the United States do not believe in God or a universal spirit, only 13% actually refer to themselves as atheists. Among those who do believe in God or a universal spirit, 81% of these nones say they are absolutely or fairly certain in this belief, compared with 96% of affiliated believers. Just over half (52%) of nones in the United States believe in life after death, with fewer believing specifically in heaven (41%) or hell (29%). Nevertheless, most American nones (74%) view the Bible as having been written by men, rather than being the word of God.

Good-quality data on the rates of belief in Canada are more difficult to come by. In an opinion poll on faith in Canada conducted by Cardus and the Angus Reid Institute (Angus Reid Institute 2017b), 72% of the 657 religious none respondents made known they did not believe in God or a higher power, and 68% noted they did not believe in life after death. In his book *Resilient Gods* (2017), Reginald Bibby distinguishes between three groups of Canadians: those who embrace religion, those who reject religion, and those somewhere in the middle. Although those who say they have no religion are found in all three of these groups, they are disproportionately (71%) found among those who reject religion. Thirteen percent of these religious rejecters say they definitely believe in God or a higher power, 21% think God or a higher power exists, and 19% believe they have been protected by a guardian angel—figures disproportionately lower than those in the "middle" or "embrace" categories (Bibby 2017, 66–67, 74).

In an older 2006 Canadian CROP opinion poll, 32% of the 430 religious none respondents reported they believed in God, another 32% said they believed we are all part of a mysterious and inexplicable force, and another 36% suggested they believed that life on Earth is a purely physical and biological phenomenon. Figure 2.2 contains these rates as well as other types of beliefs among the religiously affiliated and unaffiliated in Canada. Important to note here with the Canadian data is that not only do religious nones have a higher rate of belief in a material worldview than the religiously affiliated (a belief that life on Earth is a purely physical and biological phenomenon) but also they have a higher

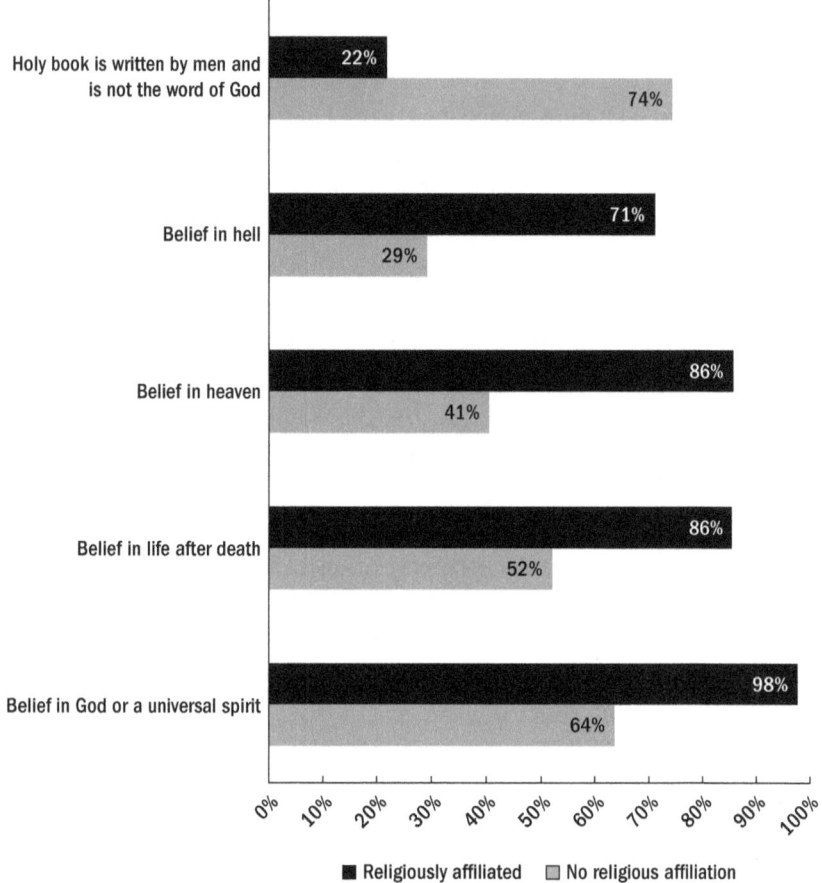

Figure 2.1. Rates of belief, USA, 2014. *Source:* (1) 2014 Pew Religious Landscape Study. N = 32,636 (hell); 34,244 (God or a universal spirit). (2) 2014 General Social Survey (for belief in life after death). N = 2,242. All estimates weighted to be representative of the general American population.

rate of belief in extraterrestrials: 47% among nones compared with 31% among the religiously affiliated. This highlights the fact that nones who do not hold traditional religious beliefs are nonetheless not devoid of beliefs altogether but rather in some cases hold alternative views and understandings of the universe.

Fortunately, many great qualitative studies have emerged in the United States of late to give us insight into what religious beliefs nones hold on to and what those beliefs mean to them (Ammerman 2014; Bengtson, Putney, and Harris 2013; Drescher 2016; Manning 2015; Zuckerman 2012). Our interview data in Canada also provides insight into how religious nones make sense of some of their beliefs. Adelaide is in her midtwenties. She has lived in several cities across western Canada. She grew up attending a Jewish synagogue with her mother and

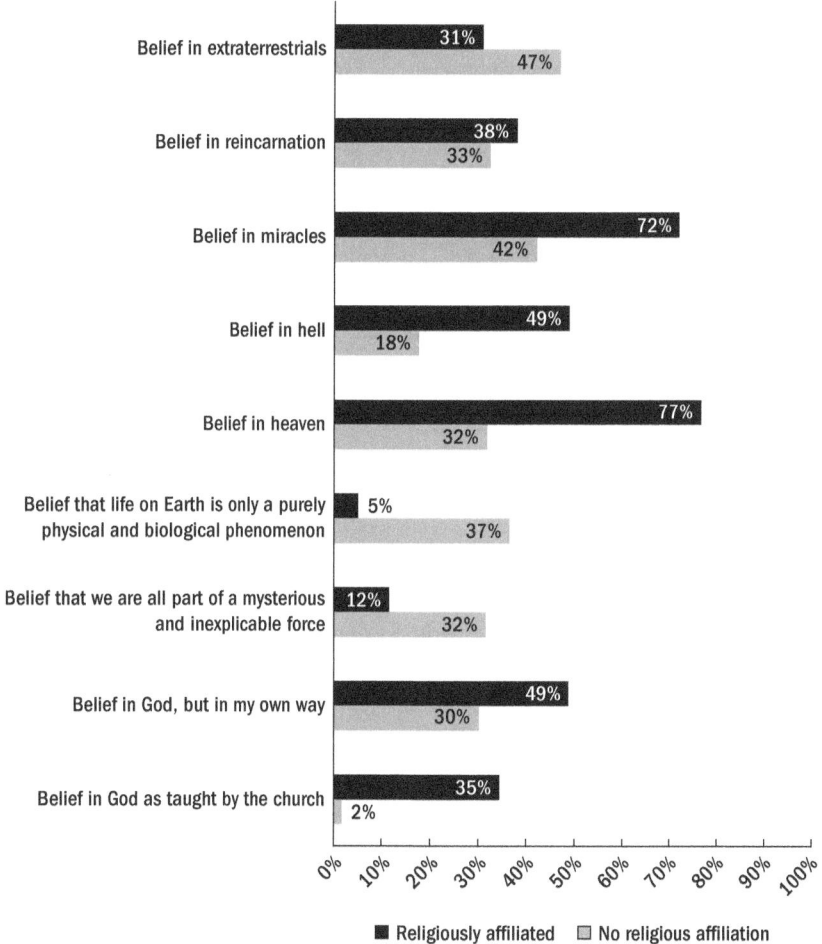

Figure 2.2. Rates of belief, Canada, 2006. *Source:* 2006 CROP survey on religious beliefs. N = 2,678. All estimates weighted to be representative of the Canadian general population.

grandmother from time to time but does not describe herself or her family as particularly religious growing up. Now married, and considering attending university to become a teacher, she said, "When someone asks me . . . 'are you religious' . . . I say one hundred percent I'm not religious, but I definitely believe in God." When probed on what this distinction means to her, reflective of other interviewees, Adelaide talked about the many good things to come from religious groups: "But what happens is that people get involved in religion and . . . make it really bad and really nasty." Later in the interview Adelaide asserted, "I think that we just couldn't have come out of nothing. I think that there's too many things that have happened, especially in my life and my friend's life . . . have happened for a reason, and you've been guided that way." She proceeded to share a story of how she ran into her now husband, an old friend that she had not seen in years, while visiting another city. She attributed that encounter to more than mere luck. Adelaide said she does not pray, but she said, "I do believe in . . . heaven, and I do believe in . . . hell . . . just be a good person, and good things are going to happen to you. Be a bad person, and bad things are going to happen to you."

Some are less confident about what they do or do not believe in. Janice, the retail worker in her midthirties whom we introduced in the last chapter, only attended a handful of religious services as a child upon invitation by friends or extended family. Currently married to someone who identifies as Catholic, and whose two children attend Catholic school, Janice acknowledged her confusion and uncertainty surrounding religious beliefs and rituals: "When it comes to the holidays, like Thanksgiving and Christmas and Easter, I don't even really understand what they're all about. . . . I know it's Jesus' birthday . . . and I know that he was born and . . . Easter . . . the dying on the cross and the resurrection. I sort of get it, but not really. . . . I'd need someone to explain that to me." Janice partially attributed her uncertainty to her lack of religious upbringing. She does believe in the afterlife, however, which "gives me a little bit of peace" when thinking of loved ones who have passed away.

Lorraine was born in England and moved to Canada at a young age, occasionally attending the Anglican Church with her siblings (not her parents) throughout her childhood years. Now in her sixties, Lorraine said she believes "in a higher force. . . . I wouldn't call it God in the way that most people would define God . . . I just feel like there has to be something outside of what happens on Earth. I do feel that we have a life force within us and when we die, that life force is released, and that it may or may not come back in another form. I don't believe in heaven or hell. I don't have a lot of strong beliefs . . . it's a little ambiguous for me, to be honest."

Indicative of some who hold less conventional beliefs, Faye, a registered nurse in her fifties, shared two stories connected to her belief in ghosts. The first was of an inebriated homeless person that she saw coming toward her, where she thought to herself, "She's going to bump into me and fall down and it's going to be embarrassing . . . so I sort of veered to avoid her bumping into me." Moments later the individual that Faye sidestepped was killed in a car accident. Faye described how a few nights later the individual who died "came to my room at night and I could see her and I guess I felt more guilty subconsciously . . . if I had only just not worried, I would have helped her or bumped into her and she wouldn't have got run over . . . then she came to my room and she didn't say anything but it was obviously her and she was just this sort of form and it was kind of dark but I just thought, she just came so that I wouldn't feel guilty anymore." Faye went on to share a story of an extended family member whose spouse recently passed away "and left things financially in a real mess. And she said she was sitting up in bed one night and . . . about a week after he died . . . and he came and actually spoke to her . . . he just said, if you need the papers for the house, they're in this drawer and he was just telling her some very practical things and she said it was wonderful."

Many nones then hold some religious or spiritual beliefs, notably in God or a higher power. However, as shown in figures 2.3 and 2.4, they often do not consider these beliefs as all that important for other aspects of their lives. In the 2010 General Social Survey, an estimated 67% of American nones indicated that they do not try to carry their beliefs into other aspects of their lives. Similarly, in Canada for the same year an estimated 67% of nones declared that religious or spiritual beliefs were not very or not at all important to how they live their lives. In line with qualitative research among some religious nones in the United States (Ammerman 2014; Manning 2015), our interviews with religious nones reveal similar sentiments, with interviewees saying something along the lines of "little to no influence." Interestingly, when we slightly pivot this

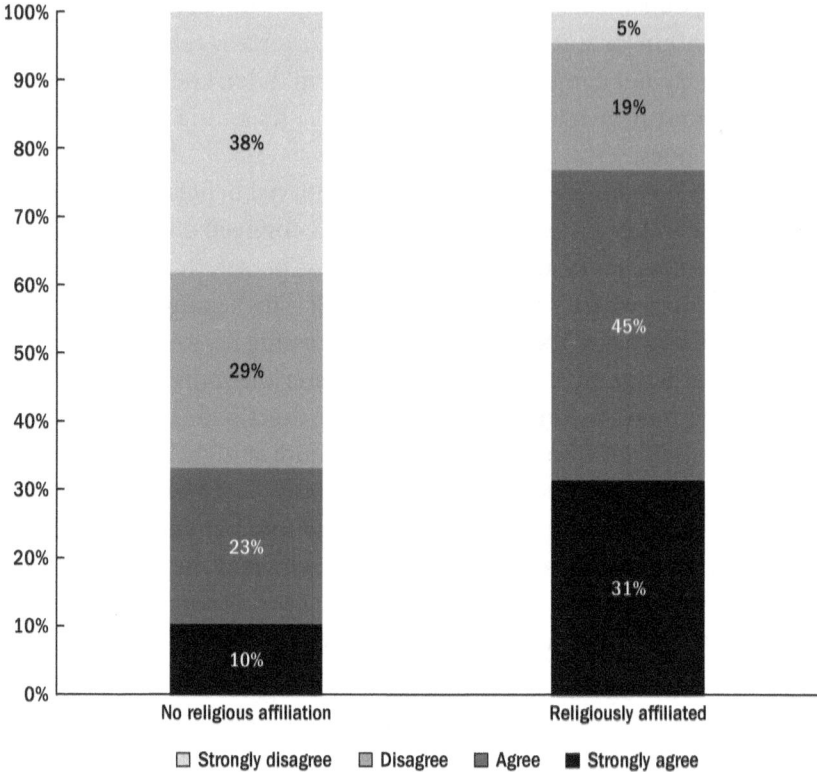

Figure 2.3. Try to carry beliefs into other dealings, USA, 2010. *Source:* 2010 USA General Social Survey. N = 2,003. All estimates weighted to be representative of general populations.

question to focus on how important their secular identity and worldview is to their lives, we received similar responses by interviewees. It seems, therefore, that overall, neither their identity as religious nones nor their various (non)religious beliefs and behaviors have any significant status in their lives. This is very different from those who identify with a religion and are actively involved in their faith, for whom religious belief, behavior, and belonging serve as key reference points in many areas of their life (see Thiessen 2015). The main exception for religious nones is likely in social contexts where they are a minority surrounded by very devout, typically conservative, religious groups—a subject we return to later in this chapter.

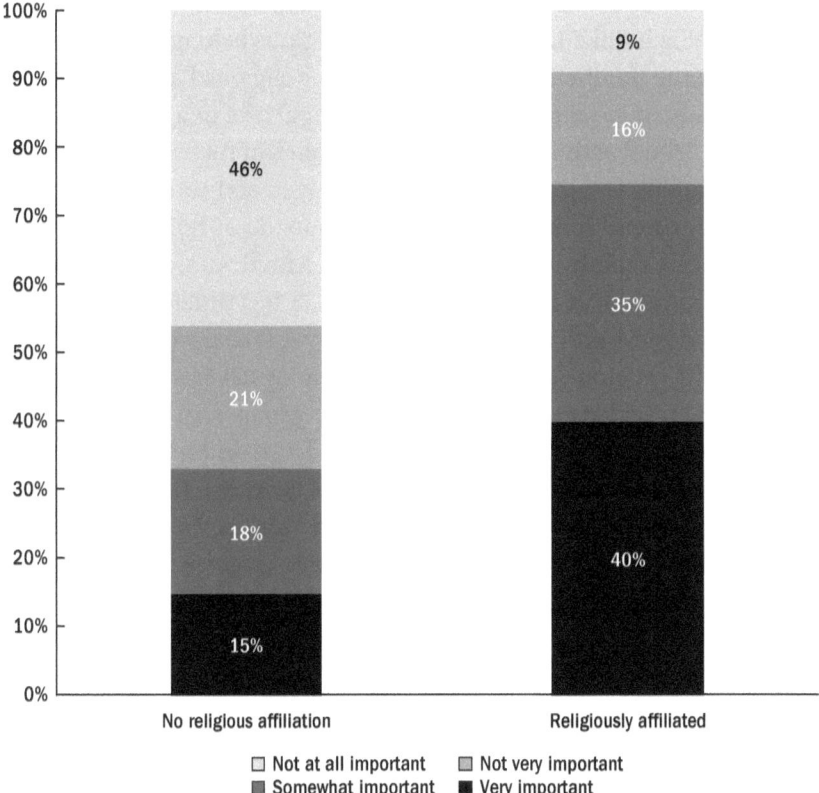

Figure 2.4. Importance of religious or spiritual beliefs in life, Canada, 2010. *Source:* 2010 Canadian General Social Survey. N = 14,653. All estimates weighted to be representative of general populations.

Religious and Spiritual Behavior without Belonging

The findings in the previous section show that, although some individuals choose not to belong to a religious group or tradition, many can and do hold religious or spiritual beliefs. In both the United States and Canada, for example, just under two-thirds of nones say they believe in God, in a higher power, in a universal spirit, or in an inexplicable force. The dimensions of believing and belonging do not always go hand in hand, although when belonging is present believing tends to follow: only 2% of the religiously affiliated in the United States in 2014 and 5% in Canada in 2006 did not believe in any form of higher power.

What then of the dimension of religious and spiritual behavior? To what extent is it linked, or not, solely to religious belonging? Figure 2.5 contains some numbers from the 2014 Pew Religious Landscape Study on how frequently religious nones say they partake in a variety of religious or spiritual activities. A handful of nones in the United States do attend religious services; participate in prayer, scripture, or religious education groups; and/or read scripture outside of religious services at least once a month. Additionally, 19% of American nones attend religious services on an infrequent basis (i.e., a few times a year). However, for the most part nones seldom or never take part in these more traditionally religious activities: 72% seldom or never attend religious services; 89% seldom or never take part in group activities related to prayer, scripture, or religious education; and 79% seldom or never read scripture outside of the context of religious services. This said, prayer and meditation are more common among nones than activities specifically linked to a religious group or tradition: 31% of American nones say they pray at least once a week, and another 7% a few times a month; 36% say they meditate at least once a month, and another 5% a few times a year.

The data on religious and spiritual behavior among the nones are not as rich in Canada as they are in the United States, but Statistics Canada's 2014 General Social Survey does give us some information in this regard (illustrated in figure 2.6). As with American nones, among Canadian nones regular attendance at religious services is extremely rare: only 2% of Canadian nones revealed they attended religious services at least once a month in 2014 (compared with 9% among nones in the United States). Seventeen percent of Canadian nones attend less frequently, and 81% not at all. Canadian nones are distinct from their American counterparts in their very low levels of religious or spiritual practice on their own, practices such as prayer and meditation: only 9% of Canadian nones divulged they undertake such practices at least once a week, only 8% less frequently, and 82% not at all. Bibby (2017, 74) documents comparable figures and trends in the aforementioned areas, including only 8% of those who "reject" religion saying table grace and only 6% reading a sacred text at least monthly. Consequently, whereas regular activities linked with religious groups are quite uncommon among both American and Canadian nones, forms of more personal spiritual activity such

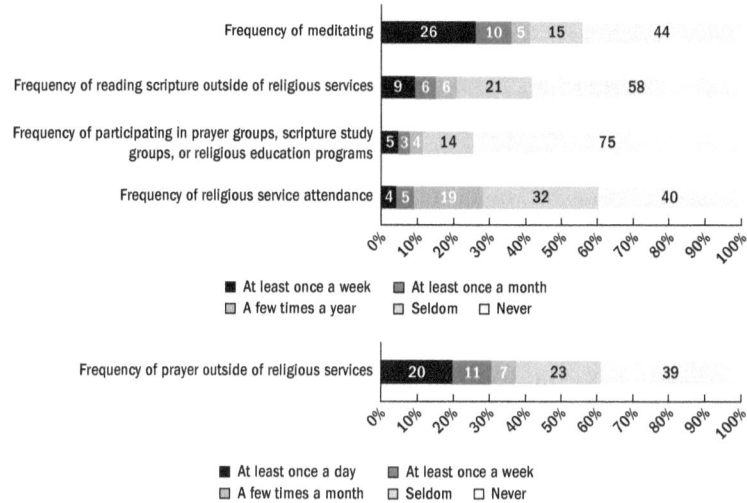

Figure 2.5. Frequency of different religious and spiritual practices, among religious nones, USA, 2014. *Source:* 2014 Pew Religious Landscape Study. N = 7,480 (meditation); 7,537 (prayer group). All estimates weighted to be representative of the USA general population.

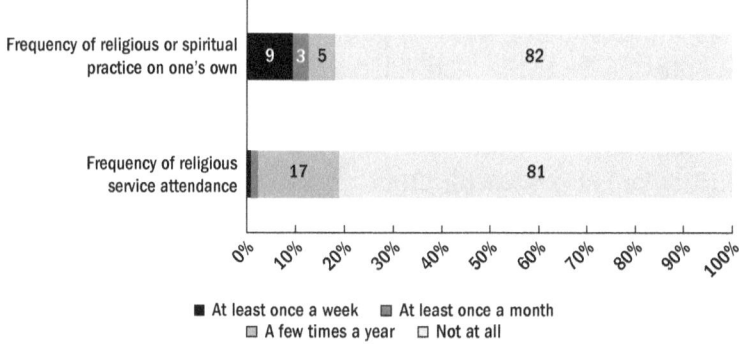

Figure 2.6. Frequency of different religious and spiritual practices, among religious nones, Canada, 2014. *Source:* 2014 Canadian General Social Survey. N = 5,600. All estimates weighted to be representative of the Canadian general population.

as prayer and meditation seem to be absent among a larger majority of nones in the Canadian context.

When we turn to interviews with religious nones, it is similarly difficult to find many concrete examples of ongoing or even sporadic religious or spiritual behavior. The same is true for some of the other qualitative research with religious nones, though a few studies stand out that do give us a better sense of religious or spiritual practices among nones (see Ammerman 2014; Drescher 2016; Lee 2015; Manning 2015). On the rare occasion when we did encounter such activity with Canadian interviewees, it was more commonly found among those raised in a religious tradition. At the same time, religious none interviewees most frequently distanced these activities from explicitly "religious" motivations or interpretations, possibly in an effort to create further space from their former religious selves.

As initially discussed in the introduction of this book, former Evangelical Darlene acknowledged attending the occasional Christmas service when she visits her mother. But she was quick to note, "I don't enjoy it." She also watches the Gaither Vocal Band on television on occasion, for the "harmony," not the lyrics, which she has a "hard time believing a lot of times."

Others like Louis, whom we saw in the previous chapter diminished his level of involvement in the Roman Catholic Church following his father's death, only attends religious services when others invite him, "just to support them, not really for me." However, Louis said he prays or gives "affirmations or thinking positive thoughts for somebody else, hoping the best for them . . . if you're thinking about somebody that's struggling or something like that, to me it's more, I hope the best for you." Peter, a lapsed Danish Lutheran who works in construction, is in his thirties and also prays for others in a similar vein to Louis. When Peter was asked to describe any other religious practices in his life, such as reading the Bible or other religious texts, he joked, "I haven't picked up a Bible since I was at a hotel . . . when I was twenty-one years old . . . it was in my way and I had to move it to get the phone book." He added, somewhat reluctantly, that he still attends an annual witch-burning ceremony connected to his Danish Lutheran roots. Acknowledging that he knows little about the religious or cultural significance of this ritual, he attended "for the party atmosphere. There's a lot of drinking and a lot of dancing, and it's just like a big party afterwards. And also partly for my kids' sake because they had a lot of games and they gave medals."

Kathy's narrative is slightly different. She grew up actively involved in the Anglican Church with her mother, while her father (United Church of Canada background) stayed at home with Kathy's brothers. Kathy's involvement faded during university as she focused on her studies. Kathy, now in her late fifties, no longer attends religious services regularly, but her husband (Catholic) does along with their children. Kathy will occasionally attend to watch her children in a church performance. This said, Kathy did attend church after her father died:

> I was struggling a little bit . . . and was trying to find . . . [a] place where I could sort of express that. And so I got to church for a short period of time, but it . . . wasn't for very long. And it just kinda seemed to help me through that moment . . . probably [giving] me a place to sit and think . . . and so if you want to call that praying, I guess you could, without the distractions of the world around me. I had two . . . kids at that point in time, both very young. Was really busy with work. And it just carved out a place where I could go, and sit, and think. You know, spend some time dealing with him, and his life, and his death.

Toward a More Substantive Understanding of the Nonreligious

From what we can measure with the survey data studied here, believing without belonging seems to be the most common phenomenon among nones in Canada and the United States, much more so than religious behavior, even more personal spiritual behavior, without belonging. On the one hand, Davie's BWB framework states that this will be the norm for the foreseeable future: in contemporary Western societies, promoting values of individual authenticity and consumerism, many will draw on a number of beliefs from a variety of sources to build and maintain their own personalized faith systems to fulfill their fundamental human needs for meaning and understanding, and will do so outside of church doors. On the other hand, the stages of decline framework, while not denying that this BWB exists, only sees this phenomenon as a temporary one, as a stepping stone toward greater declines of religion. Beliefs in the supernatural or transcendent require the least amount of practical effort from individuals, and endure the longest, even once religious and spiritual belonging and behavior have been abandoned. Yet, with no structured, institutional support for these beliefs and with many parents emphasizing antiauthoritarian styles of parenting in which they provide their children with choice in the matter, these types of beliefs become more difficult to pass on to the next generation (Bruce 2011; Manning 2015; Thiessen 2016; Voas and Crockett 2005). The need for religious or spiritual beliefs as the main sources of meaning and understanding is thus seen as socially constructed according to this framework (Bruce 2011): learnt during a child's upbringing and from the surrounding social environment, but not necessarily present in more secular contexts. We will return to this debate when we look at the different types of religious nones and their cohort trends later in this chapter.

Yet, despite the current prevalence of the BWB phenomenon in the United States and Canada, there is also a substantial portion of religious nones who are nonbelievers. Looking more specifically at the 36% of nones who say they do not believe in God or a universal spirit in 2014 in the United States (an estimated 20.8 million adults in 2014) and at the 36% of nones who think that life on Earth is purely a physical and biological phenomenon in 2006 in Canada (an estimated 2 million adults in 2006), the religious or spiritual behaviors that we can measure with our survey data are virtually nonexistent among these nonbelievers. Consequently, among the wider category of religious nones who have no religious belonging, we find this core group who have no belonging, no believing, and no religious or spiritual behavior: the nonreligious.

In recent years, there has been a burgeoning body of literature that aims to develop a more substantive understanding of these nonreligious (Beaman and Tomlins 2015; Bullivant and Lee 2012; Cimino and Smith 2014; LeDrew 2015; Lee 2015; Niose 2012; Schmidt 2016; Smith 2011; Taylor 2007; Zuckerman, Galen, and Pasquale 2016). In the new subfield of nonreligion and secular studies, researchers want to understand the nonreligious not by what they are not (religious) but by what they actually are—to move away from simple "subtraction stories" as philosopher Charles Taylor names them (2007). How do the nonreligious see and understand the world? What do they belong to, if not to a religious group or tradition? What kinds of activities do they partake in?

As we noted earlier in discussing Wayne, many who are more actively involved with religion often hold a stereotypical view of these nonreligious individuals as amoral persons lost and in search of meaning—empty vessels with no proper sense of right or wrong aimlessly and unhappily wandering the desert, waiting to be fulfilled. However, when researchers have actually interviewed nonreligious individuals, they have found that, more often than not, this view is far removed from reality (Drescher 2016; LeDrew 2015; Smith 2011). For example, religious none interviewees repeatedly conveyed that they have meaning and purpose in life. Some admitted that there are times when this is harder to come by, typically associated with stage of life realities such as in their late teen and early adult years, but overall they experience meaning and purpose through their family, relationships, and jobs. Importantly, many maintain that they, not God or a supernatural being, are responsible for bringing about this life meaning and purpose. Recalling from the last chapter, Dustin was raised in a home with an atheist father and a very scientific outlook on the world. Dustin believed "we create our own purpose . . . to contribute to the world." Unsurprisingly, survey findings by the Angus Reid Institute (2015, 14) reveal that those who "reject" religion are the most likely to attribute things like their own efforts (93%), chance (47%), or luck (35%) to determining their life outcome, versus God (8%; see also Speed, Coleman III, and Langston 2018). Other interviewees offered more general statements that "everything happens for a reason," without clearly delineating who or what is the source of life's connections. Further, when asked if they think they lack meaning, purpose, or direction in life because they do not identify with a religion or are not actively involved with a religious group, nearly all religious nones categorically responded no.

These observations are further reinforced in other survey data. Looking once again at the 2014 Pew Religious Landscape Study, 86% of the 2,860 American religious none respondents who do not believe in God or a universal spirit say they nevertheless feel a strong sense of gratitude and thankfulness in their lives at least a few times a year; 78% feel a deep sense of wonder about the universe at least a few times a year; and 67% still think about the meaning and purpose of life at least a few times a year. Among Canadians who say they "reject" religion, 69% say they often or sometimes think about the purpose of life, and 63% say they often or sometimes think about what happens after death (Bibby 2017, 83).

Of course, thinking about meaning, purpose, and understanding on the one hand and turning to religion for answers on the other are two different things. How do the nonreligious interpret and find meaning in the world around them? Science, scientific knowledge, and curiosity seem to play a big role in many of these individuals' worldview (Baker 2012; Cimino and Smith 2014; LeDrew 2015; Smith 2011; Zuckerman, Galen, and Pasquale 2016). As an indication of this in existing survey data, most nonreligious have a more positive view of the role of science in our lives. Eighty-five percent of the 136 respondents in the 2010 American GSS who say they have no religion and either do not believe in God or do not think there is any way of knowing disagree or strongly disagree that modern science does more harm than good, compared with only 55% among those respondents who are certain God exists. Seventy-five percent of the 102 nonbeliever or agnostic nones in the 2008 American GSS disagree or strongly disagree that we trust too much in science, compared with only 29% among those who are certain God exists.

For many nonreligious, especially self-identified atheists, science already has most of the answers to the ultimate concerns, such as where life comes from, what the meaning and purpose of life is, what it means to lead a good life, what happens to us after we die, and so forth. Like many other atheists interviewed, Faye, the individual we introduced earlier who believes in ghosts, also believes firmly in science: "I'm an atheist . . . I don't believe there's anything more than science and nature." For the answers that science does not already have, either there is confidence that science will have them in the not-so-distant future or there is belief that the answers are just not worth having in the first place. This does not mean that all nonreligious individuals have an in-depth knowledge and understanding of how every physical, biological, and social process works in the world around us, but many of them do hold the view that it is these processes, and only these processes, that are fundamentally at play. This scientific view is documented via qualitative research with nones in the United States as well (Zuckerman 2012).

Take the scenario of two people going for a walk in the woods together in the Rocky Mountains. Person A is actively involved in their local church and has a strong deep-seated belief in God. Person B does not belong to a religious group or tradition, does not believe in any aspect of the supernatural or transcendent, and self-identifies as an atheist. On the one hand, Person A will see and understand the natural beauty of the trees, the creeks, the lakes, the wildflowers, the wildlife, and the mountains around them as a gift from God—as incredible, wonderful, awe-inspiring, and even magical because of this. Person A does not know, and will never presume to know, how God did it, but this person fundamentally attributes all that is around them to him. Person B on the other hand will see and understand this same natural beauty around them as fundamentally the product of biological evolution, of cooperation and competition between species, with an element of chance involved. Person B will not necessarily know all the details and specific physical and biological forces at play for everything that is around them but is fairly confident that she or he could access or uncover this scientific knowledge if she or he wanted or needed to. Yet, for person B the end product of these processes that is the natural world around them is still no less incredible, full of wonder, and awe-inspiring. That evolution and chance could lead to something so beautiful and complex is in a way its "magical" character for person B. It is not surprising then, as we will uncover in greater detail shortly, that organizations such as Sunday Assembly—a "secular congregation that celebrates life"—use the phrase "wonder more" as one of its anchoring principles.

These are two very different views of the world, but both provide meaning and understanding to their respective adherents, and both are present among contemporary Americans and Canadians. To what extent a more scientific worldview is held by most or only some of the nonreligious is a question at the cutting edge of the research being conducted in nonreligion and secular studies.

Secular humanism and morality appear to be another source of guidance for many of the nonreligious (Ammerman 2014; Cimino and Smith 2007; Drescher 2016; LeDrew 2015; Smith 2011; Thiessen 2015; Zuckerman 2012; Zuckerman, Galen, and Pasquale 2016). For these individuals, although religion is one possible source of morality in our society, it is not the only source, and morality and religion do not necessarily go hand in hand (Sumerau and Cragun 2016). For example, Bibby's (2017, 68) summary of those who "reject" religion reveals that they are the most likely to maintain that it is not necessary to go to church (95%) or to believe in God (91%) to be moral and have good values. Not all people involved with a religious group are moral persons, some doing things that most would consider evil or bad, and most nonreligious people are not amoral persons. From more than one hundred interviews conducted with religious nones in the United States, Elizabeth Drescher (2016) shows that most seem to go by the Golden Rule, treating those around them as they would themselves, as a way of understanding what a good person is (see also Ammerman 2014). This can be done either through their daily interactions with others or in some cases by being part of larger social justice and welfare initiatives. We find similar observations among many interviewees in the Canadian context too. For instance, Kathy, who grew up actively involved in the Anglican Church as we learned earlier this chapter, claimed she always tries to "act ethically." When asked how she knows what the right or wrong thing to do is in any given situation, Kathy responded, "The sense is sometimes it's gut. Sometimes you just know it's not right. Sometimes . . . it's dictated by social standards around me. But a lot of it is around, 'Well, this is how . . . this was what feels good to me. I feel right about it. I can sleep at night and know I've made the right decision or done the right thing.'" However, many of the nones in Drescher's and our studies disassociate the Golden Rule from Christianity and religion. They see this way of interacting with other individuals as predating religion, as something that humankind has developed over time due to its biological and social necessity for human survival and flourishing—religion just being one manifestation of this and one way (not always the best way) of passing on this rule to the next generation.

Some—not many (Zuckerman, Galen, and Pasquale 2016, 197–226)—of the nonreligious are part of atheist, humanist, or secularist organizations, such as the American Humanist Association, American Atheists, Humanist Canada, and Sunday Assembly, in order to build, reinforce, and share their views and nonreligious identities with other like-minded individuals (Cimino and Smith 2014; LeDrew 2015; Smith 2013, 2017). Later when we develop a series of subtypes within the religious none camp, we will review some of the key findings on those connected to groups such as these. For now, it is noteworthy to us that many nonreligious do not adopt the identity label of atheist, humanist, or secularist when asked. Among the 2,860 respondents in the 2014 Pew Religious Landscape Study who say they have no religion and do not believe in God or a universal spirit, only 36% call themselves atheists or humanists; 22% say instead they are agnostics, and 42% say they are "nothing in particular." In 2017 survey data from the Canadian province of British Columbia

(Pacific Northwest Social Survey 2017),[1] 21% of the 244 respondents who say they have no religion and do not believe in God or a higher power also say they are an atheist, humanist, or secularist, compared with 28% who say they are agnostics, 22% who say they are spiritual with no religion, and 25% who say they are nothing in particular.

We argue that there are two central reasons for this limited adoption of atheist, humanist, or secularist labels, particularly the atheist descriptor, among nonbelievers. First, some are simply indifferent toward these labels, and toward issues surrounding religion, spirituality, and antitheism in general. This is particularly pronounced for those with an irreligious upbringing where parents took a hands-off approach to fostering explicit religious or secular identity, attitudes or behaviors in their children. There are a growing number of studies indicating that this indifferent group makes up a larger proportion of religious nones in Western societies, and the marginally affiliated for that matter (Bagg and Voas 2010; Zuckerman, Galen, and Pasquale 2016). These individuals simply do not think a whole lot about matters related to religion and nonreligion, and do not feel the need to either. The main focus in their lives, and main sources of meaning, appear to be what Drescher (2016) identifies as the four Fs from her many interviews with American nones: family, friends, fido (their pets), and food.

A second reason the nonreligious may not identify with the atheist label in particular is that this word conjures up a negative stigma, especially in the United States, though also noted by some interviewees in the Canadian context (Cragun et al. 2012; Pasquale 2007; Thiessen 2015). This stigma cuts in a couple of directions, including associations with "new atheists" like Richard Dawkins who seem rather aggressive and close-minded for some people's preferences, as well as a pervasive distrust among many Americans toward atheists (Edgell, Gerteis, and Hartmann 2006; Gervais, Norenzayan, and Shariff 2011; Hammer et al. 2012).

Subtypes of Religious Nones

If we think of religiosity as a multidimensional spectrum on which individuals can be anywhere from actively religious and faithful to nonreligious (nonbelieving, nonbelonging, and nonpracticing), this means that religious nones, although usually finding themselves closer to the nonreligious end of the continuum, may also be at various distances from that pole. If our research in this book were only theoretical, we could simply stick to this multidimensional continuum and work to adapt it to the nonreligion context. However, because we also want to measure some of the empirical realities related to different ways of being a religious none, we also need to develop practical measures and types within the various spectrums that can be used with survey and interview data to give us an idea of where American and Canadian nones find themselves on the continuum. Consequently, we aim to group nones into a number of subtypes, despite there always being limits to such typologies due to the variables used, the boundaries drawn between categories, and the difficulty in measuring fluidity between each category.

Despite these inherent difficulties, Joseph Baker and Buster Smith's (2015, 104) sociological research, for example, in the United States has already begun developing subtypes of nones: "Atheists tend to be the most secular overall, rejecting religion and supernaturalism more completely. Agnostics are less opposed to religion in toto than atheists, with greater openness to privatized spirituality. Agnostics are also less opposed to organized religion than both atheists and nonaffiliated believers. Nonaffiliated believers are more likely to be 'spiritual but not religious,' drawing firmer distinctions between organized religion and privatized spirituality." Building on our results so far in this chapter, from the survey data we have been analyzing we can identify a range of nones (see figure 2.7).

Although nones all find themselves at the nonbelonging end of one spectrum, they do find themselves at different points on the other believing (in supernatural agents) and behavior (linked to their worldview) continuums. We see five main subtypes of religious nones overall: (1) *involved seculars*, which includes nonbelievers who participate in organized atheist, humanist, and secularist communities (e.g., Sunday Assembly); (2) *inactive nonbelievers*, who do not believe in God or a higher power (including agnostics) and only consider themselves as slightly or not at all spiritual but are also not involved in any atheist, humanist, or secularist organizations; (3) *inactive believers*, who do believe in God or a higher power but attend religious services less than once a month and consider themselves only slightly or not at all spiritual; (4) *spiritual but not religious*, who define themselves as very or

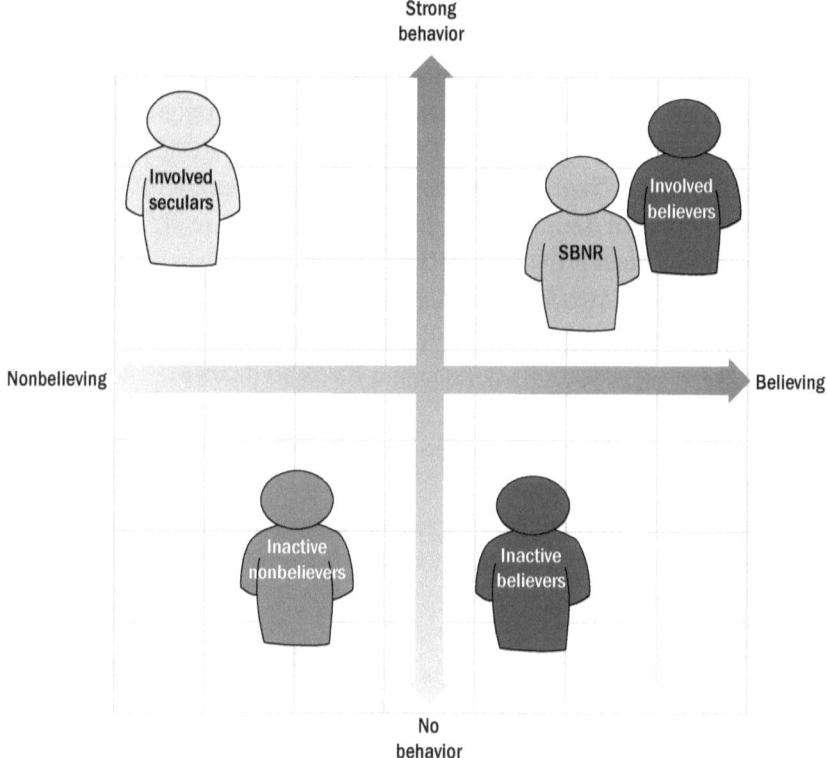

Figure 2.7. Subtypes of religious nones along believing and behavior spectrums.

moderately spiritual persons but attend religious services less than once a month; and finally, (5) *involved believers*, who do believe in God or a higher power and do attend religious services at least once a month.

Of these five subtypes, two have received more attention in the literature than others: involved secular nones and the spiritual but not religious. We summarize some of the key findings to date for these two groups, as a way to set up our discussion of the estimates and trends of the different subtypes of nones across the United States and Canada.

Involved Seculars

As referenced earlier, some religious nones across the United States and Canada actively participate in atheist, humanist, or secularist organizations, in face-to-face contexts as well as virtual ones. The primary goals are to gather with others who think similarly about the world, to reinforce their shared nonbelieving worldview, and in some cases, to actively oppose the influence and spread of religion in society (see Niose 2012).

We know that such organizations have risen in prominence and profile in the last couple of decades or so, in part due to the rise of "new atheist" authors, alongside a growing reaction against religiously motivated extremism around the world. But underneath, two opposing environmental hypotheses arise in the literature to explain the growing involvement in these types of organizations (Garcia and Blankholm 2016).

H1: Nonreligious organizations most commonly arise where larger concentrations of religious nones exist.

Alternatively, H2: These groups emerge more frequently where religious nones are a notable minority, particularly relative to a substantial Evangelical Protestant majority.

Alfredo Garcia and Joseph Blankholm (2016) tested these contrasting hypotheses in several regions across the United States and discovered that the second proposition holds empirically. Nonreligious organizations are more commonly found in regions where Evangelicalism is highest in the United States. But why? Richard Cimino and Christopher Smith (2007) assert that some religious nones become actively involved in nonreligious communities in reaction to their real or perceived minority status in society. Similar to Christian Smith's (1998) use of subcultural identity theory to explain how Evangelicals leverage an embattled narrative with the rest of secular society, those without religion are similarly constructing a narrative of marginalization against Evangelicals (also see Guenther, Mulligan, and Papp 2013). Cimino and Smith (2007) share interview data from religious nones whose interactions with Evangelicals contributed to a growing fear of the role that Evangelicals play in American society, so much so that some religious nones became more involved in nonreligious communities with the goal of strengthening the secular voice and impact in society. Stephen LeDrew (2013) adds that nonreligious organizations can be helpful spaces for atheists to "come out," particularly if they were raised in a religious tradition, and gather with other like-minded individuals. Subcultural identity theory is a useful explanation then for religious nones' decisions to form or join explicitly nonreligious communities in regions where religious belonging, belief, and behavior are highest.

Garcia and Blankholm (2016) extend their theoretical applications even further. They suggest that because Evangelicals are known for higher involvement in voluntary associations, such as church attendance or volunteer activities, religious nones who are surrounded by a predominantly Evangelical environment may similarly be spurred to look for parallel organizations to be involved in. In this way, nonreligious communities both collaborate and innovate to provide a space for religious nones to join and get involved in a secular volunteer organization.

Of course, not all atheists, humanist, and secularist communities are the same. They are diverse, with some groups positioning themselves internally and externally in different ways. Some groups, particularly staunch atheist groups, take a confrontational posture relative to religious individuals and institutions. Areas of foci include "religious criticism, critical thinking, intellectual stimulation, and advocacy of science or church-state separation more (or rather) than fostering strong communal experiences" (Zuckerman, Galen, and Pasquale 2016, 215). These groups are most commonly on display in public places where atheists and Evangelicals vie for cultural space, legitimacy, and authority.

Other nonreligious communities, such as the Sunday Assembly, are far less adversarial with conventional religious groups. Comedians Sanderson Jones and Pippa Evans, founders of the Sunday Assembly, state that the typical liturgy found in many Christian congregations is intentionally built into Sunday Assembly gatherings: announcements, singing, readings, a speaker, and financial donations. Of late, journalists, religious leaders, and scholars have documented the similar structures and forms found in Sunday Assembly and Christian church gatherings. Katie Cross (2017, 250), a practical theologian, refers to these similarities at Sunday Assembly as "vestiges of religious life." These social groups are particularly appealing to those raised in the church but who set aside their religious identification and possibly religious beliefs too.

When religious nones interviewed were asked what, if anything, they missed about their former identification and involvement in a local church (where applicable), some noted the community with other people. Janice, whom we have heard from a few times, including that she would consider greater involvement in a religious group if she found community with others, stated, "When I hear of stories about, say, how a church has gotten together and raised money to do this for this person, or this person's house . . . burnt down, and so the church has taken up a cause, and . . . they're helping rebuild her house or, and I think that my family and I do miss out on that community." Tracie, who earlier attributed her departure from the Anglican Church to intellectual disagreements, shared the following about community: "Sometimes when we go to, say, a friend's church and we sit down and have a cup of tea and there's music and all the families sitting in a row, I think that would be nice to do once a week because you don't force yourself to do that all the time. It's nice, quiet time just to be together. So I think I miss that, for sure. And there's a sense of community I miss." Still, religious nones claim that they are not willing to incur the other "baggage" outlined in earlier chapters to find community through a religious group; they can and do find community with other family, friends, neighbors, coworkers, and social clubs.

As Katie Cross learned, community is one of the main reasons people attend the Sunday Assembly, where the familiarity of its liturgy, function, and form—all the "good" things of church minus God—is a helpful bridge for some religious nones to find and experience community with others similar to themselves. At the same time, some active participants in Sunday Assembly say this organization still has a ways to go to facilitate and cultivate stronger community ties among its adherents. This is, in part, a function of meeting monthly versus weekly, alongside the lack of shared doctrine to bind one another together.

Another intriguing observation by Cross and her participants is the supposed desire by some for "pastoral care" in secular communities—leaders to talk to about life's problems, or adherents rallying together to provide meals or visits to those who are sick or gave birth to a child or lost a loved one. This extends beyond internal congregational dynamics. Building on their motto to "Live Better, Help Often, Wonder More," those in the Sunday Assembly also pursue collaborative relationships with those outside, where common interests align (e.g., volunteering at a homeless shelter).

Yet, even with membership to these various nonreligious organizations measuring in the many tens of thousands, potentially in the many hundreds of thousands (Zuckerman, Galen, and Pasquale 2016, 213), this only represents a fraction of the many millions of nonreligious individuals who surveys estimate are out there in Canada and the United States. Whereas some of the nonreligious are connected with atheist, humanist, or secularist organizations, many more appear not to be. In the 2017 Pacific Northwest Social Survey, only 5% of the 444 nonbelieving none respondents from British Columbia, Oregon, and Washington announced they took part in meetings or activities with an atheist, humanist, or secularist organization at least once in the past year.

Leading explanations as to why include that the individualist ethos is more common among religious nones versus those who are devoutly religious (see Zuckerman, Galen, and Pasquale 2016, 217–18). Further, nonreligious organizations lack many features found in religious organizations, such as "a definite and positive ideology, a centralised and formalised organisational structure, a clear system of authority, a formal procedure for resolving disputes, a *gemeinschaftlich* atmosphere and a permanent and loyal group of members" (Campbell 1971, 42). On the surface, groups like the Sunday Assembly seem to embrace many of these features, yet only time and more focused research will help us to better understand how effective or ineffective such organizational structures are for nonreligious organizations like this to be sustainable.

If we broaden our view to account for online consumption and discussion of atheist, humanist, and secularist views and materials, these forms appear to be more common than individuals actually taking part in face-to-face activities organized by these groups, although there has been no research to date systematically studying the size of these virtual communities in the United States and Canada. Consistent with other research documenting online activities (Environics 2017, 45–46), Cimino and Smith (2014) intimate that such online (and subsequent off-line) ties among the nonreligious are fairly weak and diffuse. They argue this reality reflects the tendencies among the nonreligious to selectively drop in and out of communities as they please, with low levels of long-term commitment.

The Spiritual but Not Religious (SBNR)

Scholars have given another group notable attention: those who say they are or who are identified as spiritual but not religious (SBNR). The SBNR label is mostly a scholarly one. It was first developed by Robert Fuller, a religious studies scholar, in his book *Spiritual but Not Religious: Understanding Unchurched America*, in 2001. This phrase, or ideas similar, has since become a popular term in the fields of sociology of religion and religious studies to describe those individuals who are concerned with spiritual matters but choose to pursue them away from organized religion, or in other words are unchurched (Ammerman 2014; Beaman and Beyer 2013; Chandler 2008; Drescher 2016; Fuller 2001; Heelas and Woodhead 2005; Hood Jr. 2003; Houtman and Aupers 2007; Marler and Hadaway 2002; Roof 1999; Stark, Hamburg, and Miller 2004; Watts 2018; Zinnbauer, Pargament, and Scott 1999, 901). According to this definition, "spiritual" refers to the private realm of individual seeking and bricolaging of various beliefs and practices, often centered on a holistic this-worldly view of an interconnected universe and energies, and the transcendent, which can be experienced in the body and the self once a level of heightened consciousness and authenticity are achieved. "Religious" on the other hand is associated with membership and behavior linked to a religious institution or organized religious group. Nancy Ammerman (2014) wisely points out that these two terms are used as boundary markers against one another, such that "spirituality" denotes something over and against institutional, formal, dogmatic, and authoritarian forms of religious life in contrast to personal experience and authority. Ammerman goes on to stress that religion and spirituality are not mutually exclusive terms. They overlap in many ways such that where you find religion you tend to find spirituality and vice versa.

Nevertheless, only an estimated 0.4% of Americans, for example, spontaneously use the SBNR label to describe themselves when asked what their religion is (2014 Pew Religious Landscape Study). Declared rates of SBNR go up when surveyors ask respondents specifically if they would consider themselves spiritual but not religious, rather than religious and spiritual, religious but not spiritual, or neither. For example, Angus Reid found in 2015 that 39% of the 3,041 Canadian adults they surveyed, both religiously affiliated and nonaffiliated, placed themselves in the SBNR category, as opposed to the other three available options. This SBNR rate increases only slightly to 41% among the 791 respondents who say they are inclined to reject religion (Angus Reid Institute 2015). This indicates that many people, including a substantial proportion of religious nones, are open to describing themselves as SBNR when prompted. Additionally, the finding that 18% of those who say they are inclined to embrace religion also define themselves as spiritual but not religious (Angus Reid Institute 2015) is a sign that many are more comfortable using the term "spirituality" to describe their faith than the term "religion," which has gained negative connotations for many over the last few decades.

In our interviews, very few explicitly described themselves as "spiritual but not religious." However, some, like Adelaide earlier who was adamant that she is not religious but believes in God, clearly make a distinction between religion and spirituality. As many quotations shared throughout this chapter reveal, religious nones use the language of "spirituality" to imply inclusive, experiential, and subjective qualities and boundaries that Ammerman (2014) and Drescher (2016) discuss with interviewees in the United States. As yet one further illustration, Mark, in his early forties, spends some of his free time as an artist. He offered the following link between his artistry and spirituality: "I would sit and draw and it was like meditation 'cause I realized that I'm here by myself. I'm with a piece of paper. . . . You very quickly come upon truths that you have to face . . . it comes from my soul. . . . I'm constantly searching for truth through it. . . . I don't know if that's religious but it's certainly spiritual." Elsewhere in the interview he describes his wedding, officiated by a justice of the peace who "was open to spirituality" in his backyard, "a spiritual building . . . God's planet . . . kind of the biggest spiritual building."

Corrine, whom we introduced in the previous chapter as a "cradle none," spoke in her interview about the link between nature and fitness to her spirituality: "I don't think you have to sit in a church to find [religion]. . . . I'm the closest to whatever that supreme being is whether it's God, whether it's . . . some black woman in the sky, whatever it is . . . when I'm in the mountains, and my religion is spirituality in like being outdoors and embracing that . . . *my passion is being active*, and that's where I find religion." She went on to say she feels "the most alive" in the outdoors, where she is "embraced by like mountains or trees or lakes, I just feel like the most, at ease, and at peace with myself . . . just the magnitude of just how powerful, I guess the elements are."

Regardless of whether people self-identify, solicited or unsolicited, as spiritual but not religious, there is a substantial portion of nones who have beliefs and behavior that we could classify as SBNR. For the "spiritual" component of the label, we focus here on individual self-identification as very or moderately spiritual, since the term can include a whole variety of beliefs and practices. For the "but not religious" component, we exclude individuals who frequent religious services regularly.

Estimates and Trends of the Different Types of Nones

As with all typologies, there is fluidity between and further complexity within each of the categories. But the five groupings of involved seculars, inactive nonbelievers, inactive believers, SBNR, and involved believers developed here allow us to have a general sense of nones' different approaches to believing as well as to religious and spiritual practice. Figure 2.8 contains the estimates of the size of each of the five subgroups among nones in the American states of Washington and Oregon as well as in British Columbia in Canada, where we have survey data with enough indicators to identify all five subtypes (including being able to distinguish between involved and inactive nonbelievers), as well as how this size compares with the same subgroups if measured among the religiously affiliated.

There are only small differences between the composition of religious nones in BC compared with Washington and Oregon: Washington and Oregon nones contain a slightly higher proportion of SBNR and a slightly lower proportion of inactive nonbelievers. Both involved seculars and involved believers among the nones are quite rare. Inactive nonbelieving is much more common, accounting for more than half of nones in BC and almost half in Washington and Oregon. SBNR weighs in at just over a quarter of nones in both countries and inactive believing at just under a fifth. Rates of nonbelief in general are quite high among the large group of nones in the Pacific Northwest, clocking in at an estimated 55% in BC and 52% in Washington and Oregon according to the 2017 PNSS.

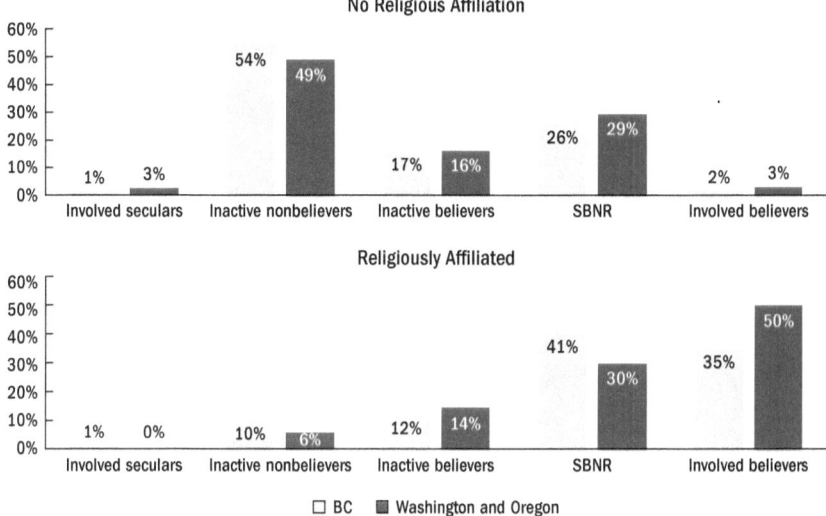

Figure 2.8. Types of religious nones and the religiously affiliated, Washington, Oregon, and British Columbia, 2017. *Source:* 2017 PNSS. N BC no religion = 355. N Washington and Oregon no religion = 314. N BC affiliated = 387. N Washington and Oregon affiliated = 438. Estimates weighted to be representative of the general BC and Washington and Oregon populations.

In fact, within the US, states that have larger religious none populations according to the 2014 Pew Religious Landscape Study are also those on average with larger groups of nonbelievers overall among the nones. Figure 2.9 illustrates this trend.[2] For example, an estimated 40% of residents in the state of Vermont say they have no religion, and 57% of these nones say they do not believe in God or a universal spirit; this compared with Alabama where an estimated 10% of residents say they have no religion, and only 18% of these nones say they do not believe in God or a universal spirit. However, there are also some exceptions to this trend, as figure 2.9 also illustrates: Rhode Island and Connecticut, for example, have lower rates of religious nones but high rates of nonbelief (over 50%) among these nones.

It would seem then that, in most regional contexts where nones have been on the rise for a longer period of time, potentially across more generations, and where they now form larger groups and are more normalized in society, there are also more nonbelieving nones. This finding

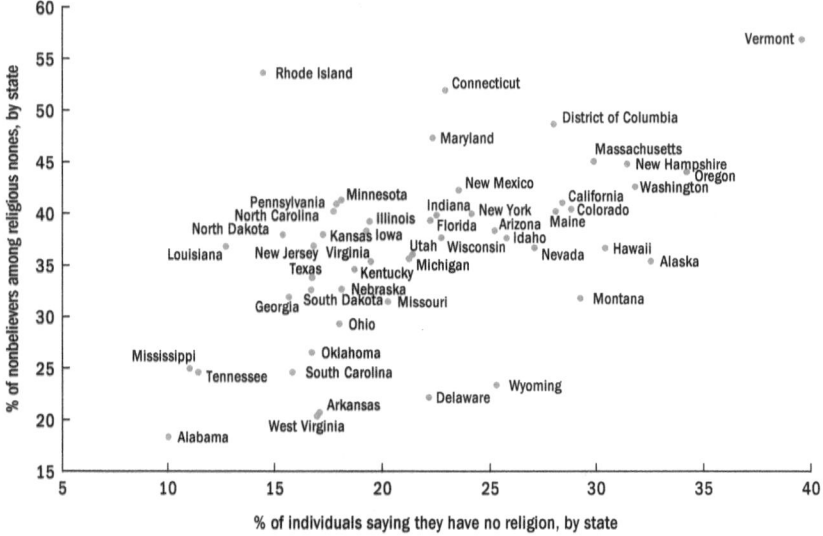

Figure 2.9. Rates of nonbelievers among the nones and rates of religious nones, by state, USA, 2014. *Source:* 2014 Pew Religious Landscape Study. Pearson correlation coefficient between x and y = 0.579***. State aggregate statistics based on N = 35,071.

supports stages of decline theory, which predicts a drop in rates of beliefs in areas where organized religion has been on the decline for a longer period of time (where there are larger groups of religious nones). However, when looking at trends over the last two decades in the United States as a whole, although the religious none population has been growing overall, there has been little shift in the internal composition of the nones. The relatively small changes in rates among the subtypes in figure 2.10 are not statistically significant (i.e., fall within each other's margins of sampling error).

With the larger sample of nones in the 2014 Pew Religious Landscape Study, we can measure good-quality estimates of the size of most of the subtypes of nones by age group for the United States. These rates are found in figure 2.11. Since spiritual self-identification is not included as a question in this survey, frequency of meditation is taken as a measure here for spirituality, it being a practice found in most spiritual traditions in a variety of forms. With this 2014 Pew data, involved and inactive nonbelievers are thus defined as those nones who do not believe in God or a universal spirit and who seldom or never meditate (24% of nones); inactive believers as nones who do believe in God or a universal spirit but attend religious services less than once a month and seldom or never meditate (30% of nones); spiritual but not religious as nones who meditate at least a few times a year but attend religious services less than once a month (37% of nones); and involved believers as nones who believe in God or a universal spirit and attend religious services at least once a month (8% of nones). Broken down by age group, we find that nonbelievers are present in higher rates among eighteen- to thirty-four-year-old nones and nones sixty-five years or older. Inactive believing is most common among fifty- to sixty-four-year-olds. SBNR is most common among thirty-five- to forty-nine-year-olds and nones sixty-five years or older. Involved believing is rare among all none age groups, and least common among nones sixty-five years or older.

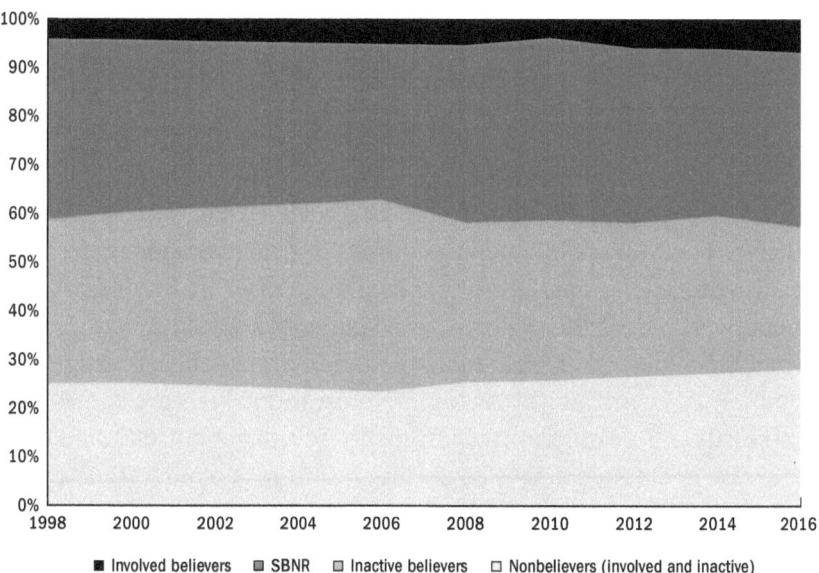

Figure 2.10. Types of religious nones among respondents who say they have no religion, USA, 1998–2016. *Source:* US GSS 1998–2016. Data missing for years 2000, 2002, and 2004; replaced with averages from 1998 and 2006. Estimates weighted to be representative of the general population. N 1998 = 165; N 2006 = 460; N 2008 = 332; N 2010 = 364; N 2012 = 378; N 2014 = 514; N 2016 = 613.

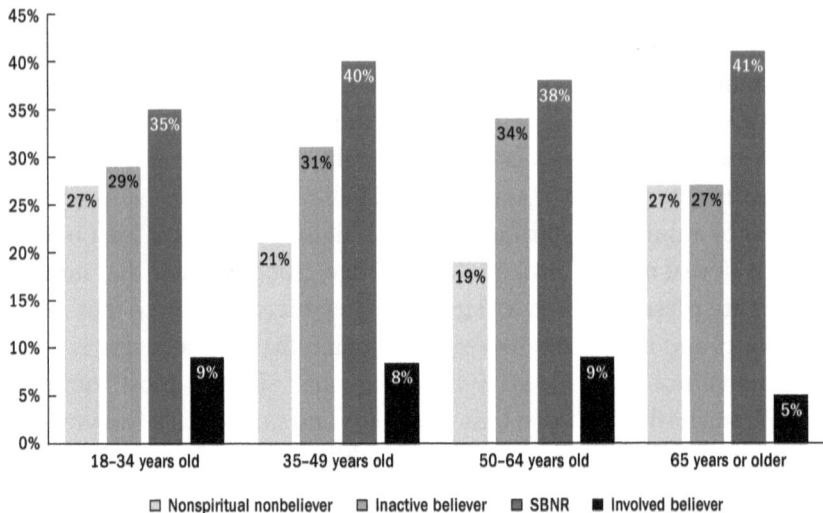

Figure 2.11. Types of religious nones among respondents who say they have no religion, by age group, USA, 2014. *Source:* 2014 Pew Religious Landscape Study. Estimates weighted to be representative of the general population. N 18–34 years = 2,651; N 35–49 years = 1,558; N 50–64 years = 1,761; N 65 years or older = 1156.

Conclusion

We will have to wait for future survey data to determine whether the few differences we do see between age groups of American nones are more permanent generational shifts, or linked more to where individuals find themselves in their life cycle. A BWB framework would state these age group differences have more to do with life cycle, nonbelief being more common in earlier adult years before most individuals are confronted with birth and death and truly begin wondering about ultimate concerns. By contrast, a stages of decline framework would argue that a more permanent generational change is at play, and current levels of nonbelief among the larger none populations of younger age groups will persist as these individuals grow older.

If the age group differences that are present are an indication of more permanent generational shifts, they are not large enough yet to affect the overall internal composition of nones between 1998 and 2016 in the

United States but may do so in future. It remains to be seen if inactive believing and SBNR will be as present later in adulthood for Gen Xers and Millennials who on average did not have as strong of a religious upbringing, and so may not assign as much importance to spiritual journeys and meaning systems, even unchurched ones.

Another important aspect of the results in this chapter is how similar many of the indicators are among the nones in both Canada and the United States: indicators such as nonbelief among the nones (if excluding belief in God, a higher power, a universal spirit, or an inexplicable force; see figures 2.1 and 2.2) as well as salience of beliefs (see figures 2.3 and 2.4). Regional distinctions across North America, such as the West Coast in general compared with the South and the Northeast, may be more crucial in terms of observing differences of believing and behavior among the nones than national differences overall (see, for example, figure 2.9). The exception here is with the activities of prayer and meditation, which we found to be present among a much larger portion of American nones than in Canada. We continue to highlight other similarities and differences between the nones from the two national contexts in the chapters still to come.

Now that we have a better understanding of some of the internal diversity among nones on various dimensions of religion, what we can begin to explore in the next chapter is how these different levels of (non)religious and (non)spiritual believing and behavior without belonging are linked to religious nones' political and social values. With the findings in this chapter, we saw that some nones are nonreligious, in that they are nonbelieving and do not have any religious or spiritual practices in their daily lives, and have developed alternative meaning systems to understand the world they live in. In the next chapter, we explore in depth how these nonreligious in Canada and the United States think socially and politically, and how this compares with inactive believing, SBNR, and involved believing nones as well as the religiously affiliated. As we will see, there are notable differences between the religiously affiliated and unaffiliated, as well as among the diverse types of religious nones. These social and political variations alert us to the complex ways that religious and secular belief, behavior, and belonging interact, distinctly shaping individuals' experiences as well as social life.

3

We Are Just as Moral . . . If Not More!

On March 23, 2018, Lou Dobbs of *Fox News* interviewed Robert Jeffress, pastor at First Baptist Church in Dallas, Texas. The interview centered on left-leaning American media that seemingly marginalize and oppress Christians in the United States, with the headline "Christianity Under Attack" splashed across the bottom of the screen. Jeffress began his comments with the following statement: "The reason this is happening is liberals know that conservative Christians are the last speed bump on the road to the godless, immoral society that liberals dream of" (Mehta 2018).

This stereotype of the individual or nation with no religion having no proper source or sense of what is right or wrong in life is commonly shared by many of those who are more actively involved with a faith group, and has a long history in both the United States and Canada (Beaman and Tomlins 2015; Bullivant and Ruse 2013; Cimino and Smith 2014; Marks 2017; Schmidt 2016). It is a perception that both of us have repeatedly encountered when speaking with faith leaders, scholars, and members of the general public about religious nones. In the previous chapter, we introduced the idea that this view of nones is not supported when we actually speak with them and ask nones questions about morality: for the most part, nones do have views, beliefs, and values about what is right and wrong but more often than not draw on sources other than religion for this morality.

Along with the personal accounts from nones that we explored in the previous chapter, the results in figure 3.1 from the 2014 Pew Religious Landscape Study in the United States help us to better understand this reality. Among American religious nones, only 32% of involved believers, 6% of the spiritual but not religious (SBNR), 6% of inactive believers, and 1% of nonbelievers identified religious teachings and beliefs as their main guiding source of morality when asked.

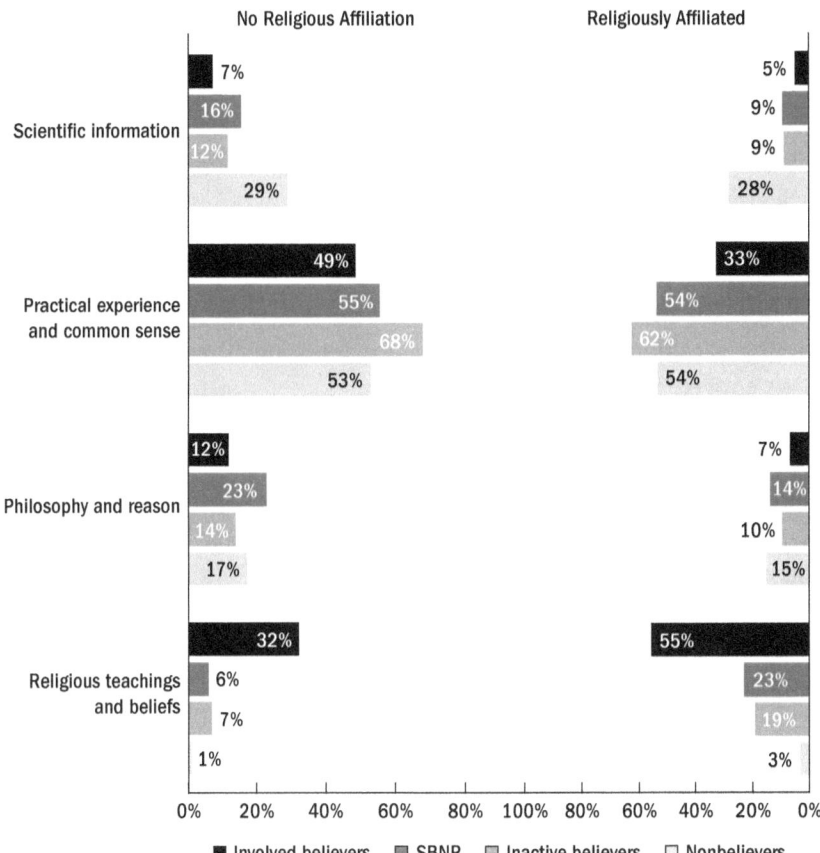

Figure 3.1. Main guiding source of morality (right and wrong) among types of religiously affiliated and nonaffiliated individuals, USA, 2014. *Source:* 2014 Pew Religious Landscape Study. N religious nones = 7,064. N religiously affiliated = 26,070.

Interestingly, these percentages are also relatively low among most of the religiously affiliated: only 23%, 19%, and 3% among the affiliated SBNRs, inactive believers, and nonbelievers respectively. However, religious teachings and beliefs are the guiding source of morality for 55% of affiliated involved believers (those attending religious services at least once a month).

By contrast, practical experience and common sense seem to be the main guiding sources of morality for a majority of nones *and* affiliated individuals—all except involved believers. Even among nonbelievers, practical experience and common sense win out. Scientific information is the main source of morality for only 29% of nonbelieving nones and 28% of nonbelieving affiliates, and philosophy and reason are the main sources of morality for only 17% of nonbelieving nones and 15% of nonbelieving affiliates.

Despite the sources of morality often being different, especially between the actively religious and those less or not at all involved with religion, views of what is right and wrong—of what people should or should not do, or what should or should not be allowed in society—often converge among nones, the marginally religious, and the actively religious. For example, a vast majority of individuals, regardless of their religious or nonreligious background, agree that committing a violent crime is wrong. At the other end of the spectrum, most people believe in helping others in need. As mentioned in the previous chapter, Elizabeth Drescher (2016) points to the Golden Rule, treating others as you would want to be treated, as shared not only by most of the religiously affiliated but also by most of the religiously unaffiliated (also see Ammerman 2014). These shared views about much of what is fundamentally right or wrong allow Canadian and American societies to function, for the most part, fairly well on a day-to-day basis: most people understanding and respecting most laws and rules in order to coexist relatively peacefully.

This said, existing research has shown that there are a number of sociopolitical issues on which many nones have distinct opinions about what is right and wrong compared with more religious individuals (Adkins et al. 2013; Ang and Petrocik 2012; Baker and Smith 2015; Hunsberger and Altemeyer 2006; Leon McDaniel, Nooruddin, and Shortle 2011; O'Neill 2001; Putnam and Campbell 2010; Rayside, Sabin, and Thomas 2017; Scheepers, Gijsberts, and Hello 2002; Smidt et al. 2010; Wilkins-Laflamme 2016b; Woodhead 2016; Zuckerman, Galen, and Pasquale 2016). Issues that have garnered a great deal of attention in this sense over the last few decades have been notably legalized abortion and same-sex marriage. A number of studies have shown nones to be on average further left of the political/ideological spectrum in the United States, Canada, and across much of the Western world on such issues (Ang and Petrocik 2012; Jelen and Wilcox 2003; Leon McDaniel, Nooruddin, and Shortle 2011; Olson, Cadge, and Harrison 2006; Putnam and Campbell 2010; Scheepers, Gijsberts, and Hello 2002; Sherkat et al. 2011; Wilkins-Laflamme 2016b).

What these studies have not done, however, is compare average attitudes between different *types* of religious nones on a wide range of social and political issues, including abortion, same-sex marriage, women in the workforce, environmental laws and spending, government aid to the disadvantaged, and immigration. In the previous chapter, we demonstrated that there is heterogeneity among the nones in terms of their believing and behavior. To what extent is this heterogeneity reflected in their issue stances as well? And how do the views of different types of religious nones resemble or differ from those of the marginally and actively religious? Does the belonging dimension matter most here, with nones of all types having different views from the religiously affiliated on these issues, or do the dimensions of believing and behavior figure more prominently? Additionally, and to follow another thread woven throughout the book so far, what regional variations do we see with regard to nones' views on such issues, especially between areas where nones make up smaller or larger portions of the overall population? This chapter is dedicated to answering these key questions.

Issue Positions among Religious Nones

As noted in the previous chapter, surveys with large enough sample sizes that ask sufficient questions about a respondent's religiosity on the dimensions of belonging, believing, and behavior to build our typology of nones are difficult to come by, especially in Canada. Surveys with large sample sizes, the needed religiosity questions, *and* variables on respondents' attitudes toward sociopolitical issues are even more difficult to find. The 2014 Pew Religious Landscape Study does have all of these variables and a large subsample of religious nones for our purposes in the United States. For Canada, the best source we currently have is the Canadian Election Studies (CES),[1] a survey series run each time there is a federal election in the country. However, with this Canadian data

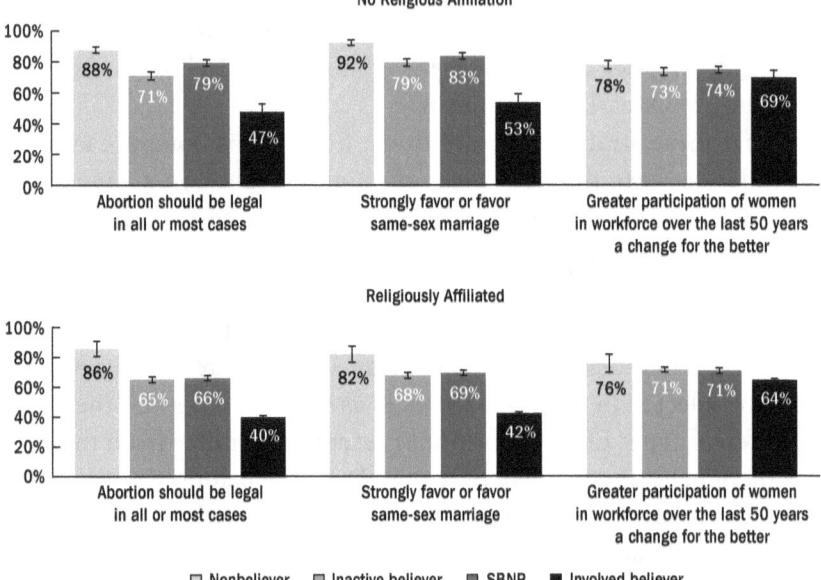

Figure 3.2.A. Predicted probabilities of left-leaning sociopolitical attitudes, USA, 2014, with CI (95%). *Source:* Data from the 2014 Pew Religious Landscape Study. Predicted probabilities generated from logit regression models with robust standard errors, while keeping the sociodemographic controls constant at their mean. Weighted to be representative of the general adult population. N abortion = 31,322. N same-sex marriage = 30,323. N women in the workforce = 32,581. Full results from these models available in table C.1 in appendix C.

we will have to limit our comparison of attitudes among religious nones overall, those who are religiously affiliated but do not consider religion important in their lives (in some ways akin to marginal affiliates), and those who are affiliated and who do consider religion to be important in their lives (in some ways similar to active affiliates).

Figures 3.2 and 3.3 contain selected results from a series of logistic regression models we generated from these data with attitudes toward abortion, same-sex marriage, women in the workforce, environmental laws and spending, government aid to the disadvantaged, and immigration, as the dependent variables; different types of religious affiliation and nonaffiliation as the main independent variables; and a series of sociodemographic controls to better isolate the effect of religiosity levels, controls that include age, gender, marital status, number of children, race (for US models only), immigrant status, level of education, and region of residence. Many of the results in the remainder of this chapter take the form of predicted probabilities of the outcome in question when keeping these sociodemographic controls constant at their means.

To briefly summarize the results from these statistical models before exploring each issue in more detail, in general religious nones tend to be more left leaning on all of the measured issues compared with those affiliated with a religion, in line with most existing research on the topic. Nevertheless, variations do exist between different types of religious

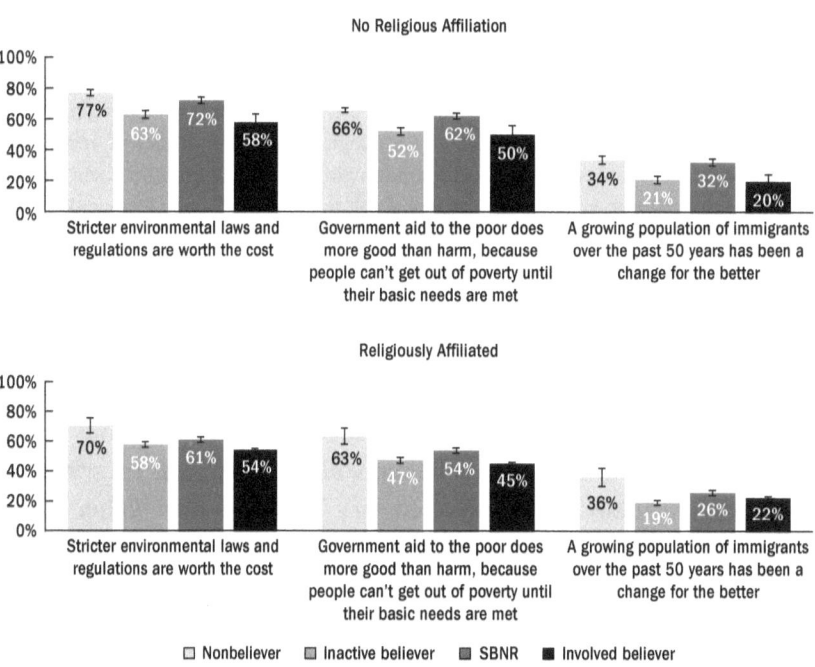

Figure 3.2.B. Predicted probabilities of left-leaning sociopolitical attitudes, USA, 2014, with CI (95%). *Source:* Data from the 2014 Pew Religious Landscape Study. Predicted probabilities generated from logit regression models with robust standard errors, while keeping the sociodemographic controls constant at their mean. Weighted to be representative of the general adult population. N poverty & immigration = 32,581. N environment = 31,724. Full results from these models available in table C.1 in appendix C.

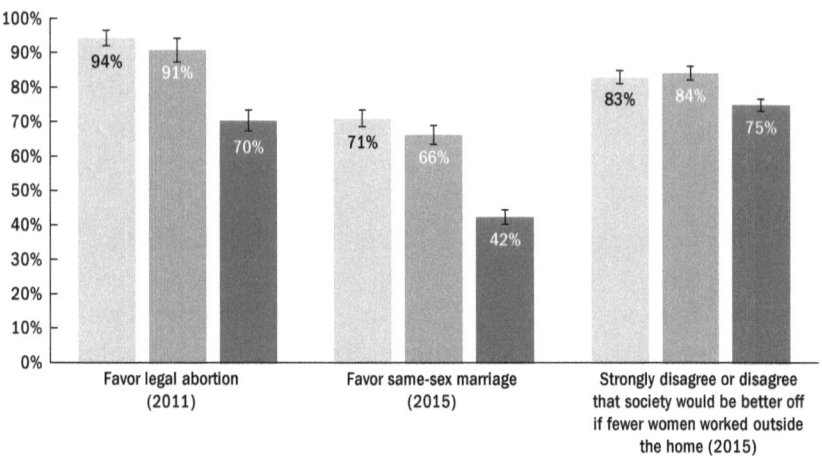

Figure 3.3.A. Predicted probabilities of left-leaning sociopolitical attitudes, Canada, 2011 and 2015, with CI (95%). *Source:* Data from the 2011 and 2015 Canadian Election Studies. Predicted probabilities generated from logit regression models with robust standard errors, while keeping the sociodemographic controls constant at their mean. Weighted to be representative of the general adult population. N abortion = 2,385. N same-sex marriage = 5,983. N women in the workforce = 5,987. Full results from these models available in table C.2 in appendix C.

nones too. Moreover, when we look more closely at social environment we find, for example, that on most issues Canadians—religious nones and the affiliated alike—tend to be more liberal than their counterparts in the United States. Rates also often vary in regions with higher versus lower proportions of religious nones residing there. We offer some explanations for these findings along the way.

Alongside this survey data, we also have interview data on some of these topics, notably abortion and same-sex marriage, with some shorter reflections on the environment as well as the government's role toward those who live in poverty. Unlike other interview data to this point, interviewees were not asked directly about the following topics. The fact that some of these topics arose as strongly for some (unsolicited) indicates to us the added significance to these views and subjects. For what it is worth, we were surprised to find very little on these topics in other qualitative research on religious nones in particular. For example, in Nancy Ammerman's (2014) *Sacred Stories, Spiritual Tribes*—a book that is probably the most informative in terms of qualitative research—she notes that on the topics of abortion and homosexuality, "despite the hot-button character of those issues, neither subject came up in more than a handful of our conversations about everyday life" with Americans across the religious spectrum (239). As with our interviews, Ammerman did not directly ask interviewees about these two topics, thus anything that was discussed emerged unprompted. Our goal in presenting these interview data is not to convey representativeness so much as to provide a sampling of the prevailing views, in people's own words, to arise across the religious continuum, from the religious nones to active religious affiliates interviewed. We hope that such data will spur further qualitative research on these topics.

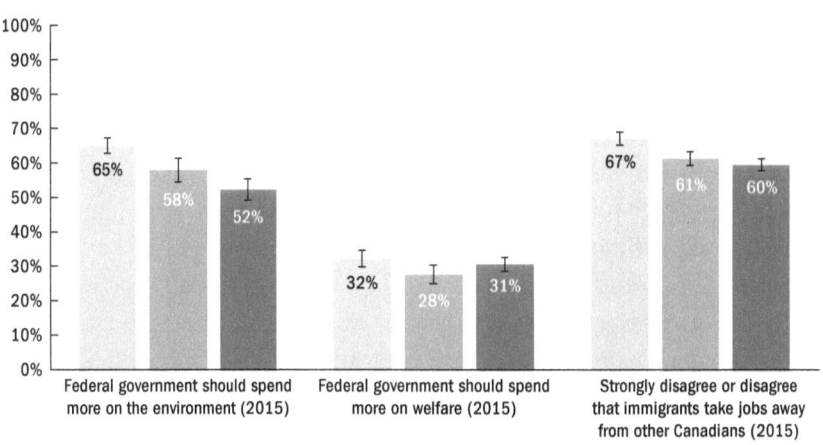

Figure 3.3.B. Predicted probabilities of left-leaning sociopolitical attitudes, Canada, 2011 and 2015, with CI (95%). *Source:* Data from the 2015 Canadian Election Study. Predicted probabilities generated from logit regression models with robust standard errors, while keeping the sociodemographic controls constant at their mean. Weighted to be representative of the general adult population. N environment = 5,870. N welfare = 5,749. N immigration = 5,932. Full results from these models available in table C.2 in appendix C.

Abortion

Let us begin this exploration of sociopolitical attitudes among nones with the issue of abortion. Previous research has studied the link between one's level of religiosity and opinions on this issue in Canada and the United States (Ang and Petrocik 2012; Jelen and Wilcox 2003; Putnam and Campbell 2010; Wilkins-Laflamme 2016b). There is wide consensus that the less religious an average respondent is, the more likely they are to be in favor of access to legal abortion. This result is also found with the survey data we analyzed. In the 2014 Pew US data, basic descriptive statistics show that 76% of those who say they have no religion also answered they are in favor of legal access to abortion, compared with 49% among those who identify with a religion. Regionally, nones in the Northeast and West United States are even more likely to support access to legal abortion, at 80% and 83% respectively, compared with those in the South (70%) and Midwest (73%). These figures reflect regional trends among Americans in general on this issue.

There is also a larger gap in these attitudes between the affiliated and unaffiliated in American states with larger none populations. We ran generalized linear multilevel mixed-effects models with the 2014 Pew Religious Landscape Study data in which individual respondents were nested within states. Results from these models indicate that an average increase of ten percentage points in the size of the religious none state population is associated with an increase of eighteen percentage points in the gap between nones' and religious affiliates' probabilities of supporting legal abortion, once respondents' age, gender, and race are controlled for.[2]

In Canada, overall support for access to legal abortion is higher than in the United States, but there still exists a gap between the nones and the affiliated. In 2011, basic descriptive statistics show that 94% of religious none respondents were in favor of legal abortion, compared with 73% among the religiously affiliated. There is little significant regional variation in support for abortion among nones across the Canadian provinces, with the exception of Prince Edward Island respondents in the 2011 CES whose probabilities of supporting legal abortion are twenty-one percentage points lower than those in the largest province of Ontario, once we control for age, gender, marital status, number of children, foreign birth, and level of education.

The results in figures 3.2 and 3.3, notably for the United States, show that the dimensions of believing and behavior seem to count for more in these differences in attitudes than actual religious (non)belonging. Once we control for the other sociodemographic variables, unaffiliated nonbelievers are the most likely to support legal abortion in the United States in 2014 (88% predicted probability of support), followed closely by affiliated nonbelievers (86% predicted probability of support). Involved believers, both affiliated and unaffiliated, are the least likely to support legal abortion at 40% and 47% predicted probabilities of support respectively. The rates of support among Canadian nones and affiliated respondents who do not consider religion to be important in their lives are also very similar, at 94% and 91% predicted probabilities of support respectively. These figures are compared with a 70% predicted likelihood of support among affiliated respondents for whom religion is important in their lives.

These findings are generally borne out in interviews too, with some variation among active religious affiliates. Kathy, a religious none (formerly Anglican) whom we met in the last chapter, shared her views on Catholics, a group that her husband and children are actively involved with: "I struggle a little bit . . . with some of their stances on issues, things like . . . abortion. They don't fit with who I am and other parts of my life." She went on to share of a church known for working with the poor but criticized by some for not "spending more time on anti-abortion work. Okay, there's something that doesn't make sense here."

The active affiliates interviewed do not generally believe in abortion. Caleb, whom we met beforehand, is a convert to Catholicism and declared, "Awarding that abortion doctor the Order of Canada is absurd and obscene." (This is a reference to Henry Morgentaler, a physician and strong advocate for abortion as an option available to women. He received the Order of Canada, the second highest medal honor of merit in Canada, for his commitment to increase healthcare options for women). Madyson, in her late twenties, married with one child, and involved in a Baptist church, said, "I wouldn't become part of a group that helps abortion."

However, other active affiliate interviewees offer a more nuanced take on the subject. Ann is a devoted Catholic in her midfifties. She critiqued

> really strong anti-abortionists . . . because it's a sin . . . as opposed to, "There's a woman in trouble. The only reason she's thinking of abortion is

because her life is so miserable or she's worried about things that, maybe, with some help, she could get past." So . . . I'm anti-abortion too, but the thing is to first look at the mother. *Why* is she thinking that, and what can you do to support her. So, really, what I always hear from their perspective is, "It's a sin to kill the unborn child." That's true. But can you please look at the one who's doing the killing first? Like, *that's* the person they need to help.

Don, a longtime highly involved conservative Protestant in his forties, and his wife have been involved with "post-abortion recovery with Catholic Family Services." Jennifer is a schoolteacher in her midthirties. She has three children and, like many of the other interviewees to speak about abortion, is also Catholic. Jennifer reflected, "I don't like abortion. But I believe that's also a decision . . . a woman makes with her doctor. You know, what's best for you . . . there's probably some things I definitely would debate with the Church." Indicative of active affiliate interviewees such as these, Nancy Ammerman (2014, 239–42) notes her surprise during qualitative research with conservatively oriented religious affiliates in the United States who only infrequently singled out abortion as problematic or were actively involved in protesting or speaking out against abortion. She expected, perhaps given the customarily highly charged climate on this topic among Evangelicals especially (and Catholics to a lesser extent) in the United States, that conservative-leaning religious people might be more vocal in their concern with and opposition to abortion.

Both the survey and interview data remind us that while there are general differences between religious nones and active religious affiliates when it comes to their attitudes toward abortion, variation exists within these groupings as well. It would be a mistake to simply assume homogeneity for either end of the (non)religious spectrum.

Same-Sex Marriage

Like their more left-leaning opinions overall on abortion, the unaffiliated are also more likely to be in favor of same-sex marriage than the religiously affiliated. Previous research has shown this (Adkins et al. 2013; Ang and Petrocik 2012; Olson, Cadge, and Harrison 2006; Putnam and Campbell 2010; Sherkat et al. 2011; Wilkins-Laflamme 2016b), and so do our results here. Looking at basic descriptive statistics, 83% of American religious nones in the 2014 Pew Religious Landscape Study support same-sex marriage (strongly favor or favor it), compared with 50% among those who identify with a religion. As with opinions on abortion, nones in the American Northeast and West have even higher levels of support for same-sex marriage, at 86% and 87% respectively, compared with nones in the South (78%) and Midwest (82%). However, unlike with attitudes toward abortion, the gap in opinions on same-sex marriage between the religiously affiliated and unaffiliated does not vary significantly based on the size of the religious none population in a given state.

In the 2015 CES, 71% of Canadian religious nones say they favor same-sex marriage, compared with 49% among the religiously affiliated. These seemingly lower levels of support for same-sex marriage in Canada than in the United States may be an artifact of how the survey question was asked in the CES, providing respondents with only three answer options (Favor, Oppose, or Don't know/no opinion) rather than a more detailed Likert scale. Consequently, respondents who do not have as strong opinions on this issue may have selected the third category in larger numbers in the CES (28% of all respondents in the 2015 CES did so). This said, the gap between the religiously affiliated and unaffiliated on this issue is still observable in Canada. This gap also does not vary significantly across Canadian regions once other sociodemographic factors are controlled for. For example, in Atlantic Canada 75% of nones support same-sex marriage, compared with 50% among the religiously affiliated; on the other side of the country in British Columbia, 70% of nones support same-sex marriage, compared with 47% among those with a religion.

Again, as with attitudes toward abortion, the dimensions of believing and behavior seem to count for more in differences in opinions on same-sex marriage in the United States according to the results in figure 3.2. Once we keep the other sociodemographic variables constant at their mean, unaffiliated nonbelievers are the most likely to support same-sex marriage, followed by unaffiliated SBNR and affiliated nonbelievers. Involved believers, both affiliated and unaffiliated, are in turn the least likely to support same-sex marriage. Likewise, in Canada in figure 3.3 nones and those who are affiliated but who do not consider religion to be important in their lives have similar predicted probabilities of supporting same-sex marriage (71% and 66% respectively), compared with the lower predicted probability of 42% found among the affiliated who consider religion to be important or very important in their lives.

As with abortion, the religious nones interviewed are the most inclined to convey left-leaning views on same-sex marriage. Joshua, a staunch atheist whose parents stopped attending the United Church of Canada when the denomination affirmed same-sex marriage, took issue with some of the following rhetoric he hears from some religious leaders in the United States: "Take any natural disaster and that being an explanation, 'Oh, that's God's wrath on homosexuals.' To me, that is deeply, deeply disturbing." Corrine, whom we've heard from a few times so far, maintained that individuals should be free to think and behave as they wish: "I think that what you believe in is totally your own right . . . I'm very, very liberal . . . I have a lot of friends who are homosexual. I have a lot of friends that are different religions, and I would never judge them any differently because of the things they do in their own head or in their own bedroom . . . it's really up to you."

No religious nones who were homosexual were interviewed, though other qualitative research makes a link between one's sexual orientation and decision to leave religious affiliation behind. Drescher (2016, 74) introduces readers to Natalie, a former Catholic and current religious none, who is also a lesbian. Natalie shares that her sexual orientation, along with other divergent views on sexuality relative to Catholicism, contributed to her "exile" from the Catholic Church. Zuckerman (2012, 64–73) shares similar findings regarding Andrew, a former Mormon, whose membership was "rescinded" once Mormon leadership found out he was gay.

Science also figures into this conversation for some religious nones, such as Samantha, whom we met earlier. She drew on her degree in science to push against religious groups that, in her mind, disregard science on this topic:

> My boyfriend's parents are very against homosexuality. . . . I've taken a lot of classes on homosexuality . . . they [boyfriend's parents] tell me that it's just a choice, but if it was a choice, then in societies where . . . it's more acceptable, there would be more homosexuality and that's not the

case. . . . I think that education kind of disproves a lot of beliefs that religious groups tend to hold as a general rule . . . it confirms to me that there's certain beliefs like that that are just outdated and they need to be updated or whatever.

Perhaps surprisingly, the active religious affiliates interviewed rarely discussed same-sex marriage in a negative light, with the exception of Rebecca, a recent high school graduate and active member of a Pentecostal congregation. She lamented that "the world's getting run by . . . secularism . . . that's scary." Rebecca continued to specify different examples of concern, including "in politics, like, gay marriage being approved and stuff, which, as a Christian . . . I imagine God would just be . . . crying." In the Canadian context, sociologists Sam Reimer and Michael Wilkinson (2015, 93) document that contrary to public perceptions that Evangelicals are consumed with the topic of same-sex marriage, very few Canadian Evangelical pastors preach on this topic.

Several interviewees connected to the United Church of Canada highlight the many progressive issues that their congregations support. Same-sex marriage is often the first area they speak of. As one example, Stephanie attended a Baptist church with a friend while growing up, stopped attending religious services in her young adult years, and later attended a United Church of Canada congregation with her husband. When asked why she started to attend a church with this denomination, Stephanie quickly responded, "They're inclusive . . . we went because we saw the rainbow . . . on the sign of the little poster that we were interested in . . . the fact . . . that they marry and that it's not seen as a negative to be a homosexual person is a really big part of it . . . I mean, just the idea that they're doing gay marriages."

The group that had the most to say about same-sex marriage was marginal religious affiliates, defined in the context of our interviews as those who identified as Christian and attended religious services mainly for religious holidays and rites of passage. Many of these interviewees formerly attended religious services nearly every week but stopped attending for a variety of reasons. Some attributed their declining involvement, or even society-wide religious declines in general, to religious groups that held conservative views on same-sex marriage. They believed religious groups should be open to everyone. Lisa attended religious services on and off throughout her life, and stopped attending when her husband passed away. At one point in the interview Lisa spoke about how religious groups treat "gay people . . . they had some big people that were . . . saying that these people are going to go to hell and I just don't . . . think that's very Christian." Monica is in her twenties and is connected to the Catholic Church. She attended religious services regularly growing up before diminishing her involvement largely due to the perceived lack of openness and inclusivity in the Catholic Church. She rattled off a list of topics where religious groups hold negative views in her mind, including homosexuality. She declares, "We're in a day and time now where . . . you're even allowed gay marriages now. . . . I think that views and fundamentals need to change within the church to sort of accommodate that." A couple of interviewees, though supportive of same-sex marriage, did not believe that religious leaders should be forced to perform weddings for same-sex couples. Richard grew up in Scandinavia and is connected to a Lutheran congregation. Now in his late thirties, he commented on same-sex marriage: "It's a very hot topic . . . my belief is a priest who . . . I wanna respect his/her belief. If they think it's wrong, they should not have to perform the ceremony. That's my belief."

Women in the Workforce

The gap in attitudes between the religiously affiliated and unaffiliated is not as pronounced on the issue of women's participation in the workforce as it is on abortion and same-sex marriage, but it is still present: basic descriptive statistics show that 75% of American nones in the 2014 Pew Religious Landscape Study agree that the greater participation of women in the workforce over the last fifty years in America has been a change for the better, compared with 65% of respondents who identify with a religion; 83% of nones in the 2015 Canadian Election Study disagree or strongly disagree that society would be better off if fewer women worked outside the home, compared with 77% of the religiously affiliated. There is no significant variation between census regions among the nones regarding their opinions on this issue. For example, an estimated 76% of American nones in the Northeast and 74% in the South supported women being part of the workforce in 2014; an estimated 83% of British Columbian nones and 79% of Atlantic Canadian nones supported women working outside the home in 2015. However, in the United States the gap in attitudes between nones and those identifying with a religion is larger in states where nones make up a larger part of the general population. For example, in Alabama where nones made up 10% of the general population in 2014, 67% of these nones support women in the workforce, compared with 62% among the religiously affiliated; in Vermont where nones made up 37% of the general population in 2014, 90% of these nones support women in the workforce, compared with 72% among those who identify with a religion.

In Canada, the province of Alberta is characterized by this wider gap between the religiously affiliated and unaffiliated: 83% of nones in Alberta support women in the workforce, compared with 68% of those who are religiously affiliated. By contrast, in Ontario 81% of nones support women in the workforce, compared with 77% of the religiously affiliated. These numbers could be affected by the proportion of religious nones in each province (as noted in our introduction, a higher proportion of nones reside in Alberta versus Ontario); by an urban-rural distinction where Alberta is more rural based versus Ontario, home to Canada's largest city of Toronto; and also by the distinct composition of Alberta's active religious affiliates, many of whom are conservative Protestants.

As can be seen with the results in figures 3.2 and 3.3, favorable attitudes toward women in the workforce follow a similar pattern as attitudes toward abortion and same-sex marriage among the different types of nones and religiously affiliated. In the United States, both unaffiliated and affiliated nonbelievers are the most likely to support women in the workforce, and unaffiliated and affiliated involved believers the least likely, once sociodemographics are controlled for. In Canada, predicted probabilities of support for women in the workforce are very similar among nones and the affiliated who do not consider religion to be important in their lives, even being slightly higher for this latter group, and are lower for the affiliated who do consider religion to be important or very important in their lives.

Attitudes toward the Environment

There is also a gap in average attitudes on environmental regulations and spending between nones and those with a religion. Basic descriptive statistics in 2014 show that an estimated 70% of nones in the United States agreed that stricter environmental laws and regulations are worth the costs they might incur on the economy, compared with an estimated 55% of the religiously affiliated. Nones in the American Northeast are even more likely to support this statement, to the tune of 75%, than those in the rest of the United States. Additionally, in states where the none population is proportionately larger, the gap in attitudes between the religiously affiliated and unaffiliated on this issue is also on average larger. For example, in Mississippi where nones made up an estimated 11% of the general population in 2014, 51% of these nones support environmental laws and regulations, compared with 50% among the religiously affiliated in the state; in Oregon where nones made up an estimated 34% of the general population in 2014, 74% of these nones support environmental laws and regulations, compared with 51% among those who identify with a religion.

In Canada in 2015, basic descriptive statistics indicate that 67% of nones felt the federal government should be spending more on the environment, compared with an estimated 55% of the religiously affiliated. Nones' probabilities in British Columbia to say this are eight percentage points higher compared with those in Ontario when age, gender, marital status, number of children, foreign birth, and level of education are controlled for. Yet the gap between the religiously affiliated and unaffiliated is similar across Canadian provinces on this issue.

Similar to attitudes toward abortion, same-sex marriage, and women in the workforce, unaffiliated and affiliated nonbelievers as well as unaffiliated SBNR in the United States are the most likely to support the cost of environmental laws and regulations; and unaffiliated and affiliated involved believers along with affiliated inactive believers, the least likely, when sociodemographics are controlled for (see figure 3.2). By contrast, in Canada in 2015 the gap between each of the three categories of affiliated and unaffiliated is roughly the same size on the issue of environmental spending (see figure 3.3).

In a slightly different framing of this subject, the qualitative components to Nancy Ammerman's (2014) research in the United States reveal that "people *outside* religious communities were half again as likely (compared to active religious participants) to include care for the earth among their list of concerns" (237) in society. Those in mainline

Protestant traditions were singled out for speaking more frequently about caring for the earth versus Catholics or conservative Protestants. Although attitudes toward the environment did not arise frequently in our interviews, they did emerge among some active religious affiliates in the United Church of Canada. As with same-sex marriage, these interviewees often singled out their denomination's commitment to the environment as a badge of honor. Henry is in his midseventies and is actively involved in his church, attending talks and lectures on a variety of topics that his church hosts. He spoke of young people and the environment in this way: "I think young people are more attuned to the social issues of today, and they want to do something. They have . . . an innate desire to help others and to understand, to stop wars and stop polluting our environment. We're here as custodians of the world, of the earth, and we're not doing that. We're just destroying everything. We're so greedy." He, like other interviewees, believed the United Church of Canada is at the forefront of religious groups positively responding to the environment. Phrases such as the following emerged: "The United Church is talking about climate change"; "a number of us . . . have tried to develop programs which make the congregation more aware of social issues: you know, development of the [Alberta] oil sands"; and "we're actually doing something to correct the environment."

Government Aid to the Disadvantaged

A gulf between the religiously affiliated and unaffiliated, especially between nonbelievers and involved believers, on issues typically split along the left/right ideological spectrum is beginning to emerge in this chapter's survey results so far. This gap is also found on the issue of government aid to the poor in the United States. In 2014, basic descriptive statistics show that an estimated 58% of American nones agreed that government aid to the poor does more good than harm, compared with an estimated 47% among those identifying with a religion. Nones in the Northeast and West are even more likely to support this statement, at 61% and 62% respectively, than nones in the South and Midwest (54% and 57%). In states where the none population is proportionately larger, the gap in attitudes on this issue between the religiously affiliated and unaffiliated is also larger. For example, in Tennessee where nones made up an estimated 11% of the general population in 2014, 58% of these nones support government aid to the poor, compared with 45% among the religiously affiliated. In Washington State, where nones represent 33% of the general population, 69% of these nones support government aid to the poor, compared with 49% among the religiously affiliated. The results in figure 3.2 show that, once again, unaffiliated and affiliated nonbelievers are the most likely to support government aid to the poor in the United States, and unaffiliated and affiliated involved believers are the least likely, once other sociodemographic variables are controlled for at their means.

In Canada in 2015, those respondents who felt the federal government should spend more on welfare were in the minority (32% overall), and this did not vary much among the three categories of the affiliated and unaffiliated (see figure 3.3). This may be because government rates of spending on welfare are already quite high in Canada, so that most do not think that more spending is required. Nones' probabilities in Prince Edward Island and British Columbia of supporting more of this type of government spending are, however, respectively twenty-eight and eleven percentage points higher than those in Ontario when other sociodemographic variables are controlled for, following regional patterns among the general population on this issue.

From our interviews, only one comment arose on the link between the government and helping those who live in poverty. This was from Beth, a marginal religious affiliate in her eighties with ties to the Lutheran church. Beth does not believe voting for a Conservative government aligns with Christian values:

> You can talk God and care for other people all you like, but people shouldn't be homeless, and I don't care if it's their own fault. Should they be dying on the street? . . . I think the prophet Jeremiah would talk a little bit about that type of thing: social issues. . . . We should never have a Conservative government any place if people followed their religious impulses or religious learning . . . and what they say they believe. I don't care whether they believe in an afterlife or not or whether they are born again or not. They should at least read the Bible and listen to it. That makes me so angry.

Beyond Beth, some religious nones highlighted their volunteer activities that included helping those economically disadvantaged. Far more active religious affiliates also highlighted their volunteering in this regard but went one step further to highlight the important contribution that religious groups make to society by helping the poor. We say more about this in the next chapter when we deal with civic engagement and religious (non)affiliation.

Attitudes toward Immigration

The last attitudinal issue that we explore in this chapter is immigration. As with the other issues, there is also a gap in how nones and those who identify with a religion feel toward immigration in the United States and Canada. In 2014 in the United States, basic descriptive statistics indicate that 33% of nones agreed that the growing number of immigrants over the past fifty years has been a change for the better, compared with 24% among the religiously affiliated. This rate among nones reaches a high of 38% in the Northeast and a low of 27% in the Midwest. However, the gap between the religiously affiliated and unaffiliated does not vary significantly in average size between states with larger or smaller none populations.

It is worth noting here that levels of outright support for immigration over the past fifty years in the United States are substantially lower than for the other sociopolitical issues addressed in this chapter so far, including among nones. Among the 35,071 American respondents in the 2014 Pew Religious Landscape Study, 26% thought that the change from immigration had been for the better; 35% thought it was a change for the worse; 30% felt that immigration had not made much of a change to US society in the past fifty years; 4% felt the changes immigration had brought have been mixed; and 5% did not know or refused to answer. In the 2014 General Social Survey in the United States, 54% of respondents overall disagreed or strongly disagreed that immigrants increase crime rates; 43% disagreed or strongly disagreed that immigrants take jobs away from Americans; and 54% agreed or strongly agreed that immigrants are good for America. Trends in the 2014 GSS data also show slightly higher levels of support for immigration among nones for these survey questions, compared with the religiously affiliated.

In Canada in 2015, basic descriptive statistics show that 66% of nones and 59% of the religiously affiliated disagreed or strongly disagreed with the statement that immigrants take jobs away from other Canadians. Moreover, nones' probabilities in the province of Quebec of supporting this statement are thirteen percentage points lower than those in Ontario when other sociodemographic variables are controlled for. Yet, as in the United States, the size of the gap between the religiously affiliated and unaffiliated on this issue does not vary significantly between Canadian regions.

The pattern between the different types of nones and the religiously affiliated in the United States is a bit different for their opinions on immigration than for the other issues explored in this chapter so far. Once other sociodemographic variables are controlled for, unaffiliated and affiliated nonbelievers are still the most likely to have more positive feelings toward immigration over the last fifty years in the United States, followed closely by the unaffiliated SBNR. However, it is religiously affiliated inactive believers who are the least likely to hold these more positive attitudes (see figure 3.2). In Canada, nones have the highest predicted probabilities of disagreeing or strongly disagreeing with the statement that immigrants take jobs away from other Canadians (67% probability), compared with a 61% probability among marginal affiliates and a 60% probability among active affiliates (see figure 3.3).

These results of a gap in attitudes toward immigrants between the religiously affiliated and unaffiliated align with those of other studies showing a trend of more negative attitudes toward immigrants among Christians, whether practicing or not, in North America and Europe (Leon McDaniel, Nooruddin, and Shortle 2011; Sahgal 2018; Scheepers, Gijsberts, and Hello 2002).

Left/Right Ideological Spectrum

To summarize thus far, religious nones find themselves on average more at the left or liberal end of the current-day political spectrum in both the United States and Canada, on issues of sexual morals and reproductive rights, gender roles, the environment, the government's role in aiding the disadvantaged, and immigration. This political leaning is also reflected in their own average self-placement on the left/right spectrum, as illustrated in figure 3.4. On a scale of zero to ten, with zero indicating

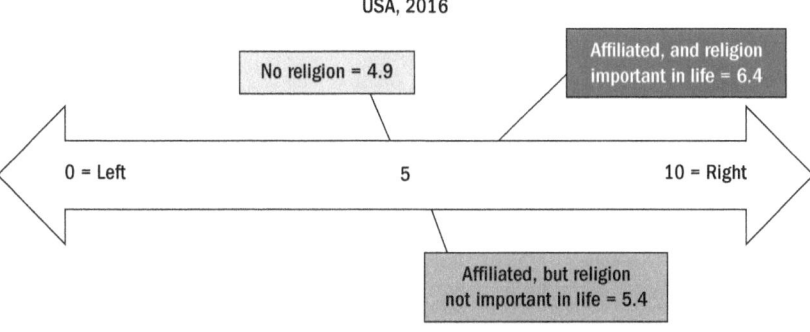

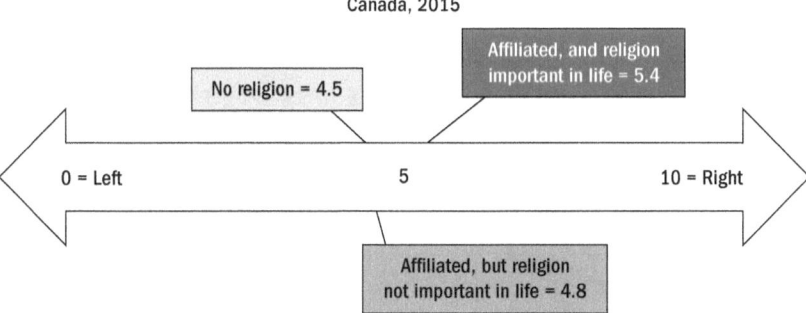

Figure 3.4. Estimated means for left/right ideological self-placement (0 = left; 10 = right), 2016 American National Election Survey and 2015 Canadian Election Survey. *Source:* Predicted means generated from OLS regression models with robust standard errors, controlling for age, gender, marital status, foreign born, level of education, and region of residence. Weighted to be representative of general adult populations. N USA = 3,356. N CND = 2,931. Full results from these models available in tables C.4 and C.5 in appendix C.

more left positioning and ten indicating more right positioning, religious nones in the 2016 American National Election Study self-placed on average at 4.9, and nones in the 2015 Canadian Election Study at 4.5, when age, gender, marital status, foreign birth, level of education, and region of residence are kept constant at their means. These figures are compared with an average self-placement of 5.4 and 4.8 among American and Canadian religiously affiliated respondents who do not consider religion to be important in their lives, and compared with 6.4 and 5.4

among American and Canadian religious affiliates who do consider religion to be important or very important in their lives.

The Importance of Social Environment

Why do we find so many more nones at the left-leaning end of the spectrum on many sociopolitical issues, and so many actively religious individuals at the right-leaning end? How might we explain variations based on higher or lower proportions of religious nones in a given region, or country in the case of Canadians seemingly being more left leaning in general versus those in the United States?

Consistent with our overarching argument to this point, socialization and the social environment in which individuals find themselves are key. During both their childhood and adult years, religious nones are much more likely to find themselves surrounded by people and living in areas characterized by more left-leaning values. As we have seen, many nones come from liberal Protestant family backgrounds in both the United States and Canada, religious traditions that have also been characterized by more liberal positions on family values, reproductive rights, gender roles and social justice. Consequently, nones are more likely to be socialized with these values growing up. This does not necessarily determine that they will share these same values as adults, but it does usually have an important influence on them. During their young adult years, many nones also find themselves attending secular colleges or universities where such liberal views are often prevalent, being discussed in classes, in clubs, and among friends on campus. Such views may also have an impact on those who are more involved with religion who attend such institutions; however, the impact on nones may be even greater since they are more likely to be primed for these views by their earlier, more left-leaning socialization at home. Virtually no empirical research exists on a university environment's influence on religious nones in this way, and so remains an important avenue for future research.

Individuals also often choose friends and partners with similar values to themselves from the available pool of people around them, and friends and partners then tend to become more like each other as they spend time together. This often further reinforces a person's ideas of what is right and wrong, since most in their circles are agreeing with these ideas. These are phenomena that sociologists Paul Lazarsfeld and Robert Merton (1954) classically group under the concept of homophily (Cheadle and Schwadel 2012; McPherson, Smith-Lovin, and Cook 2001; Olson and Perl 2011; Smith, McPherson, and Smith-Lovin 2014).

As we have noted several times in this chapter, the effect of the social environment extends to regional culture too. Nones in the generally more liberal areas of the United States, for example, such as the American Northeast and West, are more left leaning in even larger numbers on the issues of abortion, same-sex marriage, environmental laws and regulations, government aid to the poor, and immigration than those in the South and Midwest. The same logic can be applied to those in Canada versus the United States, where values of multiculturalism, diversity, and equality in many forms are engrained in Canadian cultural norms in ways not fully embraced or realized in the United States. This is why religious nones in Canada are even more liberal on at least some of the issues measured here than religious nones in the United States (similarly among the religiously affiliated), such as on abortion and immigration.

By contrast, those more actively involved with a religious group as children and in their adult years are more likely to be regularly exposed to more right-leaning values within congregations and faith groups, their family, the faith-based schools, colleges and universities they are more likely to attend, and their network of friends and acquaintances who are more likely to share their own religious identities and beliefs (Adkins et al. 2013; Nicolet and Tresch 2009; O'Neill 2001; Putnam and Campbell 2010; Raymond 2011; Reimer 2003; Smidt et al. 2010; van der Brug, Hobolt, and de Vreese 2009). To be clear, however, not all organized religious groups have more right-leaning teachings and values on sexuality, reproductive rights, family values, gender roles, and the roles and responsibilities of government in society. But on average more do than what can be found in general American and Canadian popular culture and society. Among the religiously affiliated involved believers in the 2014 Pew Religious Landscape Study, for example, 39% are Evangelical Christian, 25% are Catholic, 3% are Mormon, 2% are Jehovah's Witnesses, and 1% are Muslim. These are all traditions that tend to espouse more right-leaning values on many of the issues explored in this chapter.

Moreover, as the decline of liberal Protestant affiliation and involvement continues (Bibby 2017; Clarke and Macdonald 2017; Putnam and Campbell 2010; Sherkat 2014), the overarching gap between religious nones and the religiously affiliated on these sociopolitical markers is likely to widen. The influence of peers and teachings within the religious group is also apparent among the handful of nones who are involved believers. In the previous sections we revealed that nones who attend religious services at least once a month often have similar lower rates of left-leaning support for many issues as religiously affiliated involved believers.

The further removed an individual is from organized religion, the more on average she or he seems to hold more left-leaning attitudes. Nonbelievers, both affiliated and unaffiliated, are those who are often the most removed from organized religion, in terms of frequency of contact, beliefs, and generationally with many being irreligiously socialized. They are also those with the highest rates of left-leaning views. Even among SBNR religious nones, whom we saw in figure 3.2 are often the next most likely to hold left-leaning attitudes, their perspectives are partially informed by the SBNR label that serves as a boundary marker against organized religion. Their views could represent both an endorsement of the left-leaning values denoted earlier and a statement against what they believe organized religious groups and individuals believe. Although as indicated in figure 3.1 many nonbelievers, SBNR, and involved believers base their morality on practical experience and common sense, what this practical experience and common sense has taught them over the years can differ greatly and is strongly influenced by the familial, friendship, work, and regional social environments they find themselves in.

In areas of more advanced secularization in the United States and Canada, where indicators of organized religion are less prevalent among the general population, those larger portions of the affiliated and unaffiliated population who are less involved with organized religion appear to be even further left of the political spectrum in many cases. In contrast, the minority of those still involved with religion seem to retain their levels of right-leaning issue stances. In some cases and on some issues then, this means there is a greater distance in views between those who are more and less involved with religion. Our earlier findings in this chapter highlight that the attitude gap between the religiously affiliated and unaffiliated on many key sociopolitical issues is heightened when contrasting nonbelievers and involved believers. In some cases, such as for attitudes on abortion, women in the workforce, environmental laws and regulations, and government aid to the poor, it is also heightened between nones and the affiliated in areas where nones form a larger portion of the population. Sarah also found this for the issues of premarital sexual relations, abortion, same-sex marriage, and gender roles when comparing not just American and Canadian regions but also regions across Europe (Wilkins-Laflamme 2016b).

This polarization can also be heightened in some cases by the less and nonreligious perceiving a difference in values from those more involved with religion, and purposefully moving even further away from organized religion and its associated right-leaning values as a consequence. In chapter 1, we saw that some none interviewees identified such factors in their reasons for disaffiliating, factors that we grouped under the heading of intellectual disagreements with religion—and vice versa: those more involved with religion may perceive different, more left-leaning values in the rest of society (i.e., in places with larger proportions of religious nones) and may purposefully become more defensive of their own right-leaning values as a consequence. As mentioned earlier, Putnam and Campbell (2010), for example, understand the development of the Religious Right and the rise of the religious nones in the United States as coming from a series of value shocks and countershocks during the second half of the twentieth century. The Christian Right emerged politically in the 1980s as a reaction to the flourishing liberal sexual morals of the 1960s and 1970s, and in turn the rise of religious nones in the 1990s were a counterreaction to the Christian Right and religious fundamentalism.

Although it is not the case for every societal issue, a divide between the religious and nonreligious is present on certain issues, which in turn has the potential for causing political divisions and strife between the two groups in society as well as heightening in- versus out-group dynamics. Consequently, although many still believe that the end product of secularization is the decline in importance of religion overall, we argue rather that as the stages of decline process unfolds with organized religion in both the United States and Canada, a social divide between the growing portion of less religious individuals on the one hand and the remaining core of actively religious on the other may become more prevalent on many sociopolitical issues. The ways in which such divisions unfold vary by social context too. As we have already hinted at, and we develop in detail in chapter 5, the prominent role of Evangelicals in the United States has distinct ramifications for polarization there versus in Canada with its smaller Evangelical population and its privileged place for multiculturalism. Linking this discussion then to a central claim of ours throughout this book, these findings reinforce that advanced secularization, ongoing signs of spiritual and religious vitality for a smaller segment of a population, and polarization can and do coexist. These are not mutually exclusive phenomena but rather simultaneously exist within a larger stages of decline framework.

4

I Want Everybody to Have the Same Chance to Find Happiness

Having distinct views is one thing. Actually acting on them and being involved in one's community is another. Earlier we introduced Corrine, a religious none in her midthirties who had no religious upbringing. In line with many religious nones in the previous chapter, Corrine stated, "I'm very, very liberal, like, I have a lot of friends who are homosexual. I have a lot of friends that are different religions, and I would never judge them any differently because of the things they do in their own head or in their own bedroom." Her link to spirituality is expressed mainly through physical fitness and being in nature, which she describes as her passions in life, where she is most at peace. In these social spaces Corrine regularly volunteers her time and talents. She shared of her many volunteer activities, including for summer running races, homeless shelters, and fundraising initiatives to help increase access to education locally and internationally. Asked what motivates her to be involved in these areas, she replied, "I just want . . . everybody to have the same chance to . . . find happiness . . . we have this school in Africa, and it's just like, amazing to see these girls getting an opportunity to get an education, and have a future. . . . And homeless people here, like, having a future and not living on the street, and not being cold. . . . And then just like athletes, like, being able to like, reach their goals, and like, fulfill their dreams and things like that."

The results in the previous chapter showed us that an important number of religious nones, like Corrine, have more left-leaning attitudes on many sociopolitical issues. However, if not politically and civically engaged, their opinions may often go unnoticed. So, how engaged are religious nones when it comes to politics and to their communities in general, and how do they compare with marginally and actively religious individuals? What variations, if any, exist when it comes to political participation, charitable giving, and volunteering? Are Corrine's volunteering habits reflective of the norm or the exception among religious nones? Being more removed from organized religion for the most part, are religious nones also less involved with other political and community organizations in society? Or are a certain number instead actively involved with their communities but in different ways than more religious individuals? And what social and civic implications might be on the horizon for those in the United States and Canada, should religious nones continue to hold a sizeable proportion of the population?

Politics

To begin, the more left-leaning political positioning of many religious nones is also reflected in who they tend to vote for in national elections in the United States and Canada. For example, among nones who voted in the 2016 presidential election in the United States, an estimated 65% voted Democrat (Clinton), and only 26% voted Republican (Trump). This is compared with 36% of affiliated monthly or more frequent religious service attenders voting for Clinton, and 57% voting for Trump (estimates based on our analyses of the 2016 American National Election Study). Smidt et al. (2010) demonstrate a trend of increasing importance attributed to level of religiosity over the last several decades for Americans' voting behavior in presidential elections: the very religious in most traditions are voting increasingly Republican, and the not very religious are voting ever-more Democrat.

In the 2015 Canadian federal election, 40% of none respondents in the 2015 Canadian Election Studies (CES) voted for the Liberal Party, and 27% voted for the New Democratic Party (NDP)—both parties more left of the political spectrum. Only 18% voted for the Conservative Party. This compares with the religiously affiliated respondents in the 2015 CES who consider religion to be very important in their lives, among whom 35% voted Liberal, 16% NDP, and 38% Conservative. Sarah has shown in her previous work (Wilkins-Laflamme 2016c) that the divide in Canadian voting behavior is now much more between those who consider religion to be important in their lives (who are more likely to vote Conservative) and those who do not (who are more likely to vote NDP or Liberal). This compared with elections in the 1960s, 1970s, 1980s, and 1990s when the divide was more between

Catholics (more likely to vote Liberal in the past) and Protestants (more likely to vote Conservative in the past). Nevertheless, this religiosity effect does not seem to be the only one at play in Canadian politics, and nones and the more religious do not seem to be as split along political lines as compared with the United States. A large proportion (51%) of Canadian affiliates who say religion is very important in their lives in the 2015 CES also voted for Trudeau's Liberals or Mulcair's NDP.

As well as often being linked to *who* people vote for, some researchers argue that active religiosity is also a key catalyst for political participation in general, providing the cognitive motivation, milieus for recruitment, and material resources to facilitate involvement in political action (Djupe and Grant 2001; Greenberg 2000; Jones-Correa and Leal 2001; Putnam 2000; Smidt 2003; Verba, Schlozman, and Brady 1995). The implication at the other end of the spectrum is that religious nones are less politically engaged due to their lack of access to these networks. However, Scheufele, Nisbet, and Brossard (2003) have shown that some elements of religion, including in-group closure and fatalist worldviews, can have a negative impact on an individual's political engagement, and that by contrast some secular networks can enable such engagement effectively.

The American National Election Study and the Canadian Election Study do ask respondents a series of questions to determine how involved they are in a variety of activities directly or indirectly related to politics. Among the 1,334 and 2,723 respondents who say they have no religion in these respective 2016 and 2015 surveys, the results in figure 4.1 indicate that there is not a whole lot of difference in their levels of political participation than among marginal affiliates (affiliated with a religious group or tradition but do not consider religion to be important in their lives) and active affiliates (affiliated with a religious group or tradition and do consider religion to be important in their lives). For example, once age, gender, marital status, number of children, race, foreign birth, level of education, and region of residence are controlled for with multivariate logistic regression models, nones in the United States had a 6% chance of contributing money to a political party or candidate during the 2016 campaign, compared with a 6% chance among marginal affiliates and a 7% chance among active affiliates. In Canada, nones have

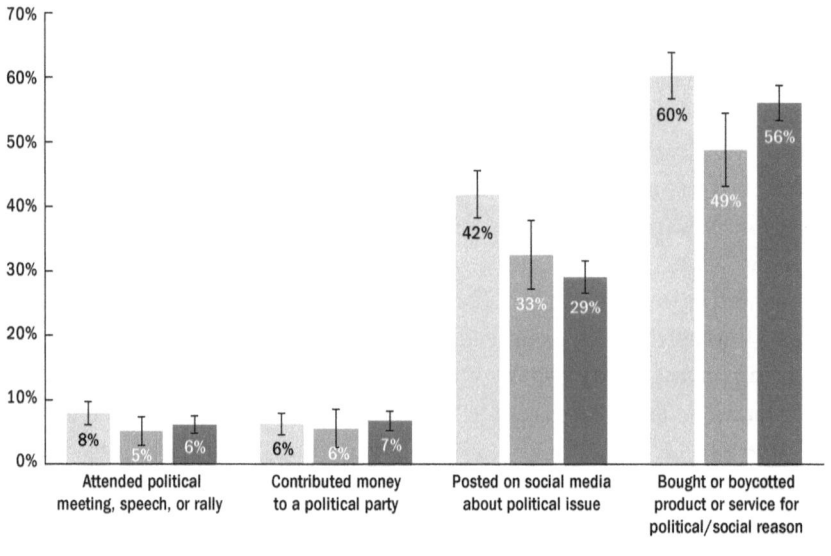

Figure 4.1.A Predicted probabilities of political engagement, USA, 2016, with CI (95%). *Source:* Data from the 2016 American National Election Study. Predicted probabilities generated from logit regression models with robust standard errors, controlling for the following covariates at their means: age, gender, marital status, number of children, race, foreign born, level of education, and region of residence. Weighted to be representative of the general adult population. N ANES 2016 = 3,480. Full results from these models available in table D.1 in appendix D.

a 14% chance of having been a member of a federal political party, compared with a 13% chance among marginal affiliates and a 14% chance among active affiliates.

The results in figure 4.1 indicate that, for all three categories of respondents, more active political participation, including attending rallies and speeches as well as donating to and being members of political parties, is not a phenomenon found among most of the general adult population. By contrast, political activities that generally require less time and resources and are often less tied to the election cycle, such as posting a political opinion on social media or buying/boycotting a product for political reasons, are more common.

One difference does stand out though between the religiously affiliated and unaffiliated in figure 4.1. In both the United States and Canada, nones are more likely to be politically engaged online and on social media, even once age is controlled for. This may be an indication that their networks that enable political engagement operate more through online portals, rather than, for example, through territorially situated congregations. Additionally, for the political participation indicators included in figure 4.1, it seems that it is marginal affiliates who often have the lowest levels of engagement, not religious nones. Marginal affiliates in both the United States and Canada are slightly less likely to buy or boycott products for political, social, or environmental reasons, and in Canada marginal affiliates are also less likely to donate money to political parties or candidates and to be involved politically online.

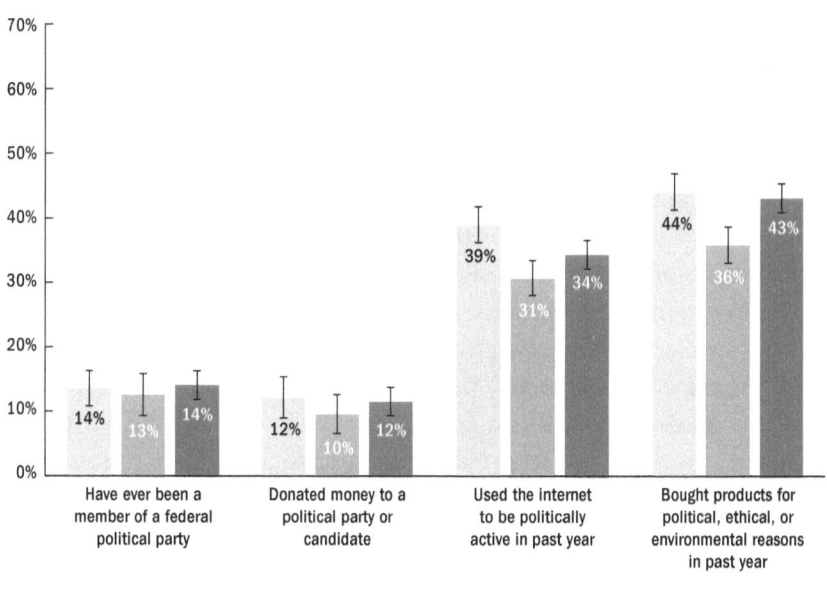

Figure 4.1.B. Predicted probabilities of political engagement, Canada, 2015, with CI (95%). *Source:* Data from the 2015 Canadian Election Study. Predicted probabilities generated from logit regression models with robust standard errors, controlling for the following covariates at their means: age, gender, marital status, number of children, foreign born, level of education, and region of residence. Weighted to be representative of the general adult population. N CES 2015 party member & donation = 2,676. N CES 2015 internet and boycott = 5,847. Full results from these models available in table D.2 in appendix D.

One possible reason for lower rates among marginal affiliates could be that these individuals are not as committed to their worldview position in general, unlike religious nones or active religious affiliates who are seemingly more definitive in their perspectives at either end of the spectrum.

There is also some regional variation in nones' political participation levels. In the United States, Northeast nones' probabilities of buying or boycotting a product or service for political or social reasons are twelve percentage points higher, and western nones ten percentage points higher, than nones in the South once other sociodemographic variables are controlled for. Whereas the gap between the nones and the religiously affiliated when it comes to their probabilities of buying or boycotting remains similar in the Midwest, South, and West, it is seventeen percentage points larger in the Northeast. We surmise that these variations reflect greater mobilization in places where there are larger proportions of religious nones, and lower activity where religious nones are fewer. In Canada, there is not a lot of variation between provinces in nones' levels of political participation, apart from in Alberta where nones' probabilities of donating to a political party or candidate are sixteen percentage points higher than nones in Ontario. Here too the regional variations in Canada might be explained by the large proportion of religious nones in Alberta, combined with the perception that Alberta is the epicenter of religious activity, notably Evangelicalism, in Canada. With the exception of the 2015 provincial election, Alberta has also been led by a conservative government for the previous half century. It could be that religious nones feel threatened in this social climate and accordingly are donating more often to political causes that they believe in, over and against the conservative religious and political environment they find themselves in, compared with nones in the rest of Canada.

Volunteering

Compared with the existing literature on (non)religion and political engagement, there is an even larger body of studies that have focused on the link between level of religiosity and charitable practices (see, notably, Angus Reid Institute 2018; Berger 2006; Borgonovi 2008; Bowen 2004; Campbell and Yonish 2003; Caputo 2009; Gibson 2008; Hall et al. 2009;

Hall 2005; Johnston 2013; Lam 2002, 2006; Lim and MacGregor 2012; Luria, Cnaan, and Boehm 2017; Monsma 2007; Parboteeah, Cullen, and Lim 2004; Perry et al. 2008; Putnam and Campbell 2010; Wuthnow 2004). Among this research, there is a general consensus of findings that point to a positive link between individual religiosity and participating in philanthropic activities. Persons with higher levels of religiosity have been repeatedly shown across many Western societies to be more likely to volunteer in their community and to give their time, money, and other available resources to nonprofit organizations (both secular and religious) than those individuals with lower or no religiosity.

A number of mechanisms have been identified in these studies as being behind this relationship. Many religious groups strongly encourage philanthropic activities both within and outside their community. Religious individuals tend to be much more involved in this congregational life, and so are also more likely to be exposed to the enabling resources and normative expectations surrounding charitable activities through their religious group (Beyerlein and Hipp 2006; Bowen 2004; Johnston 2013; Paxton, Reith, and Glanville 2014; Putnam and Campbell 2010; Wuthnow 2004). It is important to note here that, even though much of the terminology used by these studies is Christian based (congregational, etc.), these enabling mechanisms can also be present within non-Christian communities. The langar community kitchen, a staple of Sikh gurdwaras, is one example among many.

Some specific religious beliefs, values, and cognitive framing, such as the emphasis on selflessness and a sense of responsibility for helping those in need, are often the justification for engaging in philanthropic activities, and reinforce individuals' participation (Clerkin and Swiss 2013; Einolf 2011; Lam 2002; Mencken and Fitz 2013; Monsma 2007; Paxton, Reith, and Glanville 2014; Wilson and Janoski 1995; Wymer 1997). Those who are actively involved in religious activities usually also have friends, family, and acquaintances who are similarly involved. Consequently, a religious person's social network often contains many others who are volunteering and giving to charity as well as encouraging, potentially pressuring, and providing opportunities and resources to engage in these same behaviors (Becker and Dhingra 2001; Lewis, MacGregor, and Putnam 2013; Lim and MacGregor 2012; Merino 2013; Monsma 2007; Storm 2014).

These congregational life, religious values, and social network mechanisms are also not only present during an individual's adult life. Many who are actively involved in faith groups as adults were similarly active during their formative childhood years (Bengtson, Putney, and Harris 2013; Crockett and Voas 2006; Dillon and Wink 2007), and thus were often socialized in environments encouraging volunteer and charitable engagement (Hall et al. 2009; Lasby and Barr 2018; Perks and Haan 2011; Son and Wilson 2011). Nevertheless, these mechanisms are not necessarily found in equal measure among all religious traditions and faith groups. In the United States, the link between religious beliefs and volunteering has been found to be strongest among black and Evangelical Protestants (Johnston 2013); and the link between religious participation and volunteering, strongest among black and mainline Protestants (Beyerlein and Hipp 2006; Lam 2006; Paxton, Reith, and Glanville 2014; Uslaner 2002; Wilson and Janoski 1995).

Additionally, Stijn Ruiter and Nan Dirk de Graaf (2006) have found with cross-national comparisons that the effect of religiosity on volunteering appears to be stronger in more secular contexts, where congregational values and ways of life no longer permeate society but rather become solely the domain of smaller groups. In these environments, the religious beliefs, values, and norms laying the groundwork for and encouraging volunteering are instilled only among a smaller portion of the population that still has contact with faith communities, and thus the divide between the religious and the secular appears to be heightened.

One recent exception to the prevailing narrative that links higher levels of religiosity with higher rates of volunteering comes from sociologists Jacqui Frost and Penny Edgell (2018). They contend that when we examine the heterogeneity among religious nones, the picture is rather different. They suggest that atheists as well as the spiritual but not religious are more likely to volunteer for special hobby and interest groups compared with active religious affiliates. Moreover, religious nones on the whole do not seem to differ from the more religiously devout in volunteering for neighborhood associations, professional societies, literary or arts organizations, hobby groups, or political groups (see also Zuckerman, Galen, and Pasquale 2016, 206).

The data on volunteering and charitable giving we analyzed from the 2014 American General Social Survey and the 2013 Canadian General

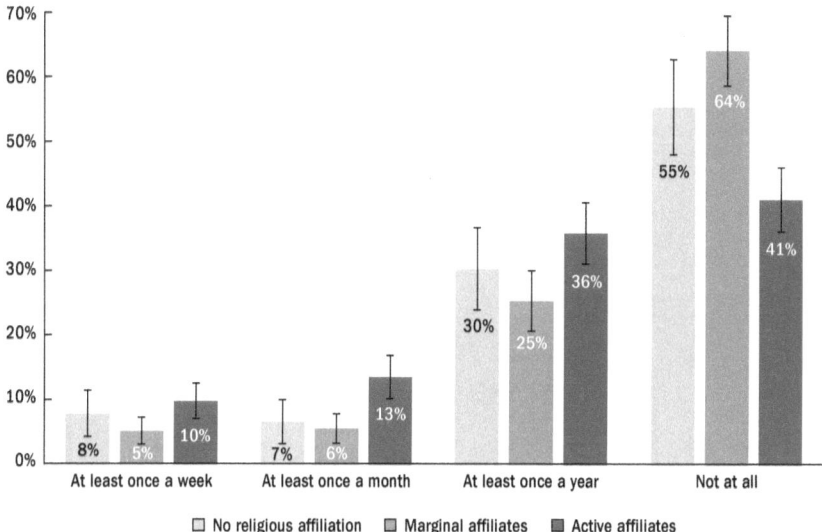

Figure 4.2.A. Predicted probabilities of frequency of volunteering in past year, USA, 2014, with CI (95%). *Source:* Data from the 2014 General Social Survey. Predicted probabilities from a multinomial logit regression model with robust standard errors, controlling for the following covariates at their means: age, gender, marital status, number of children, race, foreign born, level of education, employment status, and region of residence. Weighted to be representative of the general adult population. N = 1,249. Full results from these models available in table D.3 in appendix D.

Social Survey do show the trend of religious nones having lower rates of volunteering and charitable giving overall, especially when compared with active affiliates. However, these data sources do not allow us to compare different types of religious nones, so the comparison will have to remain among nones overall, marginal affiliates (religiously affiliated but attend religious services less than once a month), and active affiliates (religiously affiliated and attend religious services at least once a month) for this chapter. Once sociodemographics are controlled for in multivariate logistic regression models, including age, gender, marital status, number of children, race, foreign birth, level of education, employment status, and region of residence, active affiliates in the United States have a 59% probability of volunteering at least once in the year prior to the survey, compared with a 45% probability among nones and a 36% probability among marginal affiliates (see figure 4.2). In Canada,

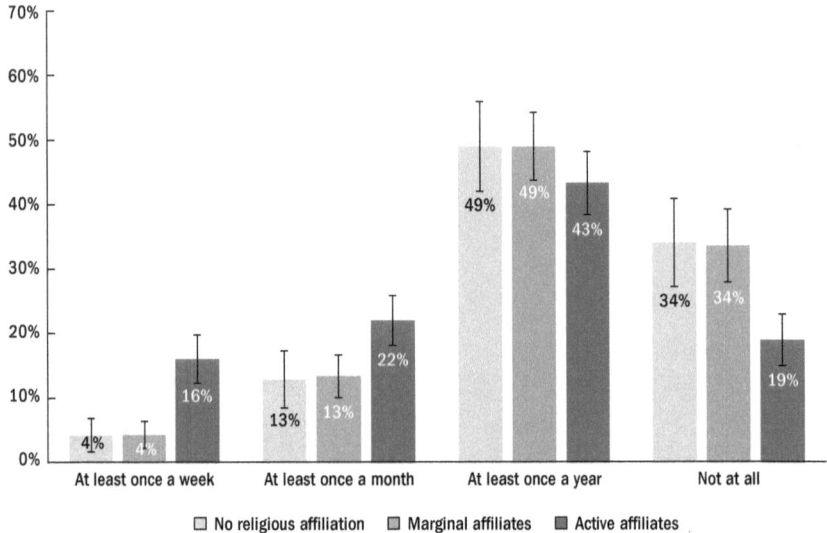

Figure 4.2.B. Predicted probabilities of frequency of charitable giving in past year, USA, 2014, with CI (95%). *Source:* Data from the 2014 General Social Survey. Predicted probabilities from a multinomial logit regression model with robust standard errors, controlling for the following covariates at their means: age, gender, marital status, number of children, race, foreign born, level of education, employment status, and region of residence. Weighted to be representative of the general adult population. N = 1,249. Full results from these models available in table D.4 in appendix D.

active affiliates have a 59% probability of volunteering in the year prior to the survey, compared with a 38% probability among both nones and marginal affiliates (see figure 4.3). This volunteer gap between the religiously affiliated and unaffiliated does not vary significantly between the four American and five Canadian Census regions. Additionally, in Canada where we can distinguish the different types of volunteering being undertaken by respondents, the gap between active affiliates and the less religious is still present when excluding volunteerism in the religion sector, in line with similar results in the United States and Canada from Robert Putnam and David Campbell (2010, 446) and Kurt Bowen (2004, 157), but the gap does become much narrower.

Among volunteers in Canada, active affiliate volunteers also give more hours on average than none and marginal affiliate volunteers: an average of 177 hours each year among active affiliate volunteers, compared with 134 hours among marginal affiliate volunteers and 152 hours among religious none volunteers. However, when volunteer hours in the religion sector are cut out from the tally, religious none volunteers then have the highest average annual hours volunteered at 149 hours, compared with 120 hours among active affiliate volunteers and 132 hours among marginal affiliate volunteers (see figure 4.3).

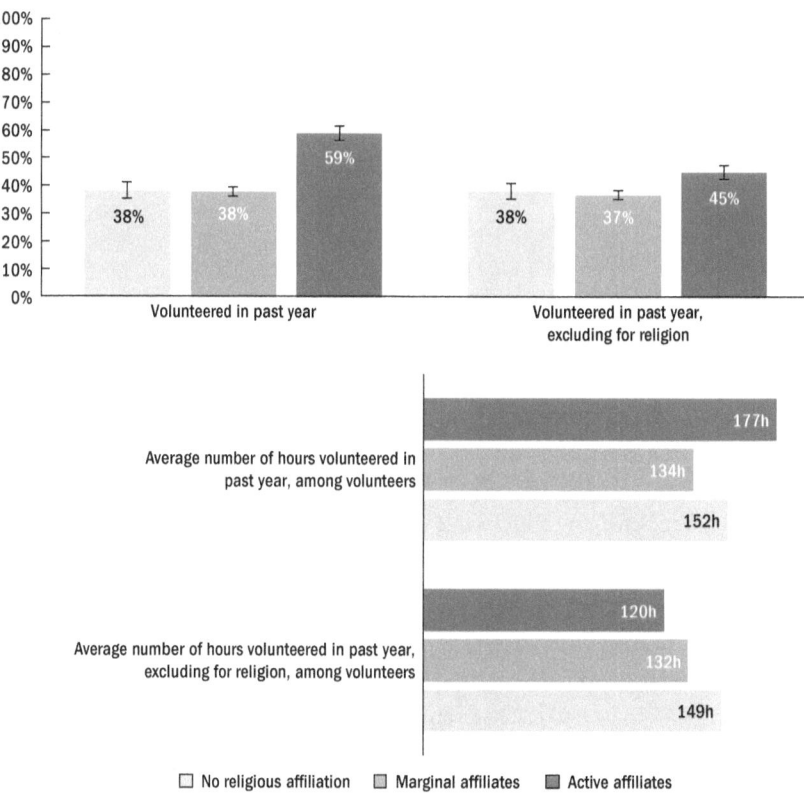

Figure 4.3.A. Predicted probabilities and means of volunteering, Canada, 2013, with CI (95%). *Source:* Data from the 2013 Canadian General Social Survey. Predicted probabilities and means generated from logit and OLS regression models with robust standard errors, controlling for the following covariates at their means: age, gender, marital status, number of children, employment status, foreign born, level of education, and region of residence. Weighted to be representative of the general adult population. N = 13,394. Full results from these models available in tables D.5 and D.6 in appendix D.

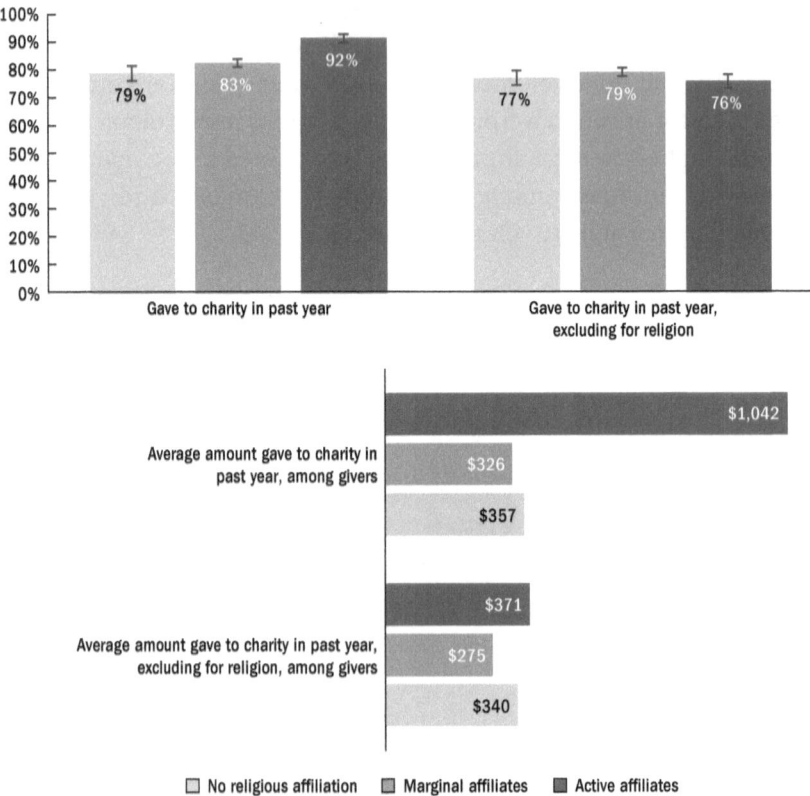

Figure 4.3.B. Predicted probabilities and means of charitable giving, Canada, 2013, with CI (95%). *Source:* Data from the 2013 Canadian General Social Survey. Predicted probabilities and means generated from logit and OLS regression models with robust standard errors, controlling for the following covariates at their means: age, gender, marital status, number of children, employment status, foreign born, level of education, and region of residence. Weighted to be representative of the general adult population. N = 13,394. Full results from these models available in tables D.7 and D.8 in appendix D.

When comparing the difference in volunteer hours outside of religious contexts between religious nones and active affiliates, keep in mind that there are fewer none volunteers versus active affiliate volunteers on the whole. In the 2013 Canadian General Social Survey (GSS) sample, religious none respondents provided 15% of all volunteer hours outside the religion sector while representing 16% of the total sample.

This compares with 33% of total volunteer hours outside the religion sector being provided by actively affiliated respondents, who represent 29% of the total sample.

Among all respondents in Canada who do volunteer their time, the most common sectors they volunteer in are generally the same: sports, culture and recreation, education and research, and social services. Religion is also among the top volunteer sectors for active affiliates, but not for marginal affiliates or nones.

On the topic of helping local communities, Nancy Ammerman (2014) cites from her qualitative fieldwork in the United States that "'helping the needy' was a common theme, but especially among those who are regular participants in religious communities . . . the importance of religious communities and spiritual engagement is significant. Only a third of nonaffiliates told stories about local volunteer work, compared to roughly half of all those who have a congregational affiliation" (220–21). In the many interviewee quotations that Ammerman provides, individual after individual reference ties to their religion or religious group as a motivating factor for volunteering or donating money to those in need. Without discrediting those with no ties to a congregation but who also volunteer or give money for charitable causes, Ammerman notes that such individuals "were less likely than their religiously active neighbors to be directly involved in any concrete effort to pursue those community betterment goals" (225). Ammerman's general distinctions between the more and less religious are helpful, yet subtle nuances still exist within these groups. For example, Elizabeth Drescher's (2016, 234–37) interviews with religious nones in the United States included George, a "Jesus Follower" who identified as a religious none to distance himself from the baggage that comes with the word "Christian." George and his family regularly volunteered with different organizations that helped those in poverty, and they did so "in Jesus' name."

During our interviews we asked our research participants whether they volunteered anywhere, if so where they volunteered and how often they volunteered. The interview findings generally align with the aforementioned survey findings. Only about 15% of active affiliate interviewees say they do not volunteer anywhere, versus around 50% of both marginal affiliates and religious nones (a handful of religious nones even laughed at the question, implying that the question was a ridiculous assertion that they might volunteer). Some of these individuals indicated that they used to volunteer but no longer do because of stage of life (e.g., young children or retired and physically unable to), and others projected that they might volunteer in the future as they become less busy.

As expected, marginal affiliates and religious nones who do volunteer concentrate their volunteer activities with secular organizations, while active religious affiliates are more likely to volunteer with religious organizations only (approximately 40%), or in both religious and secular organizations (nearly 25%). The amount of volunteering varied, with active religious affiliates most likely to say they volunteer weekly to monthly, and religious nones most likely to say they volunteered "on occasion" with event-based opportunities (e.g., annual music festival). Interviewees tend to volunteer their time in areas in which they are personally affected. The list received by interviewees is exhaustive, spanning across the areas cited earlier from the Canadian General Social Survey data.

The most instructive aspects of the interview data for us are the reasons and motivations that individuals give for their volunteering activities. Ken is in his twenties and converted to Christianity as a young adult. He volunteers in his church but is very involved outside his church too. He provided the following rationale for doing so: "I also find active involvement in community and things like that to be very important.... I'm a member of a political party. I'm affiliated with a few different ... social action-type groups, and I feel as if those are part of ... the practice. I'm kind of coming at it as, 'This is my responsibility as a Christian to work for a better world, sort of thing.' I mean, outside of that, there is, like, sort of being an ethical and morally upright person, as well."

David, a marginal affiliate in his early forties with two children, playfully joked about why he volunteers at his kids' schools: "To counterbalance school fees, school trips, to be with them.... It's going to sound bad. To have all my daughter's male friends know who I am ... [laughter] ... you know? 'I'm the dad. I'm keeping my eye on her. You mess up, you're being hammered.'" Another marginal affiliate, Erin, reflects on the volunteering and charitable activity that her family is involved in. She focused her rationale toward her children, saying, "It's a big part of their life, and we're just trying to teach them to be good people, as opposed to fitting into a box of a formal religion *and* still be a good person."

Earlier in this chapter we learned about Corrine, a religious none, who volunteers in a number of capacities locally and abroad because she wants others, notably from underprivileged and marginalized positions in society, to have a chance in life. Karen is single, in her late twenties, and has no religious upbringing or exposure. A personal invitation from a friend and an opportunity to feel good about herself was all it took to compel her to volunteer. She volunteers at a local homeless shelter: "My friend just asked me to, so I said 'yeah.' I was like, 'Oh, I got spare time.' . . . You get it over with quick. . . . It makes me feel better."

Charitable Giving

Transitioning from volunteering to charitable giving, the results in figures 4.2 and 4.3 also indicate lower overall rates of charitable giving among nones, especially when compared with active affiliates. In the United States in 2014, active affiliates had an 81% probability of giving to a charity at least once in the year prior to the survey, compared with a 66% probability among both nones and marginal affiliates once other sociodemographic variables are controlled for (see figure 4.2). In Canada in 2013, active affiliates had a 92% probability of giving to a charity in the year prior to the survey, compared with a 79% probability among nones and an 83% probability among marginal affiliates. The giving gap between the religiously affiliated and unaffiliated also does not vary significantly between the four US and five Canadian census regions. However, when looking at charitable giving only in sectors other than religion in Canada, the gap between active affiliates and the less religious disappears and the probability of a respondent giving to charity at least once in the year prior to the survey becomes relatively similar between the three groups, falling between 76% and 79%.

Among respondents who gave to charity at least once in the year prior to the 2013 Canadian General Social Survey, active affiliate givers also gave more dollars on average than none and marginal affiliate givers overall: an average of $1,042, compared with $357 and $326. However, when dollars given to religion are excluded, this gap is reduced substantially: an average of $371 among active affiliates, compared with $340 among nones and $275 among marginal affiliates. As with volunteering, the sectors that giving respondents donated the most to are relatively similar, sectors that include health, social services, and international and philanthropic intermediaries. Active affiliates also give a lot to religion, which is not the case among nones and marginal affiliates.

The results in figures 4.2 and 4.3 overall as well as in the existing literature point to active affiliates in both the United States and Canada being distinct in their higher levels of philanthropy. Lower levels of this type of community engagement among marginal affiliates (who do not come into regular contact with a place of worship) also indicates that the religious group may be key in enabling this form of activity, whether it be through the congregation, the gurdwara, the mosque, the synagogue, the temple, or in any other meeting place for faith groups.

By contrast, lower levels of philanthropic activity among marginal affiliates and religious nones are often attributed to the individualism hypothesis: those with lower levels of religiosity not only have more left-leaning values as seen in the previous chapter but also often score higher on values of individualism such as independence and self-achievement (Beyerlein and Vaisey 2013; Saroglou, Delpierre, and Dernelle 2004; Schwartz and Huismans 1995; Woodhead 2016; Zuckerman, Galen, and Pasquale 2016, 203–7), and so would be less likely to value the benefits of giving their time and resources to others. For example, in a 2017 opinion poll in Canada run by Cardus and the Angus Reid Institute (2017b), 60% of the 657 religious none respondents expressed that the best way to live one's life is to be more focused on achieving our own dreams and happiness, rather than on helping others—compared with 58% among the 1,005 marginal affiliates and 31% among the 334 active affiliates. The less religious are also not usually part of networks highly engaged in philanthropic activities that sometimes push back against the excesses of prevalent values of individualism in American and Canadian popular culture and society.

This said, many nones do seem to be learning the importance of philanthropic activity from their families, from their friends, in their schools, and potentially through government and nonprofit programs that encourage such activity. Some may also feel the need to engage more with the community to put into action their views as a counterweight to the community influence that some religious groups hold. Yet these mechanisms for enabling philanthropic activity among nones, as well as among marginal affiliates, still seem to remain less effective than those among the actively religious, indicated by the greater level of involvement from a larger proportion of active affiliates.

Interestingly, our results for both the United States and Canada indicate that, more often than not, religious nones are not those with the lowest levels of charitable volunteering and giving—marginal affiliates are. This effect is often missed in other studies, since level of religiosity is almost always treated as a linear effect, whereas our results indicate that it may often be curvilinear in that those marginal affiliates in the middle of the religiosity scale have the lowest levels of philanthropic activity overall. Perhaps being in the middle of the political/ideological spectrum and the religiosity spectrum is tied to lower levels of engagement than among those closer to either end of the spectrums who hold stronger and more distinct views, in line with what Frost and Edgell (2018) also find.

Implications for the Future of Civil Society

Since active affiliates play a large role in civil society, in both the United States and Canada where the pool of these active affiliates has shrunk over the last half century and is aging rapidly, there is worry among many scholars, faith leaders, members of nonprofits and policy makers that a whole generation of dedicated volunteers and financial givers are not being trained and replaced, by means of organized religious groups or at all. Our results in this chapter indicate that the very worst of these fears are not being fully realized: a certain proportion of nones and marginal affiliates are volunteering their time and donating their money to causes they believe in, just not at the higher rates found among active affiliates. For example, among Millennials aged fifteen to twenty-nine years old in the 2013 Canadian General Social Survey, 44% of nones, 42% of marginal affiliates, and 65% of active affiliates had volunteered in the year prior to the survey. Among eighteen- to twenty-nine-year olds in the 2014 American General Social Survey, 47% of nones, 36% of marginal affiliates, and 58% of active affiliates had volunteered at least once in the year prior to the survey. These rates are also likely to increase later in life as Millennials finish their schooling, finish raising their families, and finish with their careers (see Angus Reid Institute 2018, 17–18).

Whereas we do not find ourselves in a doomsday scenario where religious nones or members of younger generations are completely absent from civil society, in our many discussions with members of different faith groups we do hear about how many feel there are now added expectations for the shrinking pool of actively religious individuals. These sentiments are especially expressed in mainline Protestant traditions that have a vast amount of property and personnel to support amid rapidly ageing congregations and declining attendance figures. These pressures are felt in areas of philanthropy, community organization, and leadership due to the changes in civil society and in the (non)religious landscape in the United States and Canada. Between 2004 and 2013, David Lasby and Cathy Barr (2018, 30–31) show that the percentage of total donations to the religious sector in Canada is, in fact, declining (41% of total donations going to the religious sector in 2013 versus 45% in 2004), despite religious organizations being the far and away leader in receiving donations (the health sector was the next closest at 13% in 2013). In the United States, 32% of all donations went to religious organizations (followed by education, at 15%).

Some religious nones may celebrate the declining human and financial resources coming from active affiliates, at least those directed toward religious organizations—groups that some religious nones believe are harmful to society (a topic that we develop in chapter 5). Without downplaying the divisive role that some religious groups and individuals play in society, a strong empirical case can be made for the social and civic benefits that arise from the religious organizations that active affiliates give to (Ammerman 2005; Bowen 2004; Cnaan 2002; Cnaan, Boddie, and Yancey 2003; Friesen and Clieff 2014; Janzen, Chapman, and Watson 2012; Putnam and Campbell 2010; Smidt 2003; Wuthnow 2004). Religious organizations, their buildings and personnel, and millions of volunteers across the United States and Canada serve as critical hubs to serve the wider public in areas of addiction, poverty, education, immigrant and refugee settlement, childcare, and more. Active members of religious organizations also develop skills useful for the workplace or other institutional sectors in society: skills such as public speaking, teamwork, and leadership (Brady, Verba, and Schlozman 1995; Hall et al. 2009, 49; Verba, Schlozman, and Brady 1995).

Recently, scholars in both countries have started to talk about the economic "halo effect" of religious groups for society. Brian Grim and Melissa Grim (2016) offer a conservative estimate of $378 billion in annual economic contributions to the United States, with a high-end estimate of $4.7 trillion. Another study in the United States on historic sacred places in urban environments suggests that each historical sacred space contributes nearly $1.7 million annually to the local community (Partners for Sacred Places 2016). In a Toronto-based study, Mike Wood Daly (2016) reveals that every dollar that a congregation spends yields nearly five dollars' worth of services to a local community.

Given the strong evidence on the positive link among religious individuals, civil society, and local communities, it is surprising then that we hear of government and community groups gathering to discuss how to improve social or civic life without including religious groups at the table. For instance, in 2018, a civil society summit was held in Ottawa that included members of all G7 nations as well as various civil society groups across Canada, to discuss ways to create a safer, more equitable, and sustainable world. In his summary of the event, John Longhurst (2018) states, "Although a few faith-based NGOs were present, not one speaker, presenter or panelist came from a religious group, and the subject of religion didn't come up once. In a conversation after the summit, an organizer said the idea of including faith community leaders never came up in the planning. In retrospect, he acknowledged this was an oversight." Experiences such as these reinforce the ways in which Canada has become more secular over time, such that the substantial impact that religious groups make in society often seem to be nowhere on the radar for social and civic discussion and well-being.

We are not suggesting for a moment that religious groups and individuals are solely good and beneficial for society, nor are we implying that religious nones and secular organizations are bad and harmful for society (see Niose 2012). On the latter point, the data we have presented throughout this chapter suggest otherwise. As an example, secular congregations like the Sunday Assembly who exist to "Live Better, Help Often, and Wonder More" are actively involved in a variety of volunteer and charitable initiatives to benefit surrounding communities across the United States, Canada, Europe, and Australia. Other research by Frost and Edgell (2018) and Zuckerman, Galen, and Pasquale (2016) showcase the active volunteering contributions made by religious nones. Phil Zuckerman's (2008) earlier research in Scandinavia additionally documents the many positive social and civic realities to arise in a largely secular society. We are simply trying to make the case that in the United States and Canada, as the proportion of active religious affiliates decrease, there is a sizeable social and civic impact regardless of whether we focus on volunteering and charitable giving inside or outside of religious contexts.

All of this means that governments may have to play a larger role in the years to come to ensure that essential services are being provided to those in need, a role that armies of volunteers tied to faith groups used to play to a greater degree and currently continue to deliver. Religious groups are no longer enabling philanthropic activity among a majority of the Canadian and American populations, because this majority no longer comes into regular contact with religious organizations. Municipal, provincial/state, and federal governments are, however, institutions that most individuals, including religious nones, must engage with, through schools or special events, following rules and regulations, working for levels of governments, participating in government programs, or by paying taxes. State institutions could continue to expand on roles they have developed over the past century in both Canada and the United States: directly growing social services they currently provide with government employees and resources to extend to those that faith groups have traditionally provided using individual and industry tax dollars. These services once expanded to include education, welfare, and hospitals, and could in the future include more soup kitchens, shelters, immigrant settlement programs, and the like. Governments could also create or enable new networks and other innovative ways to encourage philanthropy among its population. High school student volunteer programs and tax breaks for charitable giving are examples of such indirect measures already in place in many regions across the United States and Canada. Our results in the previous chapter indicate that substantial portions of nones and marginal affiliates favor this larger role for government in providing and encouraging social services, compared with those more actively involved in faith groups who may feel it should fall more to private members and organizations within civil society such as their own groups.

Conclusion

Recall the startling words by Pastor Robert Jeffress at First Baptist Church in Dallas, at the outset of chapter 3: "Liberals know that conservative Christians are the last speed bump on the road to the godless, immoral society that liberals dream of" (Mehta 2018). Despite these words and many others like them circulating in the American, and even sometimes Canadian, contexts, findings from this chapter show that a substantial proportion of religious nones are politically and civically engaged. Religious nones like Corrine at the beginning of this chapter actively volunteer in several domains, motivated by a desire to make the world a better place and give everyone a chance to find happiness. They also donate to a variety of charitable secular organizations. Additionally, though religious nones, like religious affiliates, are not for the most part regularly active in the political sphere, they are more likely to be politically active online. By these collective markers religious nones are not necessarily amoral or immoral, as per the comments by Jeffress. To the contrary, religious nones are involved in a variety of moral and social causes.

This said, religious nones are less likely, on the whole, to volunteer or donate money when compared with active religious affiliates. Even when we distinguish these activities in religious contexts versus nonreligious ones, active affiliates make sizeable contributions in nonreligious environments. One of the surprising elements in our data is that marginal religious affiliates, not religious nones, are the least socially and civically engaged. Such differences in sociopolitical attitudes and civic engagement can have a notable impact socially and politically, and these are some of the domains that we are paying close attention to moving forward with demographic shifts among religious nones and religious affiliates in the United States and Canada.

Social cohesion and how members of each group perceive members of the other are also areas that are affected by these differences in attitudes and behavior between the nonreligious and religious. Seeing extreme and sensationalized cases in the media, the less and nonreligious may perceive the more actively religious as all intolerant right-wingers, and more religious individuals may tend to see the nonreligious as having no proper sense of community or of right and wrong due to their nonbelief. In the next chapter, we explore how these perceptions can fuel more negative attitudes among nones toward members of certain religious groups, and vice versa among the more actively religious toward nones.

5

It's Too Bad Your Parents Aren't Christian . . .

Sandra, a religious none, is in her midfifties and playfully describes herself as a "domestic goddess." She has held various part-time jobs over her lifetime and had some exposure to Evangelical Protestantism via her grandfather when she was younger. She is unsure if she believes in God, is fairly confident that there is no afterlife, and is adamantly against fundamentalist and exclusivist religious groups that are closed minded in her view. Sandra and her husband did not raise their children with any religious belief or practice in the home. When Sandra's daughter Chloe was a teenager, Chloe became actively involved in an Evangelical organization. Chloe's involvement did not initially bother her mother until Chloe noted the following comment from a fellow member of this newfound group: "It's too bad your parents aren't Christian." This statement offended Sandra and her husband. Elsewhere in the same interview, Sandra described Chloe's group as "cultish." She spoke of "blind worshipping . . . you can believe whatever you want but always keep your mind open, asking questions. As soon as anybody says to you, 'don't ask, just obey,' that to me is a huge warning sign just to back away from that. It seemed to me that it was a whole lot of just worship. . . . There was no critical thinking in it."

As should be clear now, religious nones in the United States and Canada tend to be different from those who affiliate with a religion in several important ways. Religious nones stand out based on family status (less likely to be married or to have children), gender (more likely to be male), and age (younger than those affiliated with a religion). Religious nones are more likely to be raised by parents who are also religiously unaffiliated, and who rarely if ever attend religious services. Religious nones score lower on a range of religious or spiritual belief and behavior indicators, in both institutional and noninstitutional contexts. And as we saw in the two previous chapters, the affiliated and unaffiliated hold fairly distinct sociopolitical attitudes and behaviors relative to one another, especially when comparing nonbelievers to active affiliates.

Thus far we have discussed some of the social implications to arise from these variations between the affiliated and unaffiliated, in an environment of declines in organized religion across the United States and Canada. Another important trajectory to explore, especially with a now sizeable proportion of religious nones in these two countries, is how do religious nones view those who are affiliated with a religion, and vice versa? Do religious nones hold markedly favorable or unfavorable attitudes toward some religious groups and not others, and if so, why? To what extent do members of different religious groups have pronounced positive or negative attitudes toward religious nones, and what accounts for these different attitudes? How might contextual variables, such as being a religious none in a highly devout region, intersect with these lines of inquiry?

Questions such as these have gained traction among scholars in the last decade. Some have framed this discussion in the context of "polarization." As summarized in the opening chapter, one strand of the polarization framework is that there is a widening and hostile gap between the most religious and irreligious in society (Bibby 2011; Putnam and Campbell 2010; Wilkins-Laflamme 2014, 2016b). As just one illustration, in *American Grace: How Religion Divides and Unites Us*, Putnam and Campbell (2010, 499–501) argue that while the most religious Americans may seem to be among the nicest in America (measured by their social and civic engagement), they are also among the most intolerant toward those who think and behave differently than themselves. Such intolerance may be magnified as religious nones grow and vie for greater cultural legitimacy over and against a nation historically (and still, in some respects) dominated by Evangelical Christianity.

More recently some have injected questions on religious diversity and religious nones into the conversation (see Beaman 2017; Beaman and Steele 2018). For example, how might social discourse over diversity and inclusion of religious minority groups extend (or not) to those who do not identify with any religion? How are societies negotiating sacred-secular social practices? What does it mean to pursue "deep equality" amid multiple religious and irreligious worldviews coexisting within a society?

In this chapter we turn to American and Canadian public opinion data as well as qualitative interview data with nones. We examine the level of dislike, apprehension, indifference, or respect among nones toward individuals affiliated with various religious traditions and actively practicing their faith. We also consider attitudes and perceptions among affiliates from different religious groups toward the nonreligious. Along the way we give attention to how perceptions toward the "other" are affected by region. Last, we wade into religious diversity waters insofar as Canada and the United States are navigating the role and place of religious nones in social and institutional spaces currently characterized by important levels of pluralism.

Narratives about and Perceptions toward Religious Nones

A central thread in our argument is that social context matters for how religious nones view and experience the world. Living on the West Coast in Canada or the United States versus the Canadian Maritimes or the American Midwest matters. To further illustrate this point, we now compare narratives, perceptions, and behaviors about and toward religious nones in the United States and Canada—nations with different historical narratives and trajectories concerning religion, and by extension religious nones, in society.

In the United States, "America as a Christian nation" is a well-documented historical and contemporary narrative (see, e.g., Lipset 1991; Niose 2012; Noll 1992; Schmidt 2016; Stark and Finke 1992). In 1960, Will Herberg famously documented that to "be American" was to "be religious." Not just any kind of religion. A certain kind of religion within the Judeo-Christian lineage, most notably Evangelical Christianity. In this social context religious nones were at best ignored in popular and academic discourse, and at worst vilified as outsiders to American social ideals. Just over a decade after Herberg's pronouncement, sociologist Colin Campbell's (1971) book *Toward a Sociology of Irreligion* served as a watershed moment for the academic study of religious nones. Campbell started his work by reinforcing and extending Herberg's observation of the privileged place of religion in American society: "To be nonreligious in the mid-nineteenth century was to risk not only social ostracism, petty persecution and accusations of immorality but criminal proceedings as well" (1971, 4). The widespread belief was that religion was beneficial and necessary for society to function well, and thus that irreligion was functionally problematic for individuals and society. Campbell's book opened the door to think about, dialogue, and learn about a segment of society largely ignored by scholars in a modern world dominated by religious belief, practice, and discourse. Against the backdrop of a largely religious modern context, Campbell started a conversation about how and why religious nones viewed the world in the ways that they did, and how, in turn, "the world" viewed religious nones.

Suffice to say, our discussion of religious nones in the United States today emerges in an environment with deep religious roots, where religious nones were, and still are in many regions, stigmatized as deviant outsiders. As we noted in the opening chapter, this historical context partially explains why the growth of religious nones in the United States began later than in Canada. The social stigma to say that one had no religion was incredibly high in the United States where civil religion roots run deep and, as we will note in this chapter, remains very high mainly in more devout pockets of the country.

Religious none growth started earlier and more rapidly in Canada in part because Canada's self-narrative of being a "Christian nation" was somewhat different in nature and arguably disintegrated earlier than in the United States. Especially between the mid-nineteenth and mid-twentieth centuries, English-Canadian political and public discourse was infused notably with British identity, characterized by strong ethnic ties to England, Wales, Scotland, and Ireland, the country's membership in the British Empire, and by more conservative values than in the United States (Buckner 2005; Igartua 2011; Lacombe 2002). The Anglican Church, along with the denominations that became the United Church of Canada in 1925 (Methodist Church, Presbyterian Church, Congregational Union, and Association of Local Union Churches), acted as the Protestant pillars of this national identity and collective British-Canadian memory. In French-speaking Canada during this same period, the Catholic Church became synonymous with the French-Canadian nation, acting as its main institutional, social, and religious support for survival in an otherwise Anglo-Protestant continent (Grant 1998; Noll 2006; Voisine, Hamelin, and Gagnon 1984). Until the mid-twentieth century, high proportions of Canadians identified with this small group of Protestant denominations or Catholicism, and actively attended church (more so than in the United States even). Protestant and Catholic groups played prominent roles in the provision of education, healthcare, and social services, and most political leaders were Christian (Bibby 1987, 17; Bowen 2004, 13; Clarke and Macdonald 2017; Noll 1992, 548).

However, the post–World War II decades marked the onset of a series of social changes that diminished religion's role in Canadian society. In English-speaking Canada, the collapse of the British Empire, marked notably by the independence movement in India from 1930 to 1940, the Suez Canal crisis in 1956, and Great Britain joining the European Economic Community in 1967 (Buckner 2005), helped bring an end to British-Protestant-Canadian nationalism. This form of nationalism was to be replaced by a national identity more focused on multiculturalism and religious pluralism by the end of the twentieth century. In French-speaking Canada, particularly in Quebec, the Quiet Revolution of the early 1960s brought an end to the prominent role played by the Catholic Church in most public and political affairs. The combination of religious groups weakening in public and social influence, individuals becoming less involved in religious organizations, and the progressive advancement of liberal-leaning values among more Canadians set the stage for religion—Christianity in particular—to take a less prominent place in Canadian social conscience.

As we argued earlier, one outcome tied to these changes is that religious nones developed sooner and faster in Canada versus the United States. Our interest here is in how, if at all, attitudes have changed toward religious nones in the United States and Canada more recently. Research of this kind remains in its infancy. Over the last fifteen years studies have started to emerge on this front, more so in the United States than in Canada. The first observation to note is that a range of stereotypes exist toward religious nones, which include positive, neutral, and negative perceptions (Harper 2007). But as we detail below, negative stereotypes are the most common descriptors, notably among actively religious individuals. Unsurprisingly, contextual variables such as whether religious nones are the majority or minority in a given region factor into people's perceptions.

Most research to date deals with atheists and agnostics rather than religious nones as a whole. Similar to Campbell's findings in the early 1970s, Edgell, Gerteis, and Hartmann (2006) speak of symbolic boundaries between those who are religious and atheists. The widespread social perception persists that by being religious, one is good, moral, and trustworthy. Conversely, to identify as atheist is to *not* possess these qualities. These sentiments come to the fore in many ways. For example, while Americans are more likely to vote for an atheist for president than in previous generations, still fewer than 50% of Americans in 1999 would do so (Edgell, Gerteis, and Hartmann 2006, 215; see also Baker and Smith 2015, 167). This figure is well below figures of other groups historically marginalized such as homosexuals (60%) or Jews, Catholics, or African Americans who all score around 90% (Edgell, Gerteis, and Hartmann 2006, 215). Similar observations extend to questions about social groups that agree with a person's vision of American society, or disapproval if one's child was to marry someone from another social group. Those who attend religious services more frequently, and conservative Protestants especially, are the least likely to view atheists in a positive light. Not surprisingly, in environments where religious people are a majority, distrust toward atheists is also highest (see Gervais, Norenzayan, and Shariff 2011). Edgell, Gerteis, and Hartmann (2006, 230) conclude, "Atheists are at the top of the list of groups that Americans find problematic in both public and private life, and the gap between acceptance of atheists and acceptance of other racial and religious minorities is large and persistent."

In early 2017, the Pew Research Center asked more than 4,200 adults in the United States in their American Trends Panel to rate different religious groups using a "feelings thermometer." A high score of 100 indicates the warmest and most positive feelings toward a group, while a low score of 0 reveals the coldest and least positive feelings toward a group. Jews, Catholics, mainline Protestants, and Evangelicals scored the highest, with average ratings of 66, 65, 63, and 61 respectively among all Americans. In contrast, atheists scored near the bottom (50), just above Muslims (48), based on Sarah's analyses of this Pew data. With respect to demographics, the coolest feelings toward atheists are held by those who are older, married, without a university education, of lower income strata, and living in the South. In terms of how members of specific religious groups feel toward atheists, the following data arise: Jews give them an average score of 66, Catholics a score of 48, liberal Protestants a score of 46, and Evangelical Protestants a score of 32. Not surprisingly, in 2014 individuals who personally knew an atheist rated atheists higher (average score of 50) versus those who did not (average score of 29; Pew Research Center 2014b, 10).

Slightly different questions have been asked of Canadians. A 2015 Angus Reid Institute online survey with more than three thousand adults asked about level of comfort around those who have no use for religion. Just over 40% of those who are "inclined to accept religion" say they would feel "a bit uncomfortable" (3; see also Angus Reid Institute 2017b, 15). In response to questions about perceptions on the growth of atheism in Canada, nine out of ten who embrace religion disagree that the growth of atheism is a good thing in Canada, versus one in three among those who reject religion (Angus Reid Institute 2015, 21).

Elsewhere in the survey Canadians are asked how positive, neutral, or negative they felt toward various groups. Scores of +1, 0, and −1 were assigned respectively. For example, if 30% of the population responded favorably toward a certain group, 50% responded neutrally, and 20% responded negatively; then the net score would be +10.[1] From these findings, atheists received a +4 overall image among Canadians (Angus Reid Institute 2015, 46). Evangelical Christians (+3), Sikhs (−9), Mormons (−17), and Muslims (−29) scored lower, while Roman Catholics (+35) and mainline Protestants (+36) scored more positively.

Demographically, those in Atlantic Canada and older Canadians were less positive toward atheists, while those in British Columbia and those with a university education offered lower ratings of Christian groups (Evangelicals especially, among the university-educated populace). None of these findings are surprising in light of the demographic realities that we presented in our introduction, with higher and lower rates of religiosity in different Canadian regions. If we parse out how members of different groups view atheists, intriguing disparities emerge. Due to limited sample sizes it is difficult to ascertain how members of religious traditions outside of Christianity view atheists. But within Christianity, Roman Catholics assigned a net +2 value, mainline Protestants a −6, and Evangelicals a −50.

Three initial comparative observations between the United States and Canada stand out. First, atheists are still viewed more favorably in Canada than in the United States. Canadians overall view atheists more positively than several conservative-leaning religious groups, such as

Evangelicals, Sikhs, Mormons, and Muslims. In the United States, depending on the exact wording of the question, atheists and Muslims usually score the lowest. The different contemporary historical narratives about religion in Canada and the United States are key to the discussion. Strong Evangelical overtones in the United States contribute to a fear of atheists and Muslims who threaten the "Christian nation" self-imagery. Conversely, the absence of a "Christian nation" identity, combined with the progressive reservation toward exclusivist groups amid a "multicultural, diverse, and tolerant society" framework, helps to explain atheists being viewed more favorably in Canada versus other religious traditions. Still, in both nations, atheists are not viewed as positively as the more established religious groups in each country—Catholics and mainline Protestants in both Canada and the United States, as well as Evangelicals in the United States.

Second, in both countries Evangelicals have the most reservations toward atheists (and as we detail later, the inverse is also true). Why? What are Evangelicals afraid of? What effect might the "out group" have on the "in group" that warrants these negative views? Despite the national differences in size and public presence of Evangelicals in the United States and Canada, an Evangelical subculture seems to be at work here where symbolic boundaries between "us" (Evangelicals) and "them" (atheists) are drawn (Bean 2014; Reimer 2003; Smith 1998)—namely through strict Evangelical beliefs about proselytizing outsiders, beliefs about who can obtain the afterlife, social and moral attitudes and behaviors, and isolationist tendencies within social ties or social institutions (e.g., education). These "us-them" distinctions seem to amplify negative perceptions among some Evangelicals toward the "godless other." Our observations underline previous research that shows religious ethnocentrism at work among those associated with religious fundamentalism (see Altemeyer 2003; Banyasz, Tokar, and Kaut 2016; Blogowska and Saroglou 2013; Bloom, Arikan, and Courtemanche 2015; Brandt and Reyna 2014; Goplen and Plant 2015; Leon McDaniel, Nooruddin, and Shortle 2011; Scheepers, Gijsberts, and Hello 2002), or in social milieus where those who are religious form a majority (Gervais, Norenzayan, and Shariff 2011). Evangelicalism is not as strong in Canada versus the United States, yet even media exposure to Evangelicalism in the United States can inform Canadian Evangelical perceptions about those around them (Haskell 2010).

Third, building on the symbolic boundaries drawn between Evangelicals and atheists, these boundaries also extend to more devout religious peoples in general. In Canada, those who say they are inclined to accept religion are more suspicious of those who reject religion. This finding is pronounced with those in Atlantic Canada as well as among older Canadians, who tend to be more religious on average than other Canadian regions or younger demographics (Angus Reid Institute 2015). In the United States, those who attend religious services more regularly, are older, vote Republican, or identify as conservative Protestant—variables strongly correlated with one another—are less positive toward atheists (Pew Research Center 2014b). The results in figure 5.1 show that both marginal affiliates (affiliated to a religious group or tradition but attending religious services less than once a month) and active affiliates (religiously affiliated and attending religious services at least once a month) in the United States in 2017 give their lowest feeling thermometer scores on average to atheists.

In highlighting these three initial observations, we must stress that the perceived fears of "other" groups, however defined, does not mean that such fears are necessarily warranted. Strong sociological thinking

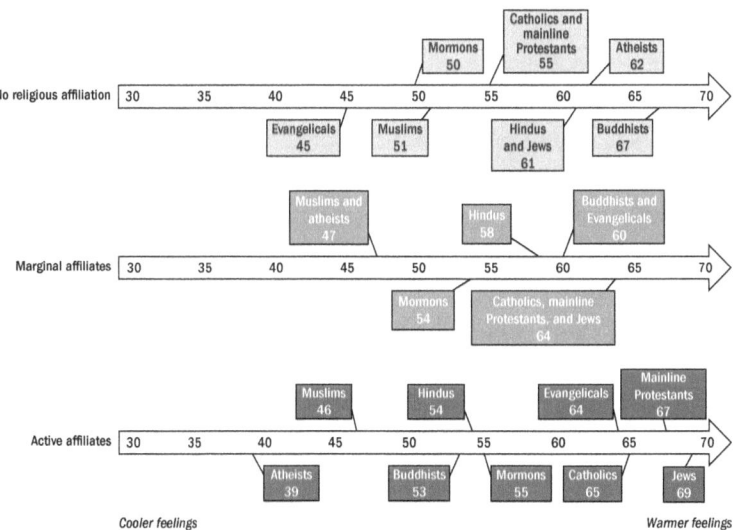

Figure 5.1. Average feeling thermometer scores, among religious nones, marginal affiliates, and active affiliates (excluding respondents with same (non)religious group when relevant), USA, Pew American Trends Panel, January 2017, N = 4,225.

should lead us to consider the sources and processes that feed such perceptions, and possibly even the incongruent perceptions that some hold. We give attention to these questions as the remainder of this chapter unfolds.

Discrimination against Religious Nones

It is one thing to hold a stereotype or prejudicial attitude toward members of another group, yet it goes one significant step further to discriminate and act on those beliefs. So what do we know about these acts of discrimination? Research into discrimination toward religious nones is unlike discrimination toward many other minority groups in society (e.g., ethnic or religious minorities) in that religious nones often lack the outward identifiers (e.g., skin color, religious attire) that cause them to stand out in the eyes of others. This being said, research by Ryan Cragun, Barry Kosmin, Ariela Keysar, Joseph Hammer, and Michael Nielsen (2012) in the United States gives us a descriptive picture into perceived discrimination toward those who say they have no religion. Their starting observation is that the majority of religious nones do *not* believe they have been personally discriminated against in the past five years due to their unaffiliation (nearly 80% of the over 1,100 sampled). Among the remaining religious nones, perceived discrimination is cited to occur in one or more of the following contexts: family, workplace, school, military, socially, or a volunteer organization. Discrimination between family members (notably when parents are religiously affiliated) and social settings stand out above the rest (see also Zimmerman et al. 2015). Unsurprisingly, by a two-to-one ratio, atheists and agnostics cite higher rates of discrimination in the past five years when compared with the rest of those who say they have no religion.

Joseph Hammer, Ryan Cragun, Karen Hwang, and Jesse Smith (2012) pick up on these findings in their discussion of anti-atheist discrimination. Based on their largely quantitative study with more than eight hundred atheists, they summarize six forms of discrimination (presented in decreasing order of occurrence, with the exception of the final "other category"): slander; coercion; social ostracism; denial of opportunities, goods, and services; hate crimes; and other. Perceived discrimination is specifically expressed in the following ways (again, in decreasing order of occurrence): anti-atheist comments in the media; expectations to participate in religious prayers or religious services against one's will; being told that atheism is wrong; and being treated differently due to a person's atheism. In response to an open-ended survey question on personal experiences of discrimination, participants shared narratives of several discrimination stressors they have confronted. These include assuming that one is (or ought to be) religious; the absence of a secular support structure; the lack of church and state separation; children discriminated against by peers and teachers or parents criticized for not raising their children with religion; expectations to tolerate others of different views without the same tolerance being reciprocated; and anticipating the social strain associated with attending rites of passage practiced by faith groups.

Interestingly, many of the examples provided by Hammer, Cragun, Hwang, and Smith (2012) point toward atheists *feeling* marginalized in society, which we distinguish as somewhat different from personally *experiencing* overt and intentional acts of discrimination. For instance, not having atheist-specific clubs to join, or the possibility of being in social settings where few other atheists are present, are lower thresholds of discrimination comparatively speaking. These are different from the following more personally felt incidences of discrimination: comments on "'being taxed to support religious programs,' witnessing state government attempts to 'infuse religion into schools, work, and public places,' being subjected to prayer at civic and other nonreligious meetings, and experiencing 'teachers who worked the importance of worship into classroom discussion as often as possible,'" or one person whose "son's mother has tried to claim [he] is unfit as a parent because he is an atheist," or another person's claim, "I dislike having to tolerate religion when most of the religious folks I'm around have little tolerance or will to understand or learn about atheism" (Hammer et al. 2012, 55). Comments such as these were more keenly expressed by those who strongly identified with their atheist identity, were "out" about their atheist identity, and came from families who embraced strict religious expectations.

Unfortunately, there is little qualitative data available to help personalize some of these experiences further in the United States or Canada.

In our interviews, some religious nones, like Sandra at the beginning of this chapter, spoke of discrimination that they personally experienced because they did not identify with a religion, or the "right religion" in the minds of others. We met Barbara previously, a religious none today who was raised Catholic but married an Anglican. She reflected on the discrimination she received in her family. She said, "I would go to a Christmas mass with mom every year. . . . I did that for quite a while, but then I got married in the Anglican church, so my mom wouldn't let me go to Catholic mass with her anymore. . . . I just thought it was really weird." Tracie is another religious none whom we introduced earlier. As a reminder, she left the Anglican tradition when her parents gave her the option to no longer attend, which became an easy decision for her due to the disconnect between her personal experiences and official church teachings. She shared one experience that she and her husband had with Evangelicals that left them with a cooler attitude toward members of this group: "Sometimes we find them offensive . . . we took the kids to . . . their friend [who] wanted them to come for the build the box thing, and they're like, 'that's awesome!' And we were all excited and I've always filled a box and then we went there and they were saying how, when they stand in the village, they only give it to the kids that are Christian and if they're not they don't give them a box. And my husband and I were, like, devastated." Later Tracie expanded on this insider-outsider narrative regarding some of her Mormon friends: "When we go to their weddings we have to sit outside because we're not actually good enough for God's eyes to watch their wedding. . . . I can't not roll my eyes when I tell you that, because they invite you because they want you there but . . ." In the next section we unpack how religious nones perceive religious groups, such as Catholics, Evangelicals, and Mormons, whom they believe are too exclusive. To be sure, as with some we have featured in this section, personally experienced discrimination due to one's religious nonaffiliation, or lack of involvement in a religious group, affects some religious nones' perceptions of religious groups.

On the whole, while these studies provide us with descriptive clues about discrimination toward nones, we know less about who is performing the discriminatory acts, the nature of the discrimination in play, or how discrimination is experienced and processed by religious nones. On these questions we need more and better data.

Perceptions by Religious Nones toward Religious Individuals and Groups

As has been demonstrated, research is clear in the United States that religious nones, mainly atheists, have perceived themselves as outsiders against the dominant (Christian) American society. How do religious nones in the United States in turn view members of different religious traditions? Far less has been published in this regard. If we go back to the Pew Research Center's 2017 "feelings thermometer" data, illustrated in figure 5.1, religious nones hold the following views toward different religious groups: nones give average scores of 67 to Buddhists, 61 to both Jews and Hindus, 55 to both Catholics and mainline Protestants, 51 to Muslims, 50 to Mormons, and 45 to Evangelical Christians (January 2017 American Trends Panel). If broken down further by the atheist subsample within the religious none category, atheists also reserve their coldest feelings for Evangelical Christians (29) and warmest feelings for Buddhists (67). Regionally, it is in the American South where religious nones and atheists more specifically give the lowest feeling thermometer scores to Evangelical Christians (an average score of 42 among the 306 religious none respondents, and an average score of 26 among the 64 atheist respondents).

In Canada, recently we have learnt a little more about how religious nones view members of different religious groups. From the 2015 Angus Reid Institute survey, referenced earlier, we see how those with no religion view members of different faith traditions: Buddhists (+38), Hindus (+8), Jews (+6), Protestants (+5), Sikhs (−9), Roman Catholics (−9), Muslims (−28), Mormons (−35), and Evangelicals (−40; Angus Reid Institute 2015, 46). Canadians were also asked about their level of comfort around religiously devout members. Just over 60% of those "inclined to reject religion" would feel uncomfortable around a religiously devout person. When asked to consider religion's impact on the world, nearly nine in ten who reject religion disagree that religion's overall impact is positive in the world, versus two in ten who embrace religion (Angus Reid Institute 2015, 22).

These latter findings are reinforced in a 2017 survey by the Angus Reid Institute (2017a), which explores the role that religious and faith communities play in an array of social initiatives (e.g., social services, community programs, immigrant and refugee settlement, health clinics, and homes for the elderly). Those described as "nonbelievers" view the impact of religious groups less favorably in these areas, above all in British Columbia and Quebec. These regional variations are not surprising, for different reasons as we introduced in our introduction. In British Columbia, where the highest rates of religious nones reside in Canada, religious nones are a (near) majority in many respects in public and social life. As such, there appears to be less sympathy toward the social and public benefits of religion; the belief is people and society get on just fine without religion. In Quebec, given its deep Catholic roots yet subsequent antagonism toward the Catholic Church in the aftermath of the Quiet Revolution, many Québécois, especially religious nones, hold negative attitudes toward the public role of religion in society.

Our read of the limited quantitative data available in the United States and Canada are that religious nones' negative sentiments for members of certain groups are intertwined with their perceptions of those groups being highly exclusive (particularly Muslims, Mormons, and Evangelicals), while holding a more positive stance toward groups that they see as more inclusive and tolerant (notably Buddhists). These quantitative findings really come to light in our interview data. To set the context, several interview questions tapped into how religious nones think and talk about different religious groups. These include perceptions of religion as a positive or negative force in society, openness to greater involvement in a religious group, perceived benefits to not identifying with a religion, and beliefs about how much control religious groups should have over people's beliefs and practices. Interviewee responses alerted us to perspectives on most of the religious groups noted above.

Reservations about "Exclusive" Groups

Catholics, Evangelicals, Muslims, Mormons, and Jehovah's Witnesses. These are the groups that nones single out as problematic for various reasons, including personally experienced discrimination from members of these groups, noted earlier. Given that Catholicism is the largest religious group in Canada, it is not surprising that Catholics were discussed the most frequently among our interviewees. One of the reasons that Catholics are singled out by religious nones is due to scandals in the Catholic Church (Thiessen 2015). As one example, Faye, whose mom left the Catholic Church after being shunned for getting divorced, singled out "all the scandal with the priests and all of that. Like, I pay attention to that." Faye continued to single out fear-based elements to Catholicism: "When you talk to people, especially in the Catholic Church that we used to go . . . there was a lot of fear stuff and I . . . could never quite believe that I needed to be afraid of something . . . I could never quite believe the hell part. Maybe the heaven part. That sounded kind of nice, but the hell? I don't think so. There's no fire burning there." Other interviewees specified areas where Catholics appear too strict, whether on birth control, abortion, baptism, marriage, or who can and cannot partake in the Eucharist. Barbara explained why she got married in an Anglican church instead of a Catholic one: "I didn't think I would do it in the Catholic Church. One, I never believed that . . . the idea that my dad had a signed piece of paper saying that he had to raise his kids Catholic . . . I never liked that idea . . . we had gone to Anglican church mass a few times, and it was just . . . more relaxed and not so strict." She continued to share her sister's experience of wanting to get married in a park and "she wanted a Catholic priest to do it, but they said no because . . . they won't go outside the church. And I'm just like, 'Well, why?' Like, that doesn't make sense to me. I think if she's wanting to get married . . . with a Catholic, you know, it should be allowed to happen . . . why would a spiritual being say that that's not ok?" As indicated earlier in this chapter, experiences like these affected Barbara's negative view of the Catholic Church today.

Evangelicals, though far smaller in size in Canada versus the United States, are still in the minds of some Canadian religious nones. This is in part because of the geographic proximity between the two nations and exposure to representations of Evangelicals in American media. For instance, awareness of scandals and hypocrisy in Evangelical settings partially contributed to some religious nones leaving behind their Christian identification, a theme we touched on previously (also see Thiessen 2015). Others, like Norman, showcased their perception of Evangelicals based on what he sees in the United States: "A lot of people . . . box themselves into a corner. Evangelical people in the States . . . they're actually waiting for the rapture to come and everybody's gonna die in a sea of blood, and they're gonna be saved? Really?" The lack of believability in seemingly outlandish and exclusive Evangelical beliefs, which partially contributed to Norman leaving behind his religious affiliation as we described before, means that members of Evangelical traditions and their beliefs do not resonate with some religious nones. Others turn to personal experiences. Sandra's story at the start of this chapter—of her daughter's Evangelical group who lamented that Sandra was not a Christian—is a reminder of how some Evangelicals, with their perceived "cultish and closed-minded" beliefs and practices, alienate religious nones. We got this sense from Darlene in the opening lines of this book too, when she discussed narrow social ties: "Evangelicals stay in . . . their own little nook."

When asked if he gains anything by not identifying with a religion, Patrick, whom we met earlier, responded by critiquing the drawbacks of exclusive attitudes and behaviors for those who identify as Muslim: "The Muslim can't marry outside your religion. . . . It's like, 'oh if I like this girl I have to become Muslim' . . . if you're a Muslim you can't marry . . . like what the hell not, like what makes me not good enough anymore? Just because I'm not in the same religion." Later, when Patrick is asked about how much control religious groups should have over people's religious beliefs and practices, he returned to talking about Muslims: "The Muslim is like not being able to marry outside your circle . . . and then . . . having your wife wear the shawl . . . you can see the control on the woman . . . like it's you have to follow this, and it's like, 'oh, it's . . . her choice' . . . yeah it's her choice because you brainwash her into thinking it was her choice." Norman went in a different direction when speaking of Muslims, highlighting their perceived divisiveness and violence within Islam: "The Muslims, the Shi'ites, and the Sunnis. It's the same guy that they're worshipping, but . . . all they can do is blow each other up."

Faye, like others, singled out Mormons for their proselytization tactics: "The people that come door to door I get a little offended by . . . it's very personal and if I want it, I'll come and find it." Mark was actively involved in the Mormon Church growing up yet went to great lengths to single out his aversion to Jehovah's Witnesses pushing their religion on to people:

> There's not a ton of people who are actually willing to sit down and talk. Lots of people are willing to sit down and tell. They come to my doors all

the time. Jehovah's Witnesses comes and are like, "lemme tell you." . . . You always wanna tell me stuff. I don't wanna be told stuff . . . I want you to hear what I have to say. If we're gonna have a conversation it should be shared. You don't wanna share. You wanna tell. . . . It's very selfishly motivated. It's always like, "I'm coming to help you." No you're not. If you were coming to help me, you wouldn't come at nine o' clock in the morning. You'd let me sleep in cause you'd know that I work hard.

These reflections on religious groups that some nones perceive as exclusive strike closer to home for some, as we noted earlier when addressing discrimination toward religious nones. Previously we introduced Lorraine, who shared her different beliefs about God as well as the afterlife, noting that she does not hold any of her beliefs too strongly. Elsewhere in her interview she discussed how much influence religious groups should or should not have over people's beliefs and practices, and tearfully shared of her strained relationship with her daughter-in-law who identifies as a Jehovah's Witness: "I do have a problem with religion dictating how people should spend their lives, spend their money, what's acceptable and what isn't. . . . I love her to pieces. . . . I respect her involvement in the church. But I have a problem with some of their beliefs, obviously. And that's been hard for me in relation to my grandchildren, especially because she's waffled, so sometimes there's Christmases, sometimes there isn't. Sometimes there's occasions, sometimes there aren't." In a different vein, when Karen, who has no religious upbringing, responded to a question about anything that would increase her chances of wanting to get involved in a religious group, she flippantly replied, "If I, like, married some guy that was religious." She went on then to disqualify certain religious groups because she perceived them to be "too much," which she later qualified to mean "too exclusive." She said, "I probably wouldn't marry a Catholic person. . . . It just seems like too much. Then my kid would have to go to Catholic. . . . Or like Jewish. I probably wouldn't marry a Jewish person cause the beliefs would be too different. . . . I wouldn't marry a Jehovah Witness . . . like, that's too much."

Why are many religious nones apprehensive of exclusive-leaning religious groups? A distinguishing variable for religious nones is they believe that they are open-minded, free, and tolerant (Thiessen 2015; Williamson and Yancey 2013). The fear and perception is that exclusive-leaning religious groups are closed-minded and intolerant toward those who view the world differently, and thus are a threat to religious nones and society overall. Sociologically, it is important to suspend judgment about these perceptions. It is difficult to say for certain if religious nones actually are as open-minded, free, and tolerant as they believe they are, or if exclusive-leaning religious groups are as closed-minded and intolerant as religious nones perceive them to be. Still, these perceptions matter because they shape people's interactions and behaviors toward others. On an individual basis, this worry may play itself out for religious nones who are stigmatized by family, friends, or coworkers. At a societal level, the worry may be that religiously inspired laws remain or come into effect on issues such as abortion, same-sex marriage, or euthanasia. Sumerau and Cragun (2016) note that this rejection of religion as bad and too exclusive among the nonreligious is also for many a process by which the boundaries of their nonreligious identities are constructed and maintained.

Openness to Religious Groups

Religious nones are not necessarily averse to all religious groups. Consistent with the quantitative findings, it was interesting to hear during interviews the distinction between some groups that they have warmer feelings toward overall, in large part because of the perceived openness and inclusivity of some traditions. Patrick, who was critical toward Muslims earlier, reflected at one point in the interview about the restrictive and "blind belief" elements to Christianity and Islam before inserting, "I mean the Buddhist . . . is something that I would identify more towards . . . because they don't have, per se, as much written . . . and then they're not as destructive as Muslim and Catholic. . . . Like that one is a lot more peaceful and it's like inner peace." Tracie similarly drew this distinction when asked if she would ever consider involvement in a religious group. She said Buddhism because she "like[s] their gentleness about the world and their beliefs that way. And a lot of the Christian history and the Muslim history there's a lot of violence."

Incidentally, when probed, neither of these individuals says they have seriously explored Buddhism. Consequently, more positive attitudes toward Buddhism among many nones may be at least in part a reflection of its distinct recent history in Western societies and pop culture: especially in the 1960s and 1970s when Eastern religions, notably Buddhism, were adopted and adapted by hippie and spiritual subcultures in white, middle-class North America as vectors for individual autonomy, quests for well-being and environmental protection as well as critiques toward consumer society and the economic growth model. Buddhism has subsequently enjoyed more positive perceptions, reinforced further by the positive public relations generated by the Tibetan Dalai Lama since the 1990s, in stark contrast, for example, to perceptions of Islam in the West (Liogier 2010; Wilkins-Laflamme 2018). Yet one wonders how familiar some religious nones are that women cannot become Buddhist monks in many of their traditions. Why the positive feelings toward a religious group that, on the surface, adopts a gendered practice that is similar to the perceived exclusive-oriented religions noted earlier? Why are some religious traditions perceived differently, despite some of their similarities? We return to some of these questions shortly.

Other interviewees spoke of their general openness to different religious traditions, particularly when talking about how they do or plan to raise their children (for more on this topic see Manning 2015; Thiessen 2016). Despite Mark leaving behind an active way of life in the Mormon tradition, and his opposition to groups imposing their faith on to him, he offered his approach to raising his children:

> We encourage them to figure out what prayer is to them. And the emphasis is on don't be afraid to feel. Don't be afraid to try and figure out what you're feeling and where it comes from. Maybe you need to go and spend some time with your friends who live the Muslim faith. I mean they're exposed to it all the time anyways. I'm finding more and more. . . . Certainly way more than when I was a kid . . . their friends are all from different faiths. They're very sensitive to it and with the political correctness they're like, they're different from us but they have the luxury to just happen to accept it and be more tolerant than definitely where we were raised. . . . So they're exposed to it and they're encouraged to follow their hearts and souls.

Joshua, a committed atheist who earlier spoke out against religious leaders who attribute natural disasters to God's wrath on homosexuals, cited several religious groups that he would be comfortable with his children exploring: "I would want to expose them to different denominations and would, probably, go to a mosque. I would take them to a synagogue. I would take them to a Baptist church. I would take them to a United church, Catholic church.... I would make it clear that I would support whatever worldview that child arrived at." Unlike Faye earlier who was critical of religious groups proselytizing at their door, Adelaide commented that "if a Jehovah's Witness comes to the door, I'll open it up. 'Okay cool, like tell me about your religion, like why do you think I should follow'... cause I'm interested in that." Adelaide's perspective is consistent with her open stance toward religious beliefs and practices, which we summarized beforehand.

To summarize, religious nones have a range of views toward different religious groups. Both quantitative and qualitative data suggest a strong reservation toward religious groups perceived to be intolerant and exclusive of others, such as Catholics, Evangelicals, Muslims, Jehovah's Witnesses, and Mormons. Conversely, some hold greater openness for groups believed to be tolerant and inclusive of others, such as Buddhists. Then there are others who appear to have a neutral posture toward religious groups regardless of how inclusive or exclusive they appear to be. What interests us next is where and why certain perceptions are developed. Again, without suggesting that any of the groups noted above are actually inclusive or exclusive, why do religious nones come to perceive other groups in a particular light?

Family and Friends: Reinforcing Perspectives

Where and how are people acquiring and developing these perceptions of religious nones and members of different religious groups? Family and friends? News media and social media? Religious groups themselves? Secular organizations? Books, articles, and influential public thought leaders? Public rituals? Laws and legal rulings? Prevailing social narratives expressed in schools, on the playground, in the local grocery store, or by politicians? "All of the above" is likely the correct answer. Since scholarly activity on religious nones remains in its infancy in the United States and Canada, little systematic research has gone into the myriad of ways that people can and do develop their views toward religious nones and vice versa. However, in step with long-standing sociological research on religious attitudes and behavior, we surmise that family and friends are key contributors. We devote a bit of space to this topic now, where there is some research on religious nones.

Social scientists have long proven that, in general, people from various demographic backgrounds (e.g., race, ethnicity, social class, and age) tend to associate most closely with those who are "like themselves" throughout their lives—as initially discussed in chapter 3, what sociologists Paul Lazarsfeld and Robert Merton classically refer to as homophily (1954). This results from a process of selection in which individuals choose friends who are similar to themselves from the available pool of persons around them, and also of socialization during which friends become more like each other over time (Cheadle and Schwadel 2012; Collins 2004). It is no different for religion. People commonly marry those with similar religious beliefs, values, and levels of involvement. Individuals frequently embrace the religion of their parents. Our closest friends tend to resemble our personal levels of religious belief, behavior, and belonging.

Beginning with the family unit, Joseph Baker and Buster Smith (2015) note that those who are not overly religious tend to marry others who are not actively religious. For example, in the United States in 2007 just over one-quarter of atheists were married to atheists, and nearly four in ten agnostics were married to agnostics, much higher than the rates of atheists and agnostics in the general American population. Additionally, these figures do not include atheists and agnostics who are married to one another, or nonbelievers who marry a "spiritual but not religious" person or another type of religious none. In the 2014 Canadian General Social Survey, 75% of religious none respondents who are either married or living in a common-law partnership say their spouse also has no religion—this compared with 6% of religious none spouses among the religiously affiliated (see also Lee et al. 2018).

Earlier we noted the growth of religious nones in the United States and Canada who are being raised with no religion, by parents who say they have no religion. We do not need to belabor that point here, other than to remind the reader that the family one is raised in plays a profound role over the attitudes and behaviors that an individual progressively acquires. For example, in the Pacific Northwest and northeastern

United States, views toward religious nones among Evangelicals are partially informed by families who wish to shelter their children from "the outside world." This may include homeschooling or faith-based schools; limiting exposure to certain music, literature, or movies; or restricting social networks to one's faith community. The inverse is true of religious nones in the American Midwest or in the Canadian Maritime provinces, for example. Parents may intentionally seek to limit their children's exposure to and interaction with members of certain religious groups that they deem to hold exclusive, repressive, or oppressive values. An additional impact of family is present for those who change their religious affiliation. As with Darlene in our opening vignette, her views as a religious none toward Evangelicals were strongly informed by her upbringing in an Evangelical home.

When we expand this discussion to one's peers, similar findings stand out in the literature (Lee 2015; Madge, Hemming, and Stenson 2014; Nemeth and Luidens 2003; Olson 1989, 1993; Ramji 2013; Wuthnow 2004). Most active religious affiliates are close friends with other active religious affiliates, and religious nones are close friends with other religious nones (Thiessen 2015, 61–62, 122). Baker and Smith (2015) note that "80% of atheists, 75% of agnostics, and 50% of nonaffiliated believers reported having at least one close friend who is 'not religious'" (165). Among the 671 respondents with no religion from British Columbia, Washington, and Oregon in the 2017 Pacific Northwest Social Survey, 54% say that three or more of their five closest friends were not religious at all. In turn, 53% of these unaffiliated respondents say that none of their five closest friends are involved in a religious group or faith community, with another 38% having only one or two such friends. Among active affiliate respondents from this same survey, 65% had three or more close friends who are involved in a religious group or faith community, 39% had no friends who were not religious at all, and 41% only had one or two friends who were not religious at all, and these findings are in regions where religious nones make up between a third and half of the general populations. Simply put, those we closely associate with provide important social milieus for shaping how we view other social groups.

An opportunity for future research exists to further study the specific mechanisms and narratives at work with our friends and families in these areas. How specifically do parents, spouses, or friends intentionally or unintentionally shape perceptions about religious nones or other religious groups? Christel Manning's book *Losing Our Religion* (2015) offers insight into five socialization strategies found among religious nones with their children. These include "non-provision" (see also Thiessen 2016); "outsourcing" religious education to a local religious group or school; "self-provision" of certain religious beliefs or practices in the home; "alternative approaches" where children are in programs to learn about different religious views and habits, and religion is openly discussed in the home; and a "return to regular religious involvement" where families become more involved in the religious tradition of the parents' younger years. Lois Lee (2015, 106–30) also speaks to this issue in the context of one's friends. She documents a range of experiences from not knowing what religion one's friends are to talking about religion at a general level but not about one's personal views and practices, intentionally locating oneself in social settings with others who are not religious, and the desire for more organized social networks to advance a nonreligious worldview. We look forward to more research like Manning's and Lee's that will develop our understanding of the mechanisms that religious nones use to pass on their worldview about other religious groups especially.

Alongside family and friends, it is worth paying attention to the role that other social domains play in shaping and informing attitudes and behaviors between religious nones and religious affiliates. For example, traditional media (see Knott, Poole, and Taira 2013), social media, law, politics, and so forth. How are social, cultural, historical, and group narratives framed, supported, and contested in these social spaces? And how do such narratives vary by social context, where religious nones are a majority versus a minority, for instance? One of the reasons religious nones in the United States and Canada might perceive some religious groups as more exclusive oriented and others as inclusive oriented could be due to media coverage. It is no secret that Muslims are predominantly portrayed in a negative light in the media, as are other conservative groups like Mormons. So too are some religious groups that "look" different, in terms of the color of their skin, their attire, and their "deviant" beliefs and practices (e.g., Sikhs). These are the kinds of questions and issues that we think scholars should give significant attention to in the future, telling us about not only the "what" but also the "how" and "why" behind people's perceptions and activities relative to those outside their (non)religious confines. In the next section we dip our toes into these waters insofar as how we might think of religious nones as part of a (religiously) diverse society.

Polarization or a Path toward Deep Equality?

Religious nones comprise a larger segment of the population in the United States and Canada today than in previous generations. This demographic shift has very real implications for social life. If we limit our analysis to people's perceptions, there are clear indicators that polarization (i.e., animosity) exists between some segments of the religiously affiliated and unaffiliated. Negative feelings are most strongly felt, mutually, between Evangelicals and atheists. In the United States, many on the whole remain suspicious of atheists; in Canada, less so. Religious nones are also more reserved about religious groups believed to be too exclusive, intolerant, and narrow. However, so far as we can tell, a smaller number of individuals on either side of the polarized continuum appear to actually behave in discriminatory ways based on their negative perceptions of the "other" (research opportunities are vast in this area).

If we zoom the lens out to an institutional level of analysis, a broader picture emerges. Some of the aforementioned groups (typically Christian groups) remain privileged and protected by those in power. Some public narratives change as demographics change. Amid social stability and change, religious and nonreligious groups also vie for cultural authority and legitimacy. Education, healthcare, public rituals, and the law are some of the institutional settings where these intersections come into play. Two examples from the past decade or so demonstrate some of these shifts and tensions. One is President Barack Obama's inaugural address in the United States in January 2009. He acknowledged the United States as "a nation of Christians and Muslims, Jews and Hindus, and non-believers" (Phillips 2009). The acknowledgment of nonbelievers was a first and was widely praised by religious nones in the United States. The second example is the atheist bus campaign that started in the United Kingdom in 2009 and then made its way to Canada and the United States. The initial campaign, "There's Probably No God. Now Stop Worrying and Enjoy Your Life," was met by a counter Christian bus campaign, "There Definitely Is a God. So Join the Christian Party and Enjoy Your Life." These ad campaigns often caused much controversy wherever they went, and some municipalities went so far as to refuse to run them. Both the support and opposition to either side of this "bus war" reveal the growing comfort for each group to speak out in support of its worldview, and in opposition to the other's.

Below we offer a couple of case studies on how religious nones are progressively gaining ground in a diverse Canadian social context. We focus on Canada where, it seems, the more established place for religious nones has opened up public discourse and policy for religious nones in a multicultural social environment. As religious nones have grown in size and stature across the United States and Canada, debates in the domain of education persist over school prayer, evolution versus creationism curriculum, public funding for faith-based schools, Christmas versus winter concerts or holidays, dedicated spaces for different religious groups, religion-specific or world religions courses, and so forth (Beaman 2017; Bouchard and Taylor 2008; Germain, Polo, and INRS-Urbanisation, culture et société 2003; Lefebvre 2005; Milot, Portier, and Willaime 2010; Rocher 2014; Rousseau 2012; Schmidt 2016). As one example, in 2013 an Ontario parent, whose two children were in a Catholic school yet did not identify as Catholic themselves (it is not clear if they were religious nones), challenged the necessity of attending mandatory religious retreats and mass (Beaman 2017). The legal ruling rendered that the children were not required to attend these events. Amid the intriguing elements to this case, the ruling stands out because of how those who do not identify with or practice a religion are singled out as part of the diverse social landscape: "The board respects the practice of diverse religious traditions within the system and individuals or groups who do not belong to an organized religion or practice a religion" (Peel District School Board 2017, 2). As with President Obama's inaugural address cited earlier, discussions of religious diversity in some settings now include space for those who do not identify with any religion.

In healthcare discussions, abortion, euthanasia, and blood transfusions are some of the issues to dominate public discourse between the actively religious and religious nones. Canadian scholars Lori Beaman and Cory Steele (2018) unpack a 2015 legal ruling in Canada in which nonreligious discourse about assisted dying (the federal Canadian government making it legal countrywide as of 2016) was apparent. They first outline a "religious approach" to assisted dying, which focuses on "a transcendental being whose will unfolds through the process of dying. Illness and suffering in this model are good, and any attempt to control the time and place of death is seen as being contrary to the sanctity of life which is ultimately attributable to that transcendent being. There is little place for human agency in this model. The wish to die is characterized as suicide and is seen as a weakness or lack of comprehension, of pain management, or of social support" (131). Terminology is very different in the recent "nonreligious" framing of the topic by the Supreme Court of Canada: "Dignity rather than suffering as the ultimate goal for human beings; an emphasis on individual agency instead of a transcendental being or notion of 'gods will'; and a move from a moral assessment to medical assessment. Simply put, the transcendence evidenced in law and enacted in the healthcare system has evolved or become an approach that can be characterized by immanence" (134). As religious nones grow in size and stature, we agree with Beaman and Steele (2018, 131) that "changes in discourse both reflect and impact on practices and debates in healthcare" and beyond.

We do not mean to suggest a uniform positive response to religious nones across various institutional spheres. Without question, it remains difficult to be a religious none, notably an atheist, in some regions of the United States and even in Canada. We simply want to highlight that in some spaces and places, discourse is broadening to account for religious nones in the diverse social milieu; in other places, typically with stronger roots and ties to a religious majority, this shift is less apparent. It is not lost on us that where groups feel more marginalized, such as atheists in the southern United States, we typically see stronger pushback from them as they oppose the religious and cultural majority. The inverse can also be true when, for example, religious groups sense they are "losing ground" to secular narratives and laws. In 2018 the federal Liberal government in Canada changed the eligibility requirements for organizations seeking funding from the Canada Summer Jobs program: "To be eligible, the *core mandate* of the organization must respect individual human rights in Canada, including the values underlying the Canadian Charter of Rights and Freedoms

(Charter), as well as other rights. *These include reproductive rights. . . . The attestation is required for the application to be considered complete and eligible for assessment*" (Canada Summer Jobs 2018, 6; italics added). Religious congregations and summer camps are two examples where millions of dollars of federal funding that are typically supplied to hire summer students were not provided to countless organizations in 2018 because they did not attest support for abortion in their grant application. In a different case, Trinity Western University, a Christian university in British Columbia, was denied accreditation for its law school in 2018 because of its required community covenant that, prior to 2018, students had to sign and that included abstaining from sex outside of a heterosexual marriage (Harris 2018). In both cases, religious groups were quite vocal about their perceived marginalized status in an increasingly secular society. Moving forward, will religious groups amplify us-them rhetoric, or will they back down, as Trinity Western University did shortly after the Supreme Court ruling, now no longer requiring students to sign a community covenant? Only time will tell.

What, then, is a possible way forward for the affiliated and unaffiliated? Religious studies scholar Lori Beaman (2014, 2017) has written extensively on religiously diverse societies. Of late she has expanded this conversation to include those who say they have no religion. Beaman draws on the concept of "deep equality," referred to here as "a vision of equality that transcends law, politics, and social policy, and that relocates equality as a process rather than a definition, and as lived rather than prescribed. It recognizes equality as an achievement of day-to-day interaction, and is traceable through agonistic respect, recognition of similarity and a simultaneous acceptance of difference, creation of community, and neighbourliness. It circulates through micro-processes of individual action and inaction and through group demonstrations of caring" (Beaman 2014, 96). Key to Beaman's (2014, 98) conceptualization is agonistic respect, which "requires an abandonment of 'rightness' and the conviction that one is imbued with the truth through some sort of transcendent authority." Beaman suggests that much of the discourse around religious diversity portrays this diversity as a problem to be solved. As such, language of tolerance or accommodation is frequently used, where the dominant "us" needs to tolerate or accommodate to "them." Instead, Beaman calls for more attention to be given to similarities between groups and successful stories of navigating difference.

At a purely descriptive level, Beaman may be right that scholars, politicians, policy makers, and everyday citizens could or should pay greater attention to where and how deep equality is unfolding, particularly in the context of religious nones. Empirically, it is far more difficult to operationalize "deep equality" values and practices, especially at a larger scale. Beaman (2017) constructively offers a series of micro-interaction examples with religious nones and members of other religious traditions—of a wedding, a marriage, a protest, and between two neighbors—where the involved parties acted kindly and compassionately toward one another, took a genuine interest in one another, and acted in ways that benefited the other. The handful of narratives provided is a helpful start. Yet at a quantitative level, how common are such interactions? Are the sample stories offered the exception or the norm? Operationalizing "deep equality" in such a way that large-scale surveys might help us to answer these questions would be a welcome contribution to the field. How might one measure this construct, or tell if individuals or groups or societies improve or regress in this regard?

Admittedly it is hard to tell from our data if deep equality is embodied, practiced, or desired. Our hunch, as with a continuum of any kind, is that those at the extremes of our discussion are unlikely to embrace "agonistic respect" toward the other—those closer to the middle, perhaps, and it may be to these middle-ground individuals that we must turn to in order to realistically find and encourage deep equality. A great opportunity awaits scholars to study in detail where deep equality is evident between the affiliated and unaffiliated. We are markedly interested in deep equality found between those in atheist and Evangelical groups. How likely is "deep equality" between atheists and Evangelicals where homophily and homogamy practices run high, characterized with strong "bonding capital" within groups and weak "bridging capital" across groups (Putnam 2000)? What steps might these groups take to strengthen their bridging capital? Where successful deep equality is experienced, what mechanisms are at work that contribute to shared values, narratives, and practices? How are these values and practices of deep equality passed on, nurtured, and sustained? Is it realistic to expect deep equality to take root across society, or is this concept mainly a utopian one? Only time and better data will help us to answer these questions, and Beaman has provided scholars a starting point for rich debate, data collection, and analysis.

Conclusion

"It's too bad your parents aren't Christian." This statement made about Chloe's mother Sandra that we encountered earlier captures a very real gap between how some of the affiliated feel toward the unaffiliated in the United States and Canada. Unsurprisingly, Sandra and other religious nones do not necessarily hold warm feelings toward the affiliated either. When we drill down, we see negative sentiments toward atheists in both the United States and Canada (but more so in the United States). Evangelicals in particular hold less positive views toward atheists. As it turns out, the feelings are mutual. Atheists are not generally fond of Evangelicals, nor are they of other religious traditions believed to be more exclusive, such as Muslims, Mormons, or Jehovah's Witnesses.

Polarization expressed in these ways matters for social and civic engagement in the United States and Canada. As William I. Thomas and Dorothy S. Thomas (1928, 572) remind us, perceptions shape our realities insofar as they become real in their consequences. With the religious none population comprising larger proportions of the population, these polarized perceptions toward and by religious nones compel us to consider how the affiliated and unaffiliated might coexist moving forward. Unless sizeable proportions of these different groups regularly interact with members of the "other" in meaningful dialogue, we have our doubts that deep equality is attainable on either side of the border. This reservation is likely stronger in the United States where the social divide is much larger, and where more seems to be at stake for the unaffiliated and some of the affiliated.

We transition now to our concluding chapter where we summarize some of the main conclusions from our findings, the implications for existing frameworks in the fields of sociology of religion and religious studies, and their implications for everyday life and for society. We also consider possible trajectories for religious nones down the road, along with areas for future study that our research opens up.

Conclusion

Darlene, Patrick, Corrine, and Sandra

At roughly one-quarter of the current population, those who say they have no religion are far more numerous in the United States and Canada than half a century ago. As we have seen, this demographic change has not been a sudden one. We have anchored our analysis in the stages of decline framework, arguing that religious none growth has transpired gradually across time and generations. Some religious nones, like Darlene, whom we met in our introduction, dropped an active religious lifestyle, leaving behind the religion of their childhood and their parents. Others, like Patrick, whom we met in chapter 1, gradually moved away from a religious identity that was not particularly salient to them or their family. Many who shed their religious affiliation then go on to have children and raise their children without religious affiliation, belief, or practice in the home, becoming religious nones raising religious nones, like Corrine in chapter 4 and Sandra in chapter 5. This latter reality is a trend that we and others have recently contended is becoming more common from one generation to the next (Bengtson, Putney, and Harris 2013; Clarke and Macdonald 2017; Thiessen and Wilkins-Laflamme 2017).

Embedded within our stages of decline framework is an understanding that religious nones come in all shapes and sizes: involved seculars, inactive nonbelievers, inactive believers, the spiritual but not religious, and religiously involved believers. Darlene, Patrick, Corrine, and Sandra are similar in that they said they have no religion, but what that identity entails varies. Darlene and Corrine most closely resemble those who say they are spiritual but not religious. Darlene, for instance, believes in God, "contemplates" life from time to time, and occasionally attends Christmas Eve services to please her mother. By her own admission, she is best known for what she is *not* rather than what she is: she is no longer religious, Evangelical, or fundamentalist. Patrick is an inactive believer. He said that he believes in God but is firm that God is not active in the world. He privileges science, reason, and human explanations for events in the world, leading one to surmise that Patrick could very easily become an inactive nonbeliever, like Sandra, over time. Sandra declared that she does not believe in God or the afterlife, despite "wishing" she could as some of those around her do to find strength in life.

Overall, inactive nonbelievers seem to be the largest group by a sizeable margin, followed by the spiritual but not religious and inactive believers (see notably figure 2.8). The size of the inactive nonbeliever group relative to the other types of religious nones could be interpreted as support for proponents of secularization theory who say that along with declines in organized religion, individuals outside of religion demonstrate low levels of spiritual beliefs. We generally agree with this theoretical interpretation; however, we diverge from ardent secularization advocates by also acknowledging the real and sizeable place of religious nones who identify as spiritual but not religious and inactive believers. We do see people leaving organized religion, and many of these individuals score low on all religiosity and spirituality indicators, but we are also witnessing changes in how some people understand and express their spirituality beyond organized religion in fairly individualistic ways, which should not necessarily be confused with religious decline and secularization. This said, as irreligious socialization becomes more widespread, it is conceivable that we might see a growth of inactive nonbelievers in subsequent generations, as people grow up with little social reinforcements for any substantive religious or spiritual belief or practice. But with the best data available to us at this point, against the backdrop of the stages of decline framework, we suggest that both secularization and individualization and spiritualization are occurring simultaneously in the United States and Canada.

Consistent with our central claims throughout, we must keep in mind that distinct social, cultural, and regional milieus factor into this discussion of heterogeneity among religious nones. A religious none growing up in a predominantly Christian environment versus a largely secular setting matters. This is why we argue that religious nones in Canada versus the United States, or the Maritime provinces and southern states versus the West Coast, have some distinct experiences and perspectives from one another. For example, we can expect, on average, there to be higher rates of inactive nonbelievers in regions with higher rates of religious nones, just as we can anticipate stronger anti-Evangelical sentiments among religious nones in places where Evangelicals are a majority.

Alongside the variation found among religious nones, several commonalities also rise to the surface on a range of social, moral, and political attitudes and behaviors. These similarities among religious nones are especially pronounced when comparing nones with the most religiously devout in society, on issues such as abortion, same-sex marriage, gender roles, immigration, and the government's role in helping the poor and the environment. In different ways presented throughout this book, Darlene, Patrick, Corrine, and Sandra showcased their left-leaning proclivities on several issues. What stands out to us is that as the religious none population grows in the United States and Canada—both nations historically (and still) dominated by those who identify as Christian—social narratives that distinguish "us" from "them" are becoming more pronounced among both the religious and irreligious (especially those further removed from organized religion, such as inactive nonbelievers). As we have seen, these groups are forming distinct subcultures and worldviews about and toward one another as well as on a range of social and civic issues. These perspectives are learned and reinforced in social settings such as the home, with one's peers and coworkers, and in larger social institutional settings.

What remains to be seen is if or how exactly these polarized perspectives will evolve in the future in different social milieus. It is clear to us that now in the United States and to a lesser extent in Canada, we are witnessing a polarized setting in many ways between active religious affiliates and religious nones—not as a bifurcation of people who identify in one of these two camps but rather the divergent and sometimes hostile views and occasional behaviors toward members of the "other" group. This development is not antithetical to the stages of decline framework. Instead it is a fulfillment of this theoretical narrative insofar as we see a shrinking core (not disappearance) of active religious affiliates—a former majority in society—alongside the growth of religious nones, with each group competing for social and cultural privilege, authority, and dominance to advance and protect its way of viewing the world.

In light of these central arguments, we draw our discussion of religious nones in the United States and Canada to a conclusion by addressing four questions. First, how does the religious none phenomenon, and all that comes with it as described in this book, intersect with broad social realities in late modern society? Second, in what ways are religious nones similar or dissimilar in the United States and Canada? Third, what might the future hold for religious nones? Should we expect them to grow, decline, or plateau, and depending on the answer, what impact might such a trajectory have in society? Fourth, what opportunities arise for further research in this field? Answers to these questions reinforce why studying religious nones in the United States and Canada is so important. With religious nones comprising a larger proportion of the population than ever before, there are real ramifications for the rest of society, in areas of politics, social justice, inequality, and social and civic engagement, to name a few. And by raising these questions in a comparative fashion between the United States and Canada, we can develop educated hunches on some possible scenarios that might be in store in the United States based on Canada's "further down the road" experience.

Late Modern Society and Religious Nones

It should be clear by now that instead of thinking of the guiding frameworks for understanding religious nones discussed earlier (stages of decline, individualization and spiritualization, and polarization) as mutually exclusive from one another, we have argued that all three of these perspectives operate in tandem with one another—with the caveat that a stages of decline explanation is the lead and most helpful one of the three. To further our case we now analyze how de-traditionalization, globalization, and expressive individualism and new tribalism (Giddens 1990, 1991, 1992)—distinct and influential elements of late modern society (the latter stages of the modern era that began in the sixteenth century)—help us to explain the social conditions that gave rise to secularization, individualization and spiritualization, and polarization among religious nones in the United States and Canada.

To begin, de-traditionalization is characterized by a people, a society, and a way of life that no longer feels bound by time, place, and tradition. Both the United States and Canada have experienced an acceleration of de-traditionalization since the world wars. The onset of urbanization, globalization, ease of travel, geographical mobility, advanced education, and technological progress and connectedness (notably the internet) means that individuals are now more than ever aware of the plurality of perspectives and choices on offer in the world; the belief that there is one correct way to live and be in the world, rooted in a local place and tradition, is a bygone perspective for many in modern Western nations. Most individuals are now socialized to value individual autonomy, freedom, and choice amid a cornucopia of options before them, from ordering at Starbucks to selecting a romantic partner and picking where they live.

Religion, a social institution historically benefiting from shared social narratives surrounding place, tradition, obligation to outside authority, and a single sacred canopy, has progressively become one institutional choice among many that individuals can choose to turn to in life. This outlook was on display with Darlene and Patrick earlier, who both spoke of the value to choose religious beliefs for themselves. At a macrolevel, with structural and social differentiation, religion—Christianity above all—has become disentangled and less central to other social institutions such as education, healthcare, politics, and law (all more so in Canada than the United States). Alongside these social changes, rationalism, empiricism, materialism, and consumption have become more important in society. As such, religion and tradition are not necessarily seen as helpful for addressing this-world concerns. Suffice to say, in line with our stages of decline thesis, traditional ties and obligations to religious affiliation, authority, or behavior have gradually become optional in late modern society for many individuals in the United States and Canada. Christian affiliation and involvement have suffered the most. The result, in part, are widespread signs of secularization, evidenced in our data with the rise of individuals choosing to say they have no religion (particularly inactive nonbelievers) and families placing less emphasis on religious socialization within the home.

Individualism, though not new to late modern society, is especially salient in contemporary social life. For Robert Bellah, Richard Madsen, William M. Sullivan, Ann Swidler, and Steven M. Tipton (1985), "expressive individualism" captures the social shift where individuals come to see themselves with a sacred and special quality, orchestrating much of their lives with themselves at the center of day-to-day life versus others or the community around them. Charles Taylor (2007) similarly speaks of an "age of authenticity," characterized by the mass turn to carefully craft and live into one's true, authentic, desired self over and against external social constraints, conditions, and authorities. Developing one's identity apart from external authority signals a "more authentic" self. Nowhere are these values more clearly expressed than in marketing and consumption habits. Individuals build a personalized identity that they wish to convey to others through what they purchase, wear, eat and drink, drive, and so forth. The consumptive options available are many, and individuals take pride as the sole authority (in their minds) over the choices they make.

As de-traditionalization and heightened value for choice and individualism contribute to secularization in some ways, these social changes also lend credence to the individualization and spiritualization thesis. For instance, parents who give their children choice over religious identity and involvement, encouraging their children to discover religion for themselves, could be interpreted as a sign that the way we approach religion is changing rather than declining in late modern society. Additionally, more than any other type of religious none that we described earlier, the spiritual but not religious (SBNR) epitomize elements of the expressive individualism and age of authenticity milieu (see Watts 2018). The SBNR marker signals for some, like Corrine, both the individual bricoleurs who have control over what beliefs and practices they will embrace and a clear boundary against institutional religion by not allowing religious groups to tell them what to believe and how to behave. For some the SBNR identity is a stable one, and for others it is a transition from once being involved in organized religion to progressively shedding all religious belief and practice. Beyond this one type, the range of ways to be a religious none reveal the fluidity and autonomy that individuals assume when constructing their identities (see Wilkinson 2018). Religious nones come in all shapes and sizes. Ironically, as much as individuals believe their choices in life are highly personalized and autonomous activities—including to say that one has no religion—the attempt to stand out as different from everyone else is a highly structured and social process (influenced, for example, by family, social media, and peers) that often results in individuals who are more alike one another than not. This observation stands out to us when comparing the collective similarities between nones within the different subtypes of religious nones described earlier, or the similarities between religious nones in different US and Canadian regions that have higher or lower proportions of religious nones around them.

Expressive individualism is not strictly an individualist phenomenon. Entire social institutions and subgroups also seek to stand out as different from one another in a globalized context. Our description and analysis of religious nones (including the different subtypes), marginal religious affiliates, and active religious affiliates along a range of social and moral issues, sociopolitical and civic engagement markers, and attitudes and actions toward one another typify the attempt to draw clear boundaries between "us" and "them." These boundaries are exasperated in the United States and Canada today as the religious none population grows, affecting many spheres of social life from gender to sexuality, the environment, and immigration. Polarization between the most secular and devout reveal a collective desire within these groups to push against competing narratives of what a good and moral society ought to look like. Such efforts would be unnecessary in a homogenous society. But with de-traditionalization, globalization, and the expanded place for individualism and choice in late modern society, religious nones in the United States and Canada are emboldened to vie for cultural legitimacy and authority against the religious perspectives and hegemony that they confront. This struggle is keenly felt in regions of the United States, and to a lesser extent in Canada, where religious nones have fewer numbers relative to Evangelicals. Will the vitriolic public tensions between the religiously affiliated and unaffiliated in the United States, which affect many corners of social life, soften over time if or when the United States becomes more secular like Canada? Only time will tell, though we envision so long as there is a sizeable committed Evangelical base in the United States, we should anticipate ongoing public strife.

If we think about these social, cultural, and historical developments in the context of the stages of decline narrative, polarization is partially a result of declining rates of active religious affiliates and the parallel rise of religious nones. Active religious affiliates, who will not disappear altogether, now experience a level of marginalization rarely if ever experienced before and are fighting in response to reassert or reclaim the cultural authority that they once held. Conversely, religious nones have grown proportionate to the overall population and have gained some cultural legitimacy in the process, depending on the region in question. Religious nones like Darlene, Patrick, and Sandra want to continue to leverage and capitalize on this momentum, and limit the influence of conservative religious groups in the process.

Comparing Religious Nones in the United States and Canada

If you ask Canadians what it means to be Canadian, most will likely respond by saying, "We are not American." Such a response is humorous to Canadians and baffling to some outsiders who take this to mean that Canada does not have its own culture. "We are not American" is obviously not a response that will suffice for describing and explaining the ways that religious nones are similar or dissimilar in Canada versus the United States. Throughout this book we have scattered several observations on this topic, and now we want to tie together these findings. A central thread in the following remarks is that in general, Canada is a more left-leaning nation (politically, morally, and economically) with weaker current-day religious roots compared with the United States. These historical and cultural variations affect our assessment of nones in both countries. At the same time, depending on the variable in question, there are sometimes marked state and provincial variations in both nations that serve as more useful comparison points versus nation-to-nation contrasts.

First, religious nones grew earlier and more rapidly in Canada than in the United States (see figure I.1). Our goal was not to sideline our core focus by tracing the history of secularization (Berger 1967; Bruce 2011; Martin 1978; Norris and Inglehart 2011; Taylor 2007) or to engage the debate over when religious decline really began (see, for example, Clarke and Macdonald 2017), as much as these discussions intersect in varied ways with the topic at hand. Instead, we waded into some of the reasons that the growth of religious nones ultimately started earlier in Canada and later in the United States. In Canada, changing ties between primarily English-speaking Western European nationalities and Protestantism as well as French Catholicism deepened Canadian values for multiculturalism and pluralism and diversity, and the absence of a sizeable and politically active conservative Christian subculture paved the way for

Canadians to say they had no religion with little fear of social shame or stigma. A central reason for the delayed onset in the rise of religious nones in the United States can be attributed to the strong place of civil religion as well as socially and politically active forms of Evangelicalism, social conditions that made it socially deviant to even consider a religious none identity. To "come out" as a religious none even thirty years ago meant that one would incur great social cost, and in many ways still does depending on where one lives in the United States. Recently the proportion of religious nones in the United States has increased dramatically as the stigma to say one does not identify with a religion diminishes somewhat.

In both countries, as we have seen, the rise of religious nones can be linked to a range of factors that caused people to leave behind their religious (mainly Christian) affiliation. In the United States, the stark increase of religious nones in the past two decades has been driven partly by a strong opposition to the Christian Right and the fusion of Evangelical Christianity and politics. Additionally, irreligious socialization now plays a growing role in the rise of nones in both the United States and Canada. While some may be tempted to project that the growth and experience of religious nones in the United States will map perfectly onto what Canada has experienced ahead of time, we would caution one to consider the distinct historical and social variables already discussed, which nuance our comparison of the two nations. At the same time, some of the overarching social changes common to both countries—such as stages of religious decline followed by irreligious socialization—do generally trend, albeit at different rates, in the same direction.

Second, the proportion of religious nones has grown over time across every region in the United States and Canada; however, the regions with the highest and lowest proportions of religious nones have remained constant over the course of recent history in both countries (see figures I.2 and I.3 in the introduction). For example, as the proportion of religious nones increases across regions in both countries, the West and Northeastern United States and British Columbia in Canada remain the hub of religious none activity, while the Midwest and South in the United States and Quebec and Atlantic Canada continue to have the lowest proportion of religious nones. We have argued that social environment makes a difference in the size and experiences of religious nones in different regions across the United States and Canada. We would be surprised to see these regional variations change substantially in the long term.

These regional comparisons factor into our third observation that religious nones are a diverse group in the United States and Canada. At the most general level, religious nones are more likely to adopt various conventional and less conventional religious and spiritual beliefs than to embrace religious or spiritual practices (public or private). When we dig a bit deeper into our five types of religious nones, regions in the United States and Canada have more in common versus a straight comparison between the United States and Canada as a whole. Regions with a longer history of higher proportions of religious nones (e.g., western Canada and United States) are more likely to have higher rates of religious nones who are inactive nonbelievers. In comparison there are higher rates of those who say they are spiritual but not religious or are inactive believers in places where religious nones are fewer.

Fourth, when we look to a range of social and moral issues, religious nones in both nations are more left-leaning than religious affiliates, especially in regions with higher proportions of religious nones. These topics include abortion, same-sex marriage, women in the workforce, the environment, government aid to the disadvantaged, and immigration. These findings remind us of the social impact that accompanies a growing and sizeable demographic of people who say they have no religion. Religious nones generally view the world differently than the religiously affiliated and are willing—along with the religiously affiliated—to vote and behave in ways consistent with their worldview. Polarization and social division are sometimes, not always, the consequence. When we compare religious nones in the United States and Canada, it turns out that religious nones north of the border, like Patrick and Corrine, are more left-leaning on the aforementioned topics than in the United States. Even those affiliated with a religion in Canada are more left-leaning than many religious affiliates in the United States. These differences can be attributed to Canada's value and practice of multiculturalism, stronger historical presence of mainline Protestantism (versus Evangelicalism in the United States), lengthier establishment of religious nones, and longer-standing political and legal policies that are left-leaning in these domains.

CONCLUSION | 181

Our fifth main insight is that Canadians generally seem warmer toward atheists and cooler toward conservative-leaning religious groups than those in the United States. Darlene, Patrick, and Sandra particularly stand out as religious nones who hold less favorable views toward conservative-leaning religious groups. In both nations, atheists and Evangelicals are highly suspicious of one another, as are more secular religious nones and more devout religious affiliates toward one another. It is hard to quantify the extent to which these polarized attitudes and perceptions manifest themselves in either country, though our hunch is that such occurrences take place more often and forcefully in the United States (e.g., consider the tensions leading up to and following the 2016 election in the United States).

One of our purposes in this book has been to compare religious nones in the United States and Canada. But in the process we have delineated observations that extrapolate to other social and historical contexts beyond these two countries. Namely, religious nones who reside in areas with a higher concentration of nones are likely to have more distinct left-leaning and secular views, experiences, and behaviors compared with religious nones who are in a minority position. And in contexts where other religious groups have a major public presence, religious nones are likely to experience social stigma in profound ways, depending on the major religious group in question, resulting in the need (and action) to seek out settings to gather with other religious nones. These observations reinforce a long-standing sociological tenet that one's localized social experiences with family, friends, neighbors, coworkers, schools, politicians, and the media shape one's sense of self and others.

The Future for Religious Nones and Society

Sociologists are not prognosticators. At the same time, we can offer plausible conjectures on possible trajectories for religious nones in the United States and Canada based on the evidence available to us in this book. Recalling from figure 1.6, interconnected factors that influence the proportional size of the religious none population include birth rates and socialization patterns, disaffiliation or reaffiliation, immigration and emigration patterns, and death rates. We have detailed the prominent role that disaffiliation has played and the growing place that irreligious socialization is playing to grow the proportion of religious nones. Might disaffiliates like Darlene or Patrick reaffiliate, or cradle nones such as Corrine convert to a religion, enough to slow, reverse, or stagnate the growth of religious nones? As we delineated from survey and interview data in chapter 1, we have our serious doubts, and even as some reaffiliation or conversion occurs, it is unlikely to match the losses experienced among the religiously affiliated.

Recent research in Canada goes one step further and provocatively intimates that there are substantial proportions of the religiously affiliated who are affiliated in name only (e.g., cultural Catholics and Protestants) but for all intents and purposes are only one step away from being religious nones (Clarke and Macdonald 2017). The implication is that those marginally attached to religious groups, who made up an estimated 35% of the American population in 2016 and 54% of the Canadian adult population in 2015 (based on our analyses of 2016 US General Social Survey [GSS] and 2015 Canadian GSS data), are making a progressive shift away from the more religiously devout toward the religious none end of the continuum. Further, these individuals are unlikely to raise their children with religion front and center, or even peripheral, to their day-to-day lives. We are inclined to agree, in line with our stages of decline framework. On the surface, given the smaller proportion of marginal affiliates in the United States compared with Canada, we anticipate that the United States will continue to lag behind Canada on some markers of the religious none experience. At the same time, Canadians have stronger ties to Catholic and mainline Protestant traditions that, historically, tend to privilege affiliation and rites of passage observances. It is conceivable then that transitions toward saying one has no religion in Canada could be slower at this point in history, comparatively speaking, and we might soon see religious none figures and experiences in the United States surpass those in Canada. We must keep the tape rolling to see how these trends unfold in both countries.

Then there are liminal nones (see Hout 2017; Lim, MacGregor, and Putnam 2010), who oscillate between identifying and not identifying with a religion. There are some indications that more liminal nones eventually land in the no religion category. Studies such as these alert us to the opportunity for longitudinal quantitative and qualitative panel research with religious nones. Where a change in religious affiliation status occurs, what contributes to such changes? Do changed identification statuses remain for a long period of time, or are they temporary? How does reaffiliation or conversion affect how people raise their children, and how do their children ultimately turn out in the short and long term? Answering such questions moves us beyond single data point discussions of reaffiliation or conversion and propel us toward a more nuanced and holistic understanding and analysis of the role that reaffiliation and conversion do or do not play among religious nones.

The proportion of religious nones in a society is about more than disaffiliation, reaffiliation, or conversion. We have described several demographic realities at work for the unaffiliated and religiously affiliated. Religious affiliates are an ageing population such that the proportionate hold of those affiliated with a religion in society may wane as religious affiliates die. However, religious nones, concentrated among younger demographics, will not necessarily fill the proportionate gap because they have lower birth rates compared with religious affiliates. On top of these demographic patterns, religious groups, especially in Canada, benefit more than religious nones from immigration, and we additionally know that immigrants, at least in the first generation, tend to have more children than those born in the United States or Canada. As we consider what possibly lies ahead for the proportion of religious nones in the United States and Canada, it is essential to keep in mind that a confluence of demographic factors influences the proportion of religious nones rather than any single measure.

Where does all of this information leave us on the possible future of religious nones in the United States and Canada? We think it is safe to expect sizeable proportions of religious nones to remain for the foreseeable future. We offer this conclusion due to the convergence of disaffiliation among both active and marginal religious affiliate populations, increased signs of irreligious socialization as the religious none population grows, and demographic trends related to age, birth rates, death rates, and immigration.

To be clear, we do not think that religious affiliation and involvement will altogether disappear, though admittedly some traditions will continue to struggle greatly. A small but stable core of religiously devout individuals exists in Canada, and a sizeable albeit shrinking core of active religious folk remains in the United States. As we have noted, there are signs that some active religious affiliates, like some religious nones, are building and advancing narratives over and against religious nones as the "other" that can sustain and possibly grow these groups. It is difficult for us to say with certainty how large religious nones will get, how small the religious affiliate ranks may diminish to, or what proportion of marginal religious affiliates will eventually become religious nones (and how long that process will generally take).

Yet on the whole we surmise that in Canada, active religious affiliates will remain the smallest group. Marginal religious affiliates will, for the foreseeable future, remain the largest group but will likely lose members over time (perhaps over generations) to the religious none camp. In the United States, the religiously devout remain a formidable force. Given the prominent place of Evangelical Christianity in American society, we anticipate that as their numbers diminish (still remaining a sizeable group), religious nones will continue to benefit. Unlike Canada, we do not see as large a middle group of marginal affiliates in the United States, mostly a function of there being fewer people with strong ties to religious traditions with roots to various state churches across Europe (e.g., Catholics, Lutherans, Presbyterians, and Episcopalians). Rather, the polarized gap between those who affiliate and are actively involved versus those who are not affiliated at all will likely dominate the religious landscape in the United States moving forward.

What of the cycle hypothesis then? Some theorize that we simply find ourselves at a low point on a normal religiosity cycle: that organized religion among a population goes through periodic highs and lows throughout history, and that we are currently in another low period that will eventually pass (see notably Stark and Finke 1992). Within this frame, religious groups are meant to hold tight and wait for a revival period to come, potentially triggered by either some natural, political, or economic disaster or some charismatic wave that will drive most to return to the pews. We are not convinced by this argument since, as seen earlier, we understand the religious none phenomenon as being tied to the fundamental social structure of late modernity. Just as one example, the terrorist attacks of September 11, 2001, were a catastrophe that reverberated across the United States and the world, and had many lasting implications for our societies since. Yet September 11 had virtually no long-term mitigating effect on the trend lines of rising religious nones illustrated in figure I.1 in the introduction. Religious revivals have happened over the course of recent American and Canadian history (think of, for example, the rise of the Christian Right or the Pentecostal and Catholic charismatic movement of the 1980s and 1990s), but as Bruce (2011) argues, the intensity of these revivals has progressively diminished over time: the trend line follows less of a cyclical pattern and more of a downward spiral. For these trends to change and for organized religion to become once more salient to a near entirety of Americans and Canadians, there would have to be a more fundamental societal shift in our opinion, affecting the phenomena of de-traditionalization and expressive individualism explored earlier in this chapter. In other words, the conditions of late modernity as a whole would have to shift. Social change on such a scale does happen, and has happened over the course of history, but may not happen for many hundreds of years yet and, when it does come, may not have the effect of driving most back to organized religion (depending on what kind of change happens, it could conceivably drive even more away). Consequently, we argue that religious nones will remain a sizeable portion of the general population for the foreseeable future and that coexistence between the religious and nonreligious is the new norm in the United States and Canada.

If we are correct, what are the potential implications for society? What could coexistence between religious nones and other religious groups entail, now that religious nones have a formidable (and still growing) place in social life? And what social and civic impact might we anticipate in the future? These are the critical "so what" questions for countless American and Canadian individuals and social institutions, as more people say they have no religion. As we have intimated, when it comes to sociopolitical and civic engagement, we do not think the sky is falling as religious nones grow and possibly stabilize in size. True, religious nones are generally less likely to volunteer or donate to charitable organizations than active religious affiliates (with some variation, depending on type of religious none and specific volunteer or giving context). Several social organizations and charities are already experiencing the drawbacks of such changes and look to the future with a degree of trepidation about their own sustainability and the well-being of those they serve. But religious nones like Corrine are not totally absent from these realms of society either—some do volunteer and donate money to different organizations. In order for religious nones, or anyone for that matter, to become more active on these fronts, different social institutions (e.g., education, politics, and family) will need to intentionally socialize and encourage widespread volunteer and charitable activity, and provide tangible opportunities for people to get involved from a young age.

It remains to be seen if an urgency will be felt in these domains to compel a society-wide push. Regardless, governments may need to become more central to filling possible gaps in the volunteer and charitable sectors as we see fewer active religious affiliates in the United States and Canada. As we demonstrated regarding government spending more to help those in poverty and the environment, religious nones are slightly more open to this possibility than active religious affiliates. In reality, Canadians have historically been more supportive than Americans of the government playing an active role in social and civic life. If this national difference persists, we could anticipate different outcomes in each nation should volunteering and charitable activity decline with a shrinking pool of active religious affiliates, with Canada possibly faring better than the United States. Nevertheless, if these volunteering and charitable gaps are not accounted for, serious questions will need to be asked across both nations. Who will provide the financial and human resources necessary to look out for refugees and immigrants, single parents, those with addictions or mental health concerns, and the impoverished? If groups such as these are not adequately supported, what other social challenges might we see in areas of education, employment, or crime? Again, we are not claiming that with the rise of religious nones we ought to set off the panic button. Yet some things will need to be adjusted in society to fill the gap historically carried by the religiously affiliated.

Polarization between religious nones and active affiliates, and atheists and Evangelicals specifically, will be significant to track in the future. As a reminder, in both the United States and Canada polarized beliefs and perceptions about the "other" exist. However, fairly rarely do such beliefs materialize into discriminatory actions toward the "other." Nevertheless, based on the beliefs and perceptions that these groups hold about the world and about one another, there is potential for more forceful social divisions to emerge in the future, in belief and possibly action. Heightened polarization is particularly possible as religious nones grow numerically and proportionately, and gain social acceptance and confidence as a "legitimate" worldview in society, combined with the loss and fear of marginalization by a diminished active religious affiliate populace. Cultural identity to each group is key to this discussion, with the religious and irreligious holding deep historical and contemporary narratives of self and other. This divide is more probable to accelerate in the United States, where Evangelicals have long enjoyed a cultural majority position in society, and who believe on religious grounds that the United States is and ought to be an openly and public Christian nation. Atheists, who have long felt marginalized and oppressed by Evangelicals, are gaining ground and, in some ways, can see and experience the pendulum swing. Both groups may thus push even stronger to spread and enforce their view of the world on to the rest of society. In Canada, groups of differing perspectives seem to have a more peaceful coexistence. This reality is partially attributable to no religious group in the last half century having a dominant public hegemony relative to religious nones in the ways experienced in the United States. Canada's stated values and practices of multiculturalism and diversity also figure prominently as politicians, legal rulings, and educators, among other social institutional spheres, consistently speak of the need for and benefit of bringing people of different views and backgrounds into the Canadian mosaic.

Broad generalizations like those we have just offered should not be interpreted as all encompassing across the United States and Canada. Other factors, such as regionalism or immigration, should also be taken into account. With respect to regionalism, the historical place of religious nones or active religious affiliates (certain kinds of active religious affiliates matter in different locales too) in a given location will influence how those groups exist and see one another. As religious affiliation demographics change, places with historically higher or lower proportions of religious nones or active religious affiliates will experience sociopolitical and civic engagement impacts differently. The same premise applies for possible polarization expressed through harmful acts between groups. Simply stated, social environment affects and is affected by these questions of social and civic engagement, coexistence, and social division. Immigration is another dynamic to consider. An influx of immigrants who are highly religious, typically within conservative-leaning traditions, and who have larger families will gradually change the demographic composition of a certain region. The ripple effect of changes like these is likely to be felt in the previously discussed contexts.

To ground this discussion in concrete realities, there are examples elsewhere of nations who are further down the religious (non)affiliation and subsequent social implications trajectory that the United States and Canada appear to be on. If we consider our stages of decline premise, might we expect the United States and Canada to follow similar paths as other nations where the proportion of religious nones are even higher? As well as the Pacific Northwest region of North America being at the forefront of these trajectories, many countries in Europe, including Great Britain, France, the Nordic countries, the Netherlands, Germany (especially Eastern Germany), the Czech Republic, and others still have large nonreligious subpopulations within their respective borders, more so currently than the United States and Canada. The same is true in Australia and New Zealand.

One of the first observations to stand out in most of these national contexts is the prevalence of a state church. Gradual religious decline occurred over generations in these locations where religion was once central and hegemonic to most aspects of social life but, over time, became less salient; religion became a cultural (rather than set apart as sacred "religious") and ritualistic fixture in society. Reasons for these shifts include many facets of modernization already discussed, such as de-traditionalization, globalization, immigration, religious and social diversity, and individualism. According to Steve Bruce (2002), one explanation for people's initial break away from the state church was the disdain toward the link between clergy and the ruling class in society. In step with other modernizing elements that affected society, as some individuals gradually diminished their connection to the state religion, it became more socially acceptable and appealing in other spheres of social life (friends, family, media, and schools) to do likewise. Bruce (2011) goes on to note that state churches reduce the strictness of their claims to stop the hemorrhaging. Unlike nations without a state church, religious affiliation figures in these countries are more widespread because *the* central religion or denomination is deeply affected by those who leave their religious affiliation behind. Relatedly, as we demonstrated earlier, religious decline for individuals tends to take a progressive shift from identifying as an active affiliate to a marginal affiliate to a religious none. Thus when we hear discussions of "C and E" folks in England (to imply Christmas and Easter rather than Church of England) or "cultural Catholics" in other state church milieus, we are mainly witnessing the gradual slide away from salient religious belonging, belief, and behavior in society.

We begin with this discussion of state churches because neither the United States nor Canada operates within a state church environment. With the exception of the strong historical link with Catholicism in Quebec, it is difficult to anticipate if or how exactly these countries may or may not follow many European countries with a state church. As for Quebec, the historically strong cultural, religious, political, and social divide between the Québécois and the rest of English-speaking North America has slowed in some ways the rise in those who say they have no religion in the province. Catholic affiliation remains deeply tied to francophone Québécois identity, despite most in the province not regularly taking part in church services and activities (Lemieux and Montminy 2000; Meunier and Wilkins-Laflamme 2011). Yet, with the Quiet Revolution of the 1960s, the predominant place of Catholicism within Quebec society has slowly weakened over time. With the proportion of religious nones in Quebec lagging behind the rest of Canada, it is worth asking if we might anticipate the floodgates opening in this respect in the future—not unlike what has been seen across many European nations with a state church. Given that religious belief and behavior in Quebec are among the lowest in Canada, might the normative expectations to identify as Catholic within the province wane over time (as we are beginning to see)? We anticipate none figures will increase, but exactly by how much is still to be determined.

In addition to state churches, in most of the national contexts with larger nonreligious populations identified earlier, the welfare state has played a much larger role in society over the last half century. It could be argued that religion becomes less critical for social and personal well-being as the government helps to look after one's basic day-to-day needs. Some might contend that this is one of the reasons the growth of religious nones started sooner and more rapidly in Canada than the United States. In Canada, the government takes a welfare-like approach with its citizens, even among conservative-leaning governments, compared to the United States. Still, the welfare state premise comes into question when we consider that the proportion of religious nones in the United States and Canada is more or less the same today, despite the different national approaches to the economic and social well-being of its citizens. The relationship between the welfare state and religious affiliation and behavior is one worth paying attention to in the years to come in both countries.

In many European nations that are further afield than the United States or Canada, there have also been important tensions surrounding religious minorities, especially more socially visible Muslim minorities, and the place of religion in the public sphere (Lefebvre 2005; Milot, Portier, and Willaime 2010; Ribberink, Achterberg, and Houtman 2017). As we have seen, such experiences and debates have also intersected, with some deciding to say they no longer affiliate with a religion in North America. Americans and Canadians are confronting these realities anew in a globalized world and appear to respond quite differently (consider the different respective responses by President Trump and Prime Minister Trudeau to Syrian refugees in 2017). At the same time, there are deeply divisive and polarizing perspectives and experiences in both nations when it comes to religious minorities, and one wonders if or when one or both nations might follow several European countries. It is too early to tell in the United States and Canada, but as religious pluralism grows within some sectors of society, might we also anticipate fewer people identifying with any religion in other sectors?

Although distinct cultural and political factors may eventually nudge the United States and Canada onto different trajectories, many European nations still offer a lens onto historically Christian societies that now function with large nonreligious populations. How well the United States or Canada map on to the stages of decline experienced elsewhere is valuable to monitor closely moving forward.

Future Research

Research into religious nones has come a long way in a relatively short period of time. Amid our advancing this conversation further, three main opportunities stand out to us to develop our collective understanding of religious nones in the United States, Canada, and abroad. First, as an extension of much work in the sociology of religion that centers on "the three Bs"—belief, behavior, and belonging—our focus on these domains does not capture all things that can be known about religious nones' approach to religion, spirituality, and secularity. A welcomed addition to the literature of late centers on "substantial seculars" and the substance of one's secularity. Nancy Ammerman (2014) and Lois Lee (2015) both helpfully provide scholars with qualitative data and insights into how religious nones learn, view, approach, practice, and experience a distinctive secular (and sometimes religious/spiritual) way of life. For example, Lee talks about the "banal" nonreligious beliefs, practices, symbols, artifacts, and assumptions that tend to go unnoticed in the private and public spheres, as expressed in domains such as greeting cards, a person's attire, popular culture (e.g., comedy shows), and books. Lee argues that these banal forms of nonreligion are important markers worth paying attention to. Ammerman draws on oral diaries and photo elicitation to highlight the ways that religious nones approach and experience religion, spirituality, and secularity in the confines of their homes, relationships, places of employment, and personal health and well-being. More exhaustive data of these kinds with each type of religious none that we delineated in chapter 2 would be advantageous.

Several questions on substantial secularity remain in our minds. How salient is the religious none identity and substantial secularity for those in question? What are the social and structural supports to develop and sustain substantial secularity? How significant are these elements of substantive secularity, personally and socially? Are the varied signs of banal nonreligion sustainable individually and collectively over time? How is substantial secularity lived out in places with higher rates of religious nones versus lower rates, and how might variations emerge in different countries around the world (e.g., predominantly Buddhist, Sikh, or Muslim regions of the world)? In the context of polarization, we need more and better data on the precise social locations and mechanisms for advancing attitudes and behaviors relative to other groups. For instance, in what settings and contexts do people learn to think positively or negatively toward another group? What are the specific mechanisms, tools, and messages used to socialize people in such a direction? Research into these areas would enable scholars to press deeper into substantive secularity and pinpoint exactly how pervasive, extensive, and influential this phenomenon really is, and where among the different types of religious nones these markers appear to be more salient than others. Moreover, such research would strengthen our capacity to compare and contrast the nuanced ways that the religiously affiliated and unaffiliated are similar or dissimilar in the functions, meanings, and experiences they attach to their religious or secular belief, behavior, and belonging.

Second, there is a burgeoning literature on religious diversity in the United States and Canada, but little of this research accounts for religious nones in the diversity conversation. Thankfully Lori Beaman's (2014, 2017, and 2018) work in Canada serves as a solid baseline for scholars around the world to meaningfully engage this subject. As we noted earlier, the field is wide open to explore how religious nones are accounted for (or not) in discussions surrounding diversity in social institutions like education, healthcare, politics, and law. Additional considerations include whether deep equality is the best or most empirically useful concept for examining this subject. If so, more research into where deep equality is found in the context of religious nones, religious diversity, and the above-mentioned institutions would be helpful. Importantly, what precise variables contribute to successful deep equality where religious nones are involved? And if deep equality is not empirically, methodologically, or practically suitable for exploring this topic, what is an appropriate alternative framework?

Third, this book has focused primarily on religious nones within a broadly Christian context. This point of departure is understandable given the religious roots in the United States and Canada that continue to affect religious identification and involvement today; Christianity remains, by a large margin, the leading religious identifier among citizens in both countries. Against this backdrop, the United States and Canada are seeing greater proportions of people identifying with religious traditions outside of Christianity. How do these changing trends intersect with our understanding and analysis of religious nones in these two nations? For instance, how widespread are Muslims, Mormons, Sikhs, or Jews in the United States and Canada who are leaving behind their religious identification in favor of saying they have no religion? How are their processes and narratives of setting aside their former religious affiliation similar or different to the majority of those at the center of our study? Of the types of nones that we have described, where would members of these other traditions fit, or do we need a different framework that is more all encompassing or narrower for different traditions?

Questions like these extend beyond the United States and Canada. As we noted in our introduction, saying that one has no religion is historically and culturally located. In some contexts (e.g., China) the "no religion" identification option implies a binary distinction between religion and something else (e.g., culture) that does not exist in local vernacular. In other global contexts religion, ethnicity, and culture are fused together in such a way that people say they identify with a religion, though perhaps do so to signal their ethnic and cultural identification—to be Israeli is to be Jewish, to be Turkish is to be Muslim, or to be Filipino is to be Catholic. Then there are settings (e.g., Saudi Arabia, Egypt, or Iran) where leaving one's religion comes at a great personal and social cost, sometimes even death. Although religious nones are not growing by leaps and bounds in the United States and Canada due to immigration, some religious nones do migrate to these countries from each of the aforementioned contexts, sometimes seeking or creating a secular diaspora in turn. How, if at all, are their perceptions and experiences different from religious nones born and raised in the United States or Canada? What does identifying as a religious none mean to them? This discussion of religious nones from around the world reminds us that studying religious nones in a global context entails that scholars pay careful attention to the historical, social, and cultural particularities that religious nones are exposed to, all the while seeking common language for describing and explaining religious none experiences around the world.

What Now?

As sociologists who both have a fair bit of professional contact with groups outside the academy (e.g., media, policy makers, religious groups, and atheist, humanist, and secularist groups), we anticipate that some reading this book will want to know what should be done with this information. Those in the media and in government likely have a stronger interest in the social, moral, political, and civic implications of a growing religious none population, along with the polarized perspectives between the unaffiliated and affiliated. What should we do in society to ensure peaceful and equitable coexistence among the different groups described in this book? Educators, politicians, lawmakers, and healthcare professionals may also have an interest in what should be done about religious and secular diversity in their respective domains. Religious groups undoubtedly want to know what can be done to enable some religious nones, like Darlene and Patrick, to return to their group, or those without much or any religious background, like Corrine and Sandra, to consider joining their group. Some religious groups may also have an interest in how to counteract some of their larger social concerns (as defined by those groups) associated with the rise of religious nones. By contrast, atheist, humanist, and secularist groups may focus on how to draw even more people away from religious groups, as well as to draw in many inactive religious nones to become active contributors with the expressed interest of creating a sense of community, of sharing aspects of their worldview and potentially curbing religious influence in society.

The following statement may disappoint some or all members in these various groups, but it is not for us as sociologists to say what any should or should not do with these data (see, for example, Berger 1963). We are not frontline practitioners who, for better or worse, possess a different level of familiarity and knowledge of these topics than we do as scholars and researchers. What we offer to the conversation is an outside sociological perspective based on empirical data and analysis on an array of social perceptions, behaviors, and realities, which in our view is invaluable for practitioners to grasp before reasonably considering what they could or should do with this information. For example, if religious groups think that by simply changing their supply of religion (what they provide in terms of beliefs and activities) they will attract religious nones, the quantitative and qualitative data available to us would suggest that, on the whole, such thinking is likely flawed. If groups at either end of the polarized spectrum delineated earlier downplay the role that family plays in growing and socializing members into their group, then our data should give them pause to think again.

If any advice is worth giving from this study, it is for readers to carefully pay attention to what the data and analysis reveal and do not reveal, rather than what they wish the data would uncover. Only in understanding how people think about and perceive the world—which has been our central task in this book—can the reader truly have a sound starting point for then processing what the contents of this book mean for their particular interests. On that front, we are eager to contribute, listen, and learn how this research intersects with various audiences of diverse interests. We hope this book becomes an important empirical and analytical base for thoughtful, informed, and reasoned dialogue on religious nones in the United States, Canada, and further afield.

ACKNOWLEDGMENTS

We had a blast writing this book together, which included numerous occasions where we shared our ideas with others who offered constructive feedback along the way.

When we started to explore the possibility of this book, we approached Phil Zuckerman at Pitzer College who kindly met with us for a video call conversation to hear our ideas, offer recommendations, and ultimately endorse our project as part of the NYUP Secular Studies series. Since that conversation, Phil has provided additional insights and consistent enthusiasm for our work. Phil, thank you for being so generous with your time and expertise, exemplifying the ideal of established scholars who contribute meaningful peer feedback for the advancement of knowledge in our discipline.

From June to December 2018 we both received sabbaticals from our home institutions—Ambrose University and the University of Waterloo. During this period, we spent some time at the Centre for Studies in Religion and Society (CSRS) in Victoria, British Columbia. This beautiful and inspiring place enabled us to research, brainstorm, write, and present various components of the book. We were also embedded in a fantastic learning community of scholars who were grappling with different aspects of religious life around the world; this group offered useful insights to our presentations and discussions, which helped to shape our conclusion chapter in particular. Our special thanks to Paul Bramadat, director of the CSRS, for inviting and including us in the center's activities. We value the interdisciplinary and diverse focus of the center's work. We hope to return again.

We want to express our gratitude for the following funding sources, which aided our work on religious nones: Ambrose University, Jack Shand Research Award (from the Society for the Scientific Study of Religion), and the University of Waterloo. Without these partners, it would have been difficult to complete this project.

Most of the quantitative analyses and results found in this book would not have been possible without many organizations making their survey data files freely available to researchers for download. We would sincerely like to thank Statistics Canada, the Pew Research Center, the research teams producing the American National Election Study, the Canadian Election Study, the American General Social Survey and the Project Canada Surveys, the Angus Reid Institute, Cardus, and CROP Inc. for their open access policies and willingness to share when it comes to their data. This open access to high-quality quantitative data has allowed us to strengthen our collective understanding of religious nones in the United States and Canada.

As we progressed in the project, we gave several conference presentations across Canada, the United States, and Europe, along with a range of public lectures outside of formal academic settings. We tested hunches and floated possible interpretations, and our colleagues and audiences met us with the rigor and candor that one could only hope for in settings like these. Such exchanges strengthened our thinking and analysis throughout the project. Ryan Cragun from the University of Tampa in particular has been a strong colleague and friend throughout this project.

Last, we want to thank the anonymous reviewers who offered helpful feedback to strengthen the manuscript. Additionally, the great team at New York University Press has been a delight to work with. Namely, Jennifer Hammer (editor) and Amy Klopfenstein (in marketing) have ensured that the writing and review process was straightforward, and that the word gets out for others to hear about our book and hopefully pick it up and have a read.

APPENDIX A: INTERVIEW GUIDE USED IN SEMISTRUCTURED INTERVIEWS WITH RELIGIOUS NONES

(1) Description of Project and Demographic Information
   a. How old are you?
   b. What is your highest level of completed education?
   c. What type of occupation are you currently involved in?
   d. Are you married? If so, how long have you been married?
   e. Do you have any children? If so, how many, and how old are they?
(2) Tell Me a Bit about Your Upbringing
   a. Where did you grow up? Did you have any siblings? What were your parents' occupations while you were growing up?
   b. Growing up, was your family affiliated with any religious group? If so, which group? If not, skip to questions g, h, and i.
   c. How often did your family attend religious services?
   d. Aside from religious services, what other religious activities, if any, were you involved in? What religious activities did you do at home?
   e. Would you describe your family as religious? Explain.
   f. Growing up, how much of a difference would you say religious beliefs and practices made on your family's life? Your life personally?
   g. (Only for those **not** raised in a religious home) Did your family ever talk about religion or spirituality? Was there any evidence of religious belief or practice in your home growing up?
   h. (Only for those **not** raised in a religious home) Were you ever exposed to religious belief and/or practice outside of your home growing up (e.g., neighbors, school, or extended family)?
   i. (Only for those **not** raised in a religious home) Would you describe yourself as religious growing up? If so, in what way? Explain.

      j. Thinking back to when you moved out of your family's place, what effect, if any, did that have on your (ir)religious journey? Did your interest in religion increase, decrease, or stay the same? Did your level of involvement in secular/religious organizations increase, decrease, or remain the same?
(3) Current (Ir)religious Affiliation, Beliefs, Practices, and Level of Importance Attributed to Each
    a. At present, are you affiliated with any religious group?
    b. How often do you attend religious services?
    c. How did you decide to affiliate (or not affiliate) with this group?
    d. Could you indicate for me how important your religious affiliation (or affiliation as a religious none) is relative to other aspects of your life (e.g., family, job, or social activities)? Explain.
    e. Have you ever seriously considered affiliating or getting involved with any other congregation, denomination, or religious group? Why or why not?
    f. Tell me about any religious/spiritual/secular beliefs that you hold as well as any religious/spiritual/secular practices that you participate in. Probe the following too:
        i. Would you identify yourself as an atheist (God does not exist), agnostic (do not definitively believe or disbelieve that God exists), or theist (God does exist)? Do you believe in a supernatural power or deity?
        ii. Do you believe in the afterlife? If so, do you desire life after death? What do you think is required to obtain life after death?
        iii. Do you believe that you have meaning, purpose, and direction in life? If so, what is the source of that meaning and direction?
        iv. Do you associate with any particular thinker or set of readings or group that influences your approach to religion, spirituality, or secularity? If so, do you agree and abide by all that they prescribe, or do you hold to some teachings and reject others?
        v. If married, did you get married in a church and/or did you include any religious/spiritual elements in the service? If not married, do you plan to get married in a church and/or to include any religious/spiritual elements in the service? Do

you plan to have your funeral in a church and/or to include any religious/spiritual elements in the service?
  vi. If you have children someday, how will you raise them? Will you give them a religious upbringing? Will you take/send them to church? Why/why not?
  vii. How much of a difference would you say your religious/spiritual/secular beliefs and practices make to your life? If a great difference, in what way? If not much of a difference, why not? Explain.
  viii. How confident are you in the religious/secular beliefs and practices that you adopt?
(4) Religious Costs and Rewards
  a. Do you think you gain anything in particular by not identifying with a religion?
  b. Keeping in mind some of these benefits, what are some of the sacrifices that you have made along the way? In other words, what are the "costs" associated with obtaining these benefits? (Are there any "costs" for not belonging to a religious group or attending religious services regularly?)
(5) Dependable and Responsive
  a. Do you have a sense that you can depend on God and/or another spiritual entity? If so, how? Can you provide an example? If not, why?
  b. Do you believe that God and/or another spiritual entity is concerned about, and acts on behalf of, humans? Explain.
(6) Role of Others in Shaping One's (Ir)religious Life
  a. Would you say that (ir)religious beliefs and practices are primarily up to the individual to develop and foster, or should this occur in the context of other people? If shared with others, what sort of activities do you have in mind? How are these beliefs reflected in your (ir)religious journey?
  b. How influential do you think (ir)religious groups should be in shaping people's religious beliefs and practices? How influential is your (non)religious group/identity in shaping your religious beliefs and practices?
  c. Of your closest friends, how many of them identify similar to you, as a religious none?

(7) Secularization and Greater Involvement
   a. There is some research that suggests that attendance at religious services is on the decline. Presuming for a moment that this is true, what do you think explains this?
   b. Would you consider the possibility of being more involved in a religious group if you found it to be worthwhile for you or your family?
   c. If participants are interested in greater involvement, what factors do you think would make greater participation more worthwhile? If participants are not interested in greater involvement, why not (and then skip to question [f])?
   d. If religious groups received the responses that you have just provided and they adjusted their supply of religion to provide some of the things that you mention, how likely would you be to increase your level of participation?
   e. For yourself (if they desire greater involvement), are there any efforts that you have made to find a suitable congregation to participate in, one that meets some of your criteria? If so, describe one of those instances.
   f. (If this has not come up yet . . .) If you have children someday, how will you raise them? Will you give them an (ir)religious upbringing? Will you take/send them to church? Why/why not?
(8) Religious Involvement in the Context of Other Social Involvements
   a. Overall, do you think that religion is a positive or a negative social force in society? Explain.
   b. Do you believe that people need religion in order to be moral or ethical beings?
   c. Are there other organizations, social activities, or volunteer initiatives that you dedicate your time to? If so, what does this commitment entail? (If they have trouble thinking of any, suggest things like sports activities, book clubs, political activities, social protests or movements, and regular meetings with friends and family.)
   d. How important are these involvements for you? Is there any correlation between these involvements and your religious

involvements? Put another way, does your religious involvement influence the type or amount of time given to other activities, or would you be more involved in church activities if you were not involved in any of the above activities?
e. Anything you want to add?

APPENDIX B: FURTHER STATISTICAL RESULTS FROM CHAPTER 2

TABLE B.1. Results from a multilevel logit regression model for being a nonbeliever, among religious nones, USA, 2014

	Odds ratio	Std. Err.
Fixed effects		
Age (5-year age groups)	.992***	.001
Female	.523***	.028
Black (reference category = White)	.164***	.024
Hispanic (reference category = White)	.481***	.043
Other race (reference category = White)	.718***	.068
Percentage of religious nones at state level	1.025***	.007
Individual-level constant	.751†	.126
State-level constant estimate	.204***	.048

Source: 2014 Pew Religious Landscape Study. N = 6,968. N groups = 51. LR test vs. logit model = 10.85***.
***: $p \leq .001$; †: $p \leq .1$

APPENDIX C: FURTHER STATISTICAL RESULTS FROM CHAPTER 3

TABLE C.1. Marginal effects on favoring legal abortion, same-sex marriage, women in the workforce, environmental laws and regulations, government aid to the poor, and immigration, USA, 2014

	Favor legal abortion $N = 31,322$ Pseudo $R^2 = .117$		Favor same-sex marriage $N = 30,323$ Pseudo $R^2 = .180$		Favor women in the workforce $N = 32,581$ Pseudo $R^2 = .035$	
	dydx	SE	dydx	SE	dydx	SE
Reference category = affiliated involved believers						
Unaffiliated nonbeliever	.497***	.019	.530***	.022	.137***	.017
Unaffiliated inactive believer	.275***	.014	.315***	.014	.086***	.014
Unaffiliated SBNR	.368***	.014	.367***	.014	.099***	.013
Unaffiliated involved believer	.064**	.024	.086***	.023	.047†	.025
Affiliated nonbeliever	.462***	.044	.346***	.035	.112***	.035
Affiliated inactive believer	.217***	.009	.200***	.009	.064***	.009
Affiliated SBNR	.226***	.009	.214***	.009	.060***	.010
Age (5-year groups)	.002***	.000	−.003***	.000	−.002***	.000
Female	.046***	.007	.110***	.006	.053***	.006
Common law (ref. married)	.079***	.015	.126***	.015	.038**	.014
Sep./divorced (ref. married)	.042***	.010	.025**	.010	.016†	.010
Widowed (ref. married)	−.016	.013	−.010	.012	−.005	.012
Never married (ref. married)	.023*	.011	.050***	.010	.005	.010
Number of children	−.029***	.003	−.023***	.002	−.017***	.002
Black (ref. White)	.086***	.012	−.044***	.011	.035***	.011
Hispanic (ref. White)	−.014	.012	.044***	.012	.052***	.012
Other race (ref. White)	.047***	.014	−.014	.014	−.011	.014
Foreign born	−.047***	.012	−.030**	.011	.044***	.012
University education	.118***	.006	.148***	.006	.106***	.007
Northeast (ref. South)	.089***	.010	.113***	.009	.008	.009
Midwest (ref. South)	.004	.009	.051***	.008	−.014†	.008

Source: 2014 Pew Religious Landscape Study. Robust SE. ***: $p<=.001$; **: $p<=.01$; *: $p<=.05$; †: $p<=.1$

TABLE C.1. (continued)

	Favor environmental laws and regulations $N = 31,724$ Pseudo $R^2 = .045$		Favor government aid to the poor $N = 32,581$ Pseudo $R^2 = .042$		Favor immigration $N = 32,581$ Pseudo $R^2 = .102$	
	dydx	SE	dydx	SE	dydx	SE
Reference category = affiliated involved believers						
West (ref. South)	.056***	.009	.080***	.008	.003	.009
Unaffiliated nonbeliever	.238***	.017	.202***	.015	.098***	.012
Unaffiliated inactive believer	.082***	.014	.067***	.014	−.014	.012
Unaffiliated SBNR	.179***	.014	.162***	.013	.085***	.010
Unaffiliated involved believer	.032	.026	.047†	.026	−.029	.022
Affiliated nonbeliever	.160***	.034	.176***	.034	.115***	.025
Affiliated inactive believer	.033***	.010	.023*	.010	−.033***	.009
Affiliated SBNR	.063***	.010	.084***	.010	.032***	.009
Age (5-year groups)	−.001***	.000	.000	.000	−.002***	.000
Female	.089***	.007	.081***	.007	−.030***	.006
Common law (ref. married)	.048***	.015	.096***	.014	.017	.011
Sep./divorced (ref. married)	.038***	.010	.091***	.010	.004	.009
Widowed (ref. married)	.027*	.013	.049***	.013	−.012	.013
Never married (ref. married)	.017	.011	.074***	.011	.026**	.009
Number of children	−.020***	.003	−.004	.003	−.012***	.002
Black (ref. White)	.084***	.012	.218***	.012	.077***	.010
Hispanic (ref. White)	.037**	.012	.081***	.012	.110***	.009
Other race (ref. White)	.022	.015	.072***	.014	.038***	.012
Foreign born	.041***	.012	.025*	.012	.155***	.009
University education	.123***	.007	.072***	.007	.164***	.005
Northeast (ref. South)	.058***	.010	.050***	.010	.032***	.008
Midwest (ref. South)	.012	.009	.028**	.009	.007	.008
West (ref. South)	.015†	.009	.046***	.009	.019*	.008

Source: 2014 Pew Religious Landscape Study. Robust SE. ***: p<=.001; **: p<=.01; *: p<=.05; †: p<=.1

TABLE C.2. Marginal effects on favoring legal abortion, same-sex marriage, women in the workforce, government spending on the environment, government spending on welfare, and immigrants, Canada, 2011 and 2015

	Favor legal abortion (2011) N = 2,385 Pseudo R^2 = .138		Favor same-sex marriage (2015) N = 5,983 Pseudo R^2 = .126		Favor women in the workforce (2015) N = 5,987 Pseudo R^2 = .030	
	dydx	SE	dydx	SE	dydx	SE
Reference category = active affiliates						
No religious affiliation	.292***	.033	.249***	.015	.079***	.015
Marginal affiliates	.213***	.033	.203***	.015	.092***	.015
Age	−.002**	.001	−.004***	.000	−.001	.000
Female	.032†	.019	.146***	.013	.048***	.012
Common law (ref. married)	—	—	.078***	.022	−.005	.019
Sep./divorced (ref. married)	.101**	.034	.030	.021	.005	.019
Widowed (ref. married)	.006	.033	−.010	.026	−.011	.022
Never married (ref. married)	−.025	.032	.051*	.020	−.017	.018
At least one child in home	−.058*	.027	—	—	—	—
Foreign born	−.035	.028	−.137***	.020	−.088***	.016
University education	.055*	.022	.097***	.014	.067***	.013
Nfld & Labrador (ref. Ontario)	−.041	.041	.012	.049	.052	.044
PEI (ref. Ontario)	−.082*	.041	.084	.055	−.066	.046
Nova Scotia (ref. Ontario)	−.062	.043	.036	.033	−.016	.030
New Brunswick (ref. Ontario)	−.100*	.040	−.010	.037	−.043	.031
Quebec (ref. Ontario)	.097***	.026	.039*	.017	−.001	.015
Manitoba (ref. Ontario)	−.098**	.036	.010	.031	−.027	.026
Saskatchewan (ref. Ontario)	−.089**	.035	−.086*	.040	.001	.034
Alberta (ref. Ontario)	−.091*	.038	−.056†	.029	−.063*	.025
British Columbia (ref. Ontario)	.035	.034	−.007	.021	−.004	.018

Source: 2011 and 2015 Canadian Election Studies. Robust SE. ***: p<=.001; **: p<=.01; *: p<=.05; †: p<=.1

TABLE C.2. (*continued*)

	Favor more government spending on the environment N = 5,870 Pseudo R² = .026		Favor more government spending on welfare N = 5,749 Pseudo R² = .027		Immigrants do not take jobs away from Canadians N = 5,932 Pseudo R² = .067	
	dydx	SE	dydx	SE	dydx	SE
Reference category = active affiliates						
No religious affiliation	.125***	.018	.017	.017	.072***	.017
Marginal affiliates	.054**	.018	−.028†	.017	.016	.017
Age	−.000	.001	.001*	.000	−.000	.001
Female	.055***	.014	.037**	.014	−.032*	.014
Common law (ref. married)	.043†	.023	.054*	.022	−.068***	.021
Sep./divorced (ref. married)	.050*	.023	.113***	.021	−.057**	.021
Widowed (ref. married)	.026	.029	.046†	.028	−.053†	.028
Never married (ref. married)	.099***	.022	.171***	.019	−.018	.021
Foreign born	.006	.022	.060**	.020	.166***	.022
University education	.082***	.015	.022	.014	.221***	.014
Nfld & Labrador (ref. Ontario)	−.020	.054	.035	.051	−.031	.050
PEI (ref. Ontario)	.015	.060	.193***	.051	−.048	.058
Nova Scotia (ref. Ontario)	.028	.037	.081*	.034	−.007	.036
New Brunswick (ref. Ontario)	.049	.040	.024	.038	−.105**	.036
Quebec (ref. Ontario)	.027	.018	.040*	.017	.132***	.017
Manitoba (ref. Ontario)	.003	.033	−.010	.033	.019	.032
Saskatchewan (ref. Ontario)	.002	.041	−.012	.042	−.027	.040
Alberta (ref. Ontario)	−.059†	.032	−.037	.034	.029	.029
British Columbia (ref. Ontario)	.034	.023	.090***	.021	.020	.022

Source: 2011 and 2015 Canadian Election Studies. Robust SE. ***: p<=.001; **: p<=.01; *: p<=.05; †: p<=.1

TABLE C.3. Individual-level and state-level effects on favoring abortion, same-sex marriage, women in the workforce, environmental laws and regulations, government aid to the poor, and immigration, USA, 2014

	Favor legal abortion N = 32,377 LR test vs. logit model = 364***		Favor same-sex marriage N = 31,320 LR test vs. logit model = 480***		Favor women in the workforce N = 33,754 LR test vs. logit model = 66***	
	Odds ratios	SE	Odds ratios	SE	Odds ratios	SE
Fixed effects						
No religious affiliation* Percentage of religious nones at state level	1.019*	.007	1.009	.007	1.018***	.006
No religious affiliation	2.552***	.423	3.762***	.630	1.047	.132
Age (5-year age groups)	1.001	.001	.978***	.001	.988***	.001
Female	1.139***	.027	1.522***	.038	1.248***	.030
Black (reference category = White)	1.129**	.047	.574***	.025	1.085†	.046
Hispanic (reference category = White)	.632***	.025	.809***	.035	1.110*	.047
Other race (reference category = White)	1.162**	.057	.863**	.045	.978	.047
Percentage of religious nones at state level	1.038***	.008	1.046***	.009	1.011*	.004
Individual-level constant	.407***	.069	1.015	.200	2.394***	.253
State-level constant estimate	.312***	.035	.370***	.041	.160***	.023
State-level random slopes no religious affiliation estimate	.162**	.052	.128*	.054	.000	.121

Source: 2014 Pew Religious Landscape Study. N groups = 51. ***: $p<=.001$; **: $p<=.01$; *: $p<=.05$; †: $p<=.1$

TABLE C.3. (*continued*)

	Favor environmental laws and regulations N = 32,782 LR test vs. logit model = 246***		Favor government aid to the poor N = 33,754 LR test vs. logit model = 108***		Favor immigration N = 33,754 LR test vs. logit model = 175***	
	Odds ratios	SE	Odds ratios	SE	Odds ratios	SE
Fixed effects						
No religious affiliation* Percentage of religious nones at state level	1.016**	.005	1.014**	.005	1.004	.006
No religious affiliation	1.407**	.175	1.361**	.162	1.361*	.178
Age (5-year age groups)	.992***	.001	1.000	.001	.987***	.001
Female	1.531***	.036	1.384***	.031	.845***	.022
Black (reference category = White)	1.372***	.057	2.512***	.103	1.268***	.055
Hispanic (reference category = White)	1.077†	.043	1.337***	.051	1.838***	.073
Other race (reference category = White)	1.087†	.051	1.339***	.060	1.407***	.068
Percentage of religious nones at state level	1.015*	.007	1.019***	.005	1.021***	.006
Individual-level constant	.984	.153	.425***	.050	.358***	.053
State-level constant estimate	.283***	.033	.195***	.026	.251***	.031
State-level random slopes no religious affiliation estimate	.038	.148	.056	.060	.046***	.072

Source: 2014 Pew Religious Landscape Study. N groups = 51. ***: p<=.001; **: p<=.01; *: p<=.05; †: p<=.1

TABLE C.4. Effects on ideological left/right self-placement, USA, 2016

	β	SE
Reference category = active affiliates		
No religious affiliation	−1.396***	.116
Marginal affiliates	−.882***	.151
Age	.010**	.003
Female (ref. male)	−.091	.101
Other gender (ref. male)	−2.087*	.023
Marital status: widowed (ref. married)	−.275	.207
Marital status: divorced (ref. married)	−.141	.150
Marital status: separated (ref. married)	.093	.374
Marital status: never married (ref. married)	−.155	.135
Foreign born	.110	.165
University education	−.859***	.097
Northeast (ref. South)	−.687***	.142
Midwest (ref. South)	−.352**	.131
West (ref. South)	−.626***	.132
Model intercept	6.588***	.207

Source: 2016 American National Election Study. Robust SE. N = 3,356. R^2 = .138. ***: p<=.001; **: p<=.01; *: p<=.05; ': p<=.1

TABLE C.5. Effects on ideological left/right self-placement, Canada, 2015

	β	SE
Reference category = active affiliates		
No religious affiliation	−.926***	.104
Marginal affiliates	−.585***	.100
Age	.007*	.003
Female	−.456***	.084
Marital status: common law partnership (ref. married)	−.232†	.129
Marital status: divorced (ref. married)	−.234	.147
Marital status: separated (ref. married)	−.885***	.277
Marital status: widowed (ref. married)	−.159	.203
Marital status: never married (ref. married)	−.441***	.119
Foreign born	.150	.126
University education	−.389***	.091
Newfoundland & Labrador (ref. Ontario)	−.512	.439
Prince Edward Island (ref. Ontario)	−.747†	.395
Nova Scotia (ref. Ontario)	.091	.232
New Brunswick (ref. Ontario)	.032	.226
Quebec (ref. Ontario)	−.197*	.099
Manitoba (ref. Ontario)	−.227	.228
Saskatchewan (ref. Ontario)	−.041	.284
Alberta (ref. Ontario)	.158	.162
British Columbia (ref. Ontario)	−.269*	.133
Model intercept	*5.635****	*.215*

Source: 2015 Canadian Election Study. Robust SE. N = 2,931. R^2 = .078. ***: p<=.001; **: p<=.01; *: p<=.05; †: p<=.1

APPENDIX D: FURTHER STATISTICAL RESULTS FROM CHAPTER 4

TABLE D.1. Marginal effects on political participation indicators, USA, 2016

	Attended political meeting, speech, or rally $N = 3,480$ Pseudo $R^2 = .033$		Contributed money to a political party $N = 3,480$ Pseudo $R^2 = .060$	
	dydx	SE	dydx	SE
Reference category = active affiliates				
No religious affiliation	.018	.011	−.006	.012
Marginal affiliates	−.012	.018	−.014	.020
Age	.000	.000	.002***	.000
Female (ref. male)	−.006	.011	−.023*	.011
Other gender (ref. male)	.138**	.050	.075	.083
Marital status: widowed (ref. married)	.044†	.025	−.001	.021
Marital status: divorced (ref. married)	−.012	.018	−.014	.018
Marital status: separated (ref. married)	−.020	.035	−.051	.038
Marital status: never married (ref. married)	.027*	.013	.026†	.014
Foreign born	−.043*	.021	−.004	.019
University education	.034***	.010	.036***	.010
Northeast (ref. South)	−.008	.016	.006	.016
Midwest (ref. South)	−.021	.014	−.054***	.016
West (ref. South)	.010	.013	.001	.014

Source: 2016 American National Election Study. Robust SE. ***: p<=.001; **: p<=.01; *: p<=.05; †: p<=.1

TABLE D.1. (*continued*)

	Posted on social media about political issue $N = 3,478$ Pseudo $R^2 = .043$		Bought or boycotted product or service for political/social reason $N = 3,469$ Pseudo $R^2 = .022$	
	dydx	SE	dydx	SE
Reference category = active affiliates				
No religious affiliation	.120***	.021	.041†	.023
Marginal affiliates	.035	.030	−.070*	.031
Age	−.005***	.001	−.001	.001
Female (ref. male)	.037†	.019	.037†	.020
Other gender (ref. male)	.109	.147	.041	.183
Marital status: widowed (ref. married)	−.041	.046	.000	.045
Marital status: divorced (ref. married)	.025	.028	−.010	.030
Marital status: separated (ref. married)	−.058	.067	−.146*	.067
Marital status: never married (ref. married)	−.024	.025	.041	.027
Foreign born	−.066*	.034	−.051	.035
University education	.038*	.019	.123***	.020
Northeast (ref. South)	.002	.028	−.009	.030
Midwest (ref. South)	−.022	.025	−.030	.026
West (ref. South)	−.012	.025	.030	.027

Source: 2016 American National Election Study. Robust SE. ***: p<=.001; **: p<=.01; *: p<=.05; †: p<=.1

TABLE D.2. Marginal effects on political participation indicators, Canada, 2015

	Been a member of a federal political party $N = 2,676$ Pseudo $R^2 = .095$		Donated money to a political party or candidate $N = 2,681$ Pseudo $R^2 = .096$	
	dydx	SE	dydx	SE
Reference category = active affiliates				
No religious affiliation	−.005	.018	.007	.021
Marginal affiliates	−.016	.022	−.023	.022
Age	.006***	.001	.004***	.001
Female	−.036*	.015	−.028†	.015
Marital status: living with a partner (ref. married)	.005	.029	−.006	.028
Marital status: divorced (ref. married)	.044†	.026	−.022	.029
Marital status: separated (ref. married)	.031	.044	.003	.044
Marital status: widowed (ref. married)	−.016	.023	−.065**	.024
Marital status: never married (ref. married)	−.019	.028	.012	.031
Foreign born	−.023	.022	.012	.023
University education	.090***	.015	.111***	.016
Newfoundland & Labrador (ref. Ontario)	−.119*	.053	−.099*	.049
Prince Edward Island (ref. Ontario)	−.029	.037	−.010	.041
Nova Scotia (ref. Ontario)	.015	.034	−.038	.035
New Brunswick (ref. Ontario)	−.042	.043	−.071*	.049
Quebec (ref. Ontario)	−.029	.023	−.054*	.023
Manitoba (ref. Ontario)	.026	.029	−.001	.031
Saskatchewan (ref. Ontario)	.032	.031	.070**	.027
Alberta (ref. Ontario)	.059*	.026	.083*	.034
British Columbia (ref. Ontario)	.012	.023	.019	.021

Source: 2015 Canadian Election Study. Robust SE. ***: p<=.001; **: p<=.01; *: p<=.05; †: p<=.1

TABLE D.2. (*continued*)

	Use the internet to be politically active N = 5,914 Pseudo R^2 = .063		Bought products for political, ethical, or environmental reasons N = 5,847 Pseudo R^2 = .044	
	dydx	SE	dydx	SE
Reference category = active affiliates				
No religious affiliation	.043*	.017	.010	.018
Marginal affiliates	−.035*	.017	−.070***	.018
Age	−.006***	.000	−.002***	.001
Female	.001	.014	.055***	.014
Marital status: living with a partner (ref. married)	.013	.021	.011	.023
Marital status: divorced (ref. married)	.027	.025	.024	.025
Marital status: separated (ref. married)	.058	.038	.054	.040
Marital status: widowed (ref. married)	−.038	.033	−.004	.029
Marital status: never married (ref. married)	.033†	.020	−.030	.022
Foreign born	−.011	.021	−.047*	.022
University education	.113***	.014	.183***	.014
Newfoundland & Labrador (ref. Ontario)	−.172**	.055	−.123*	.055
Prince Edward Island (ref. Ontario)	.029	.055	.004	.060
Nova Scotia (ref. Ontario)	.030	.035	.007	.036
New Brunswick (ref. Ontario)	−.002	.036	−.105**	.040
Quebec (ref. Ontario)	−.074***	.018	−.072***	.018
Manitoba (ref. Ontario)	.040	.030	−.023	.033
Saskatchewan (ref. Ontario)	−.049	.039	−.036	.043
Alberta (ref. Ontario)	.033	.030	.009	.031
British Columbia (ref. Ontario)	.023	.022	.045†	.023

Source: 2015 Canadian Election Study. Robust SE. ***: $p<=.001$; **: $p<=.01$; *: $p<=.05$; †: $p<=.1$

TABLE D.3. Marginal effects on frequency of volunteerism, USA, 2014

	Volunteering at least once a week		Volunteering at least once a month	
	dydx	SE	dydx	SE
Reference category = active affiliates				
No religious affiliation	−.016	.024	−.068*	.030
Marginal affiliates	−.045*	.020	−.079***	.023
Age	.001	.001	−.001	.001
Female (ref. male)	.017	.017	.023	.020
Marital status: widowed (ref. married)	−.005	.031	.050	.035
Marital status: divorced (ref. married)	.024	.023	.037	.027
Marital status: separated (ref. married)	−.062	.056	−.005	.051
Marital status: never married (ref. married)	.009	.025	−.028	.033
Number of children	−.001	.007	.009	.007
Foreign born	−.006	.026	.061*	.028
Black (ref. White)	.006	.025	−.052†	.031
Other race (ref. White)	.009	.031	−.069†	.037
University education	.028	.017	.075***	.019
New England (ref. South Atlantic)	.039	.037	.061	.041
Middle Atlantic (ref. South Atlantic)	.031	.030	.008	.031
E. N. Central (ref. South Atlantic)	−.018	.029	.014	.032
W. N. Central (ref. South Atlantic)	−.045	.042	.054	.037
E. S. Central (ref. South Atlantic)	.012	.040	.005	.048
W. S. Central (ref. South Atlantic)	.031	.029	−.051	.041
Mountain (ref. South Atlantic)	.011	.033	.010	.036
Pacific (ref. South Atlantic)	.016	.029	−.027	.037

Source: 2014 American General Social Survey. Robust SE. Pseudo R^2 = .082. N = 1,249. ***: $p<=.001$; **: $p<=.01$; *: $p<=.05$; †: $p<=.1$

TABLE D.3. (continued)

	Volunteering at least once a year		Never volunteered	
	dydx	SE	dydx	SE
Reference category = active affiliates				
No religious affiliation	−.034	.039	.128**	.041
Marginal affiliates	−.083*	.034	.207***	.033
Age	−.004***	.001	.004***	.001
Female (ref. male)	.045	.028	−.085**	.029
Marital status: widowed (ref. married)	−.158*	.071	.113†	.066
Marital status: divorced (ref. married)	−.038	.044	−.022	.045
Marital status: separated (ref. married)	.005	.074	.061	.076
Marital status: never married (ref. married)	−.082*	.040	.100*	.044
Number of children	−.007	.011	−.001	.011
Foreign born	−.096†	.050	.042	.048
Black (ref. White)	.029	.043	.017	.045
Other race (ref. White)	−.015	.055	.075	.056
University education	.118***	.030	−.220***	.031
New England (ref. South Atlantic)	.060	.071	−.161*	.077
Middle Atlantic (ref. South Atlantic)	.045	.051	−.084	.053
E. N. Central (ref. South Atlantic)	.057	.046	−.054	.048
W. N. Central (ref. South Atlantic)	−.011	.064	.001	.068
E. S. Central (ref. South Atlantic)	−.026	.069	.009	.069
W. S. Central (ref. South Atlantic)	−.029	.055	.049	.057
Mountain (ref. South Atlantic)	.064	.054	−.085	.057
Pacific (ref. South Atlantic)	−.048	.050	.059	.052

Source: 2014 American General Social Survey. Robust SE. Pseudo R^2 = .082. N = 1,249. ***: p<=.001; **: p<=.01; *: p<=.05; †: p<=.1

TABLE D.4. Marginal effects on frequency of charitable giving, USA, 2014

	Give at least once a week		Give at least once a month	
	dydx	SE	dydx	SE
Reference category = active affiliates				
No religious affiliation	−.118***	.034	−.072*	.033
Marginal affiliates	−.118***	.025	−.067**	.025
Age	.001†	.001	.001	.001
Female (ref. male)	−.022	.019	−.014	.023
Marital status: widowed (ref. married)	−.035	.043	−.012	.043
Marital status: divorced (ref. married)	−.039	.029	−.047	.035
Marital status: separated (ref. married)	−.045	.053	.004	.063
Marital status: never married (ref. married)	−.066*	.032	−.063†	.033
Number of children	.005	.006	.001	.008
Foreign born	−.046	.034	−.047	.038
Black (ref. White)	−.049†	.033	−.105**	.041
Other race (ref. White)	.053	.036	.003	.043
University education	−.005	.019	.116***	.023
New England (ref. South Atlantic)	−.056	.058	.017	.052
Middle Atlantic (ref. South Atlantic)	.015	.032	−.055	.042
E. N. Central (ref. South Atlantic)	−.005	.031	−.047	.038
W. N. Central (ref. South Atlantic)	−.031	.040	−.039	.050
E. S. Central (ref. South Atlantic)	.045	.038	−.072	.058
W. S. Central (ref. South Atlantic)	−.025	.035	.004	.041
Mountain (ref. South Atlantic)	.036	.034	−.027	.043
Pacific (ref. South Atlantic)	−.006	.039	−.036	.039

Source: 2014 American General Social Survey. Robust SE. N = 1,251. Pseudo R^2 = .106. ***: p<=.001; **: p<=.01; *: p<=.05; †: p<=.1

TABLE D.4. (*continued*)

	Give at least once a year		Never given	
	dydx	SE	dydx	SE
Reference category = active affiliates				
No religious affiliation	.055	.043	.135***	.037
Marginal affiliates	.054	.035	.131***	.033
Age	.001	.001	−.003**	.001
Female (ref. male)	.086**	.030	−.049†	.027
Marital status: widowed (ref. married)	.111†	.066	−.063	.063
Marital status: divorced (ref. married)	−.004	.047	.091*	.041
Marital status: separated (ref. married)	−.100	.087	.141*	.064
Marital status: never married (ref. married)	−.039	.045	.168***	.037
Number of children	−.035**	.011	.028**	.009
Foreign born	−.024	.050	.117**	.041
Black (ref. White)	.036	.047	.118***	.036
Other race (ref. White)	−.058	.058	.002	.049
University education	−.003	.035	−.108***	.033
New England (ref. South Atlantic)	.116	.079	−.077	.074
Middle Atlantic (ref. South Atlantic)	.063	.054	−.022	.048
E. N. Central (ref. South Atlantic)	.086†	.050	−.034	.045
W. N. Central (ref. South Atlantic)	.117	.073	−.047	.067
E. S. Central (ref. South Atlantic)	.077	.072	−.050	.066
W. S. Central (ref. South Atlantic)	−.021	.057	.042	.051
Mountain (ref. South Atlantic)	.027	.061	−.035	.053
Pacific (ref. South Atlantic)	.045	.054	−.003	.050

Source: 2014 American General Social Survey. Robust SE. N = 1,251. Pseudo R^2 = .106. ***: $p<=.001$; **: $p<=.01$; *: $p<=.05$; †: $p<=.1$

TABLE D.5. Marginal effects on volunteering, Canada, 2013

	Volunteer at least once a year—all sectors N = 13,394 Pseudo R² = .066		Volunteer at least once a year—excluding religion sector N = 13,394 Pseudo R² = .048	
	dydx	SE	dydx	SE
Reference category = active affiliates				
No religious affiliation	−.188***	.019	−.063***	.019
Marginal affiliates	−.193***	.014	−.077***	.014
Age	−.003***	.000	−.003***	.000
Female	.022†	.012	.021†	.012
Marital status: living with a partner (ref. married)	−.045*	.020	−.035†	.020
Marital status: divorced (ref. married)	−.106***	.022	−.088***	.022
Marital status: separated (ref. married)	−.099**	.035	−.096**	.034
Marital status: widowed (ref. married)	−.019	.023	−.018	.023
Marital status: never married (ref. married)	−.036*	.018	−.032†	.017
Foreign born	−.146***	.016	−.144***	.016
University education	.156***	.014	.155***	.013
Newfoundland & Labrador (ref. Ontario)	.011	.024	.021	.023
Prince Edward Island (ref. Ontario)	.030	.024	.034	.024
Nova Scotia (ref. Ontario)	.054*	.021	.038†	.021
New Brunswick (ref. Ontario)	−.050*	.021	−.048*	.021
Quebec (ref. Ontario)	−.097***	.016	−.089***	.016
Manitoba (ref. Ontario)	.068***	.021	.046†	.021
Saskatchewan (ref. Ontario)	.096***	.023	.101***	.023
Alberta (ref. Ontario)	.046*	.022	.038†	.022
British Columbia (ref. Ontario)	.070***	.019	.062***	.019

Source: 2013 Canadian Election Study. Robust SE. ***: p<=.001; **: p<=.01; *: p<=.05; †: p<=.1

TABLE D.6. Effects on hours volunteered, among volunteers, Canada, 2013

	Number of hours volunteered—all sectors $N = 7,056$ $R^2 = .028$		Number of hours volunteered—excluding religion sector $N = 7,056$ $R^2 = .018$	
	β	SE	β	SE
Reference category = active affiliates				
No religious affiliation	−25.037	17.949	28.900†	17.573
Marginal affiliates	−42.354***	11.733	12.076	11.211
Age	1.900***	.453	1.454***	.447
Female	−17.036†	9.753	−21.340*	9.458
Marital status: living with a partner (ref. married)	−3.895	13.593	−1.613	13.551
Marital status: divorced (ref. married)	11.448	22.261	21.928	21.427
Marital status: separated (ref. married)	1.444	25.136	8.977	25.833
Marital status: widowed (ref. married)	22.207	16.862	17.374	15.967
Marital status: never married (ref. married)	27.710	20.268	24.131	20.015
Foreign born	−1.603	14.484	−5.167	14.170
University education	21.913*	10.297	24.587*	10.067
Employed full time	−38.645**	14.363	−39.833**	14.089
Newfoundland & Labrador (ref. Ontario)	−22.331	16.732	−23.450	15.010
Prince Edward Island (ref. Ontario)	10.232	21.417	7.214	20.318
Nova Scotia (ref. Ontario)	22.331	26.187	21.701	25.759
New Brunswick (ref. Ontario)	6.866	19.606	5.521	19.189
Quebec (ref. Ontario)	−36.617**	12.747	−31.022*	12.408
Manitoba (ref. Ontario)	−8.718	19.953	−3.305	19.471
Saskatchewan (ref. Ontario)	−21.645	15.246	−23.240†	13.773
Alberta (ref. Ontario)	−2.412	18.714	−4.236	17.919
British Columbia (ref. Ontario)	−23.937†	14.179	−23.067†	13.943
Model intercept	132.414***	31.911	95.376**	31.469

Source: 2013 Canadian Election Study. Robust SE. ***: p<=.001; **: p<=.01; *: p<=.05; †: p<=.1

TABLE D.7. Marginal effects on charitable giving, Canada, 2013

	Gave to charity at least once a year—all sectors N = 13,394 Pseudo R^2 = .086		Gave to charity at least once a year—excluding religion sector N = 13,394 Pseudo R^2 = .060	
	dydx	SE	dydx	SE
Reference category = active affiliates				
No religious affiliation	−.143***	.017	.013	.017
Marginal affiliates	−.111***	.015	.032*	.014
Age	.001*	.000	.001**	.000
Female	.024*	.010	.038***	.011
Marital status: living with a partner (ref. married)	−.055***	.017	−.028	.020
Marital status: divorced (ref. married)	−.077***	.020	−.062**	.022
Marital status: separated (ref. married)	−.120***	.025	−.131***	.029
Marital status: widowed (ref. married)	−.083***	.017	−.106***	.022
Marital status: never married (ref. married)	−.147***	.013	−.150***	.014
Foreign born	−.059***	.013	−.088***	.014
University education	.069***	.013	.098***	.014
Newfoundland & Labrador (ref. Ontario)	.027	.024	.050*	.025
Prince Edward Island (ref. Ontario)	−.017	.022	.022	.023
Nova Scotia (ref. Ontario)	.003	.019	.024	.022
New Brunswick (ref. Ontario)	−.018	.019	−.009	.021
Quebec (ref. Ontario)	−.021	.014	−.028†	.016
Manitoba (ref. Ontario)	.004	.018	.000	.020
Saskatchewan (ref. Ontario)	.005	.021	.025	.023
Alberta (ref. Ontario)	.034†	.019	.049*	.021
British Columbia (ref. Ontario)	−.040**	.016	−.049**	.017

Source: 2013 Canadian Election Study. Robust SE. ***: p<=.001; **: p<=.01; *: p<=.05; †: p<=.1

TABLE D.8. Effects on amount (in CND$) given to charity, among givers, Canada, 2013

	Amount (in CND$) given to charity—all sectors N = 11,528 R² = .076		Amount (in CND$) given to charity—excluding religion sector N = 11,528 R² = .035	
	β	SE	β	SE
Reference category = active affiliates				
No religious affiliation	−685.446***	75.584	−30.706	59.690
Marginal affiliates	−716.345***	52.249	−95.587**	32.261
Age	10.506***	1.257	6.563***	.790
Female	−99.515**	38.522	−86.575***	26.844
Marital status: living with a partner (ref. married)	−10.298	70.442	−6.269	38.137
Marital status: divorced (ref. married)	71.739	119.483	107.109	110.128
Marital status: separated (ref. married)	−195.689***	50.755	−96.369**	33.955
Marital status: widowed (ref. married)	−124.841**	45.014	−30.332	36.847
Marital status: never married (ref. married)	18.034	53.888	24.907	33.512
Foreign born	−125.886*	53.852	−119.507***	33.188
University education	410.414***	46.725	275.809***	29.799
Employed full time	190.118***	36.320	123.675***	23.398
Newfoundland & Labrador (ref. Ontario)	−204.736***	44.561	−145.422***	27.128
Prince Edward Island (ref. Ontario)	−130.157*	52.062	−84.250*	33.588
Nova Scotia (ref. Ontario)	−120.597**	42.915	−108.905***	28.393
New Brunswick (ref. Ontario)	−201.313***	39.679	−152.695***	26.879
Quebec (ref. Ontario)	−189.971***	47.071	−131.752***	25.404
Manitoba (ref. Ontario)	148.486	101.188	79.691	72.254
Saskatchewan (ref. Ontario)	122.623	79.180	64.164	70.942
Alberta (ref. Ontario)	355.353***	86.861	248.678***	68.708
British Columbia (ref. Ontario)	157.806*	69.762	47.428	39.118
Model intercept	431.024***	96.960	2.292	59.442

Source: 2013 Canadian Election Study. Robust SE. ***: $p<=.001$; **: $p<=.01$; *: $p<=.05$; †: $p<=.1$

NOTES

CHAPTER 1. I'M DONE . . . AND I'M NOT GOING BACK!
1 However, Skirbekk et al. (2012) indicate that a longer duration of stay among mainland Chinese immigrants is associated with higher levels of identification with Christianity and Buddhism.
2 Statistics Canada, 2006 Census, accessed June 20, 2017, www.statcan.gc.ca.
3 See Zuckerman, Galen, and Pasquale (2016) for estimates of world region nonreligious populations.
4 Religious affiliation in the American GSS is asked as, "What is your religious preference? Is it Protestant, Catholic, Jewish, some other religion, or no religion?"

CHAPTER 2. NONES OF ALL SHAPES AND SIZES
1 Data for the Pacific Northwest Social Survey (PNSS) were collected online during the month of October 2017 from respondents living in British Columbia, Oregon, or the state of Washington. This was done by a research team of which Sarah was part, and led by Paul Bramadat at the Centre for Studies in Religion and Society at the University of Victoria (www.uvic.ca/research/centres/csrs). The University of Waterloo's Survey Research Centre (https://uwaterloo.ca/survey-research-centre) managed the data collection, and the sample of respondents was drawn from the Léger group's online panel (http://leger360.com/en-ca/subscribeNow). More information about this survey can be found at https://uwspace.uwaterloo.ca/handle/10012/13406.
2 A hierarchical generalized linear model was run using the 2014 Pew Religious Landscape Study, with individuals nested within US states (group level), to confirm this finding once controlling for age, gender, and race as fixed effects. This model estimates that with an increase of ten percentage points in the size of the religious none population at the state level, the probability of an average religious none respondent not believing in God or a universal spirit increases by twenty-five percentage points. Full results of this model are available in table B.1 in appendix B.

CHAPTER 3. WE ARE JUST AS MORAL . . . IF NOT MORE!
1 The CES surveys are run across the ten provinces during each federal election in Canada. In more recent years, these surveys have taken a three-wave format: a series of questions asked by means of telephone interviews during the election

campaign period, just after election day, and then through a self-completion mail-back questionnaire (turned online questionnaire since 2011). For more information, visit the CES website: https://ces-eec.arts.ubc.ca/english-section/home.

2 Full results from these multilevel models for all six US issue positions are available in table C.3 in appendix C.

CHAPTER 5. IT'S TOO BAD YOUR PARENTS AREN'T CHRISTIAN . . .

1 A side but not insignificant observation here is that in 2009 and 2013 Angus Reid was involved in surveys that measured Canadian attitudes toward different religious groups (Angus Reid Global 2013), yet religious nones are nowhere to be found in these surveys. This omission and recent addition is a possible sign of the shift that has taken place to pay greater attention to this growing segment of the Canadian population.

BIBLIOGRAPHY

Achterberg, Peter, Dick Houtman, Stef Aupers, Willem de Koster, Peter Mascini, and Jerpen van der Waal. 2009. "A Christian Cancellation of the Secularist Truce? Waning Christian Religiosity and Waxing Religious Deprivatization in the West." *Journal for the Scientific Study of Religion* 48:687–701.

Adams, Michael. 2006. *Sex in the Snow: The Surprising Revolution in Canadian Social Values*. Toronto: Penguin.

Adkins, Todd, Geoffrey C. Layman, David E. Campbell, and John C. Green. 2013. "Religious Group Cues and Citizen Policy Attitudes in the United States." *Politics and Religion* 6:235–63.

Albanese, Catherine L. 1990. *Nature Religion in America: From the Algonkian Indians to the New Age*. Chicago: University of Chicago Press.

Altemeyer, Bob. 2003. "Why Do Religious Fundamentalists Tend to be Prejudiced?" *International Journal for the Psychology of Religion* 13:17–28.

Altemeyer, Bob, and Bruce Hunsberger. 1997. *Amazing Conversions: Why Some Turn to Faith and Others Abandon Religion*. Amherst, NY: Prometheus Books.

American National Election Study. 2016. University of Michigan and Stanford University. ANES 2016 Time Series Study. Ann Arbor, MI: Inter-University Consortium for Political and Social Research (distributor), 2017-09-19. https://doi.org/10.3886/ICPSR36824.v2.

Ammerman, Nancy. 2005. *Pillars of Faith: American Congregations and Their Partners*. Berkeley: University of California Press.

———. 2014. *Sacred Stories, Spiritual Tribes: Finding Religion in Everyday Life*. New York: Oxford University Press.

Ang, Adrian, and John R. Petrocik. 2012. "Religion, Religiosity, and the Moral Divide in Canadian Politics." *Politics and Religion* 5 (1): 103–32.

Angus Reid Global. 2013. "Canadians View Non-Christian Religions with Uncertainty, Dislike." Accessed March 21, 2018. http://angusreid.com.

Angus Reid Institute. 2015. "Religion and Faith in Canada Today: Strong Belief, Ambivalence and Rejection Define Our Views." Accessed June 17, 2016. http://angusreid.org.

———. 2017a. "Canada at 150: Religion Seen to Have Played a Positive Role in Local Communities, Less So on the National Stage." Accessed September 28, 2017. http://angusreid.org.

———. 2017b. "A Spectrum of Spirituality: Canadians Keep the Faith to Varying Degrees, but Few Reject It Entirely." Accessed September 28, 2017. http://angusreid.org.

———. 2018. "Most Take Pride in Canadian NGO's Development Work Abroad, Express Frustration over Continued Suffering." Accessed July 19, 2018. http://angusreid.org.

Arweck, Elisabeth, and Eleanor Nesbitt. 2010. "Growing Up in a Mixed-Faith Family: Intact or Fractured Chain of Memory?" In *Religion and Youth*, edited by Sylvia Collins-Mayo and Pink Dandelion, 167–74. Aldershot, UK: Ashgate.

Bagg, Samuel, and David Voas. 2010. "The Triumph of Indifference: Irreligion in British Society." In *Atheism and Secularity*, vol. 2: *Global Expressions*, edited by Phil Zuckerman, 91–111. Santa Barbara, CA: Praeger.

Bahr, Howard M. 1970. "Aging and Religious Disaffiliation." *Social Forces* 49 (1): 59–71.

Baker, Joseph O'Brian. 2012. "Perceptions of Science and American Secularism." *Sociological Perspectives* 55 (1): 167–88.

Baker, Joseph O'Brian, Jonathan Hill, and Nathaniel Porter. 2016. "Assessing Measures of Religion and Secularity with Crowdsourced Data from Amazon's Mechanical Turk." Paper presented at the Society for the Scientific Study of Religion's annual meeting. Atlanta.

Baker, Joseph O'Brian, and Buster G. Smith. 2009. "None Too Simple: Examining Issues of Religious Nonbelief and Nonbelonging in the United States." *Journal for the Scientific Study of Religion* 48 (4): 719–33.

———. 2015. *American Secularism: Cultural Contours of Nonreligious Belief Systems*. New York: New York University Press.

Banyasz, Alissa M., David M. Tokar, and Kevin P. Kaut. 2016. "Predicting Religious Ethnocentrism: Evidence for a Partial Mediation Model." *Psychology of Religion and Spirituality* 8 (1): 25–34.

Barman, Jean. 2008. *British Columbia: Spirit of the People*. Madeira Park, BC: Harbour.

Beaman, Lori. 2014. "Deep Equality as an Alternative to Accommodation and Tolerance." *Nordic Journal of Religion and Society* 27 (2): 89–111.

———. 2017. "Religious Diversity in the Public Sphere: The Canadian Case." *Religions* 8: 259.

———. 2018. *Deep Equality in an Era of Religious Diversity*. New York: Oxford University Press.

Beaman, Lori, and Peter Beyer. 2013. "Betwixt and Between: A Canadian Perspective on the Challenges of Researching the Spiritual but Not Religious." In *Social Identities between the Sacred and the Secular*, edited by Abby Day, Giselle Vincett, and Christopher R. Cotter, 127–42. Farnham, UK: Ashgate.

Beaman, Lori, and Cory Steele. 2018. "Transcendence/Religion to Immanence/Nonreligion." *International Journal of Human Rights in Healthcare* 11 (2): 129–43.

Beaman, Lori, and Steven Tomlins, eds. 2015. *Atheist Identities: Spaces and Social Contexts*. New York: Springer.

Bean, Lydia. 2014. *The Politics of Evangelical Identity: Local Churches and Partisan Divides in the United States and Canada*. Princeton, NJ: Princeton University Press.

Becker, Penny Edgell, and Pawan H. Dhingra. 2001. "Religious Involvement and Volunteering: Implications for Civil Society." *Sociology of Religion* 62 (3): 315–35.

Bellah, Robert, Richard Madsen, William M. Sullivan, Ann Swidler, and Steven M. Tipton. 1985. *Habits of the Heart: Individualism and Commitment in American Life*. Berkeley, CA: University of California Press.

Bengtson, Vern L., Norella M. Putney, and Susan Harris. 2013. *Families and Faith: How Religion Is Passed Down across Generations*. New York: Oxford University Press.

Berger, Ida E. 2006. "The Influence of Religion on Philanthropy in Canada." *Voluntas: International Journal of Voluntary and Nonprofit Organizations* 17:110–27.

Berger, Peter. 1963. *Invitation to Sociology: A Humanistic Perspective*. New York: Knopf Doubleday.

———. 1967. *The Sacred Canopy: Elements of Sociological Theory of Religion*. Garden City, NY: Doubleday.

Beyer, Peter, and Rubina Ramji, eds. 2013. *Growing Up Canadian: Muslims, Hindus, Buddhists*. Montreal, QC: McGill-Queen's University Press.

Beyerlein, Kraig, and John R. Hipp. 2006. "From Pews to Participation: The Effect of Congregation Activity and Context on Bridging Civic Engagement." *Social Problems* 53 (1): 97–117.

Beyerlein, Kraig, and Stephen Vaisey. 2013. "Individualism Revisited: Moral Worldviews and Civic Engagement." *Poetics* 41 (4): 384–406.

Bibby, Reginald. 1987. *Fragmented Gods: The Poverty and Potential of Religion in Canada*. Toronto: Stoddart.

———. 2011. *Beyond the Gods and Back: Religion's Demise and Rise and Why It Matters*. Lethbridge, AB: Project Canada Books.

———. 2017. *Resilient Gods: Being Pro-Religious, Low Religious, or No Religious in Canada*. Vancouver, BC: University of British Columbia Press.

Bibby, Reginald, and Andrew Grenville. 2013. "The Christmas Onlys: A Wakeup Bell for Canada's Religious Groups." Accessed January 21, 2014. http://reginaldbibby.com.

Bibby, Reginald, Sarah Russell, and Ron Rolheiser. 2009. *The Emerging Millennials: How Canada's Newest Generation Is Responding to Change and Choice*. Lethbridge, AB: Project Canada Books.

Block, Tina. 2005. "'Going to Church Just Never Even Occurred to Me': Women and Secularism in the Pacific Northwest, 1950–1975." *Pacific Northwest Quarterly* 96:61–68.

———. 2010. "Religion, Irreligion, and the Difference Place Makes: The Case of the Postwar Pacific Northwest." *Social History* 43:1–30.

———. 2017. *The Secular Northwest: Religion and Irreligion in Everyday Postwar Life*. Vancouver: University of British Columbia Press.

Blogowska, Joanna, and Vassilis Saroglou. 2013. "For Better or Worse: Fundamentalists' Attitudes toward Outgroups as a Function of Exposure to Authoritative Religious Texts." *International Journal for the Psychology of Religion* 23 (2): 103–25.

Bloom, Pazit Ben-Nun, Gizem Arikan, and Marie Courtemanche. 2015. "Religious Social Identity, Religious Belief, and Anti-Immigration Sentiment." *American Political Science Review* 109 (2): 203–21.

Borgonovi, Francesca. 2008. "Divided We Stand, United We Fall: Religious Pluralism, Giving, and Volunteering." *American Sociological Review* 73:105–28.
Bouchard, Gérard, and Charles Taylor. 2008. *Fonder l'avenir. Le temps de la conciliation. Rapport final intégral*. Commission de consultation sur les pratiques d'accommodement reliées aux différences culturelles, Quebec.
Bowen, Kurt. 2004. *Christians in a Secular World: The Canadian Experience*. Montreal, QC: McGill-Queen's University Press.
Brady, H. E., S. Verba, and K. Schlozman. 1995. "Beyond SES: A Resource Model of Political Participation." *American Political Science Review* 89:271–94.
Bramadat, Paul. 2016. "The Past and Future of Religion in Cascadia: Tectonic Shifts in the Best Place on Earth." Paper presented at the Sites of Memory: Religion, Multiculturalism and the Demands of the Past conference, University of Toronto, September 16, 2016.
Bramadat, Paul, and David Seljak, eds. 2005. *Religion and Ethnicity in Canada*. Toronto: Pearson.
Brandt, Mark J., and Christine Reyna. 2014. "To Love or Hate Thy Neighbor: The Role of Authoritarianism and Traditionalism in Explaining the Link between Fundamentalism and Racial Prejudice." *Political Psychology* 35 (2): 207–23.
Brown, Callum G. 2013. "The Twentieth Century." In *The Oxford Handbook of Atheism*, edited by Stephen Bullivant and Michael Ruse, 229–44. New York: Oxford University Press.
Bruce, Steve. 2002. *God Is Dead: Secularization in the West*. Malden, MA: Blackwell.
———. 2011. *Secularization: In Defence of an Unfashionable Theory*. New York: Oxford University Press.
Bruce, Steve, and Tony Glendinning. 2003. "Religious Beliefs and Differences." In *Devolution: Scottish Answers to Scottish Questions*, edited by C. Bromley, J. Curtice, K. Hinds, and A. Park, 86–115. Edinburgh, UK: Edinburgh University Press.
Buckner, Phillip, ed. 2005. *Canada and the End of Empire*. Vancouver: University of British Columbia Press.
Bullivant, Stephen. 2008a. "Introducing Irreligious Experiences." *Implicit Religion* 11 (1): 7–24.
———. 2008b. "Research Note: Sociology and the Study of Atheism." *Journal of Contemporary Religion* 23 (3): 363–68.
———. 2017. "The 'No Religion' Population of Britain." Accessed June 21, 2017. www.stmarys.ac.uk.
Bullivant, Stephen, and Lois Lee. 2012. "Interdisciplinary Studies of Non-Religion and Secularity: The State of the Union." *Journal of Contemporary Religion* 27:19–27.
Bullivant, Stephen, and Michael Ruse, eds. 2013. *The Oxford Handbook of Atheism*. New York: Oxford University Press.
Bunting, Robert. 1997. *The Pacific Raincoast: Environment and Culture in an American Eden, 1778–1900*. Lawrence: University Press of Kansas.
Cadge, Wendy, and Elaine H. Ecklund. 2006. "Religious Service Attendance among Immigrants: Evidence from the New Immigrant Survey—Pilot." *American Behavioral Scientist* 49 (11): 1574–95.

Campbell, Colin. 1971. *Toward a Sociology of Irreligion*. London: Macmillan.
Campbell, David E., and Steven J. Yonish. 2003. "Religion and Volunteering in America." In *Religion as Social Capital: Producing the Common Good*, edited by Corwin E. Smidt, 87–106. Waco, TX: Baylor University Press.
Canada Summer Jobs. 2018. "Canada Summer Jobs 2018: Creating Jobs, Strengthening Communities; Applicant Guide." Accessed February 13, 2018. https://www.canada.ca.
Caputo, Richard K. 2009. "Religious Capital and Intergenerational Transmission of Volunteering as Correlates of Civic Engagement." *Nonprofit and Voluntary Sector Quarterly* 38:983–1002.
Casanova, José. 1994. *Public Religions in the Modern World*. Chicago: University of Chicago Press.
Chandler, Siobhan. 2008. "The Social Ethic of Religiously Unaffiliated Spirituality." *Religion Compass* 2:240–56.
Cheadle, Jacob E., and Philip Schwadel. 2012. "The 'Friendship Dynamics of Religion,' or the 'Religious Dynamics of Friendship'? A Social Network Analysis of Adolescents Who Attend Small Schools." *Social Science Research* 41:1198–212.
Cimino, Richard, and Christopher Smith. 2007. "Secular Humanism and Atheism beyond Progressive Secularism." *Sociology of Religion* 68 (4): 407–24.
———. 2014. *Atheist Awakening: Secular Activism and Community in America*. New York: Oxford University Press.
Clarke, Brian, and Stuart Macdonald. 2017. *Leaving Christianity: Changing Allegiances in Canada since 1945*. Montreal, QC: McGill-Queen's University Press.
Clerkin, Richard M., and James E. Swiss. 2013. "Religious Motivations and Social Service Volunteers: The Interaction of Differing Religious Motivations, Satisfaction, and Repeat Volunteering." *Interdisciplinary Journal of Research on Religion* 9:1–19.
Clydesdale, Tim. 2007. *The First Year Out: Understanding American Teens after High School*. Chicago: University of Chicago Press.
Cnaan, Ram A. 2002. *The Invisible Caring Hand: American Congregations and the Provision of Welfare*. New York: New York University Press.
Cnaan, Ram, Stephanie Boddie, and Gaynor Yancey. 2003. "Bowling Alone but Serving Together: The Congregational Norm of Community Involvement." In *Religion as Social Capital: Producing the Common Good*, edited by Corwin Smidt, 19–31. Waco, TX: Baylor University Press.
Collins, Randall. 2004. *Interaction Ritual Chains*. Princeton, NJ: Princeton University Press.
Collins-Mayo, Sylvia, and Pink Dandelion, eds. 2010. *Religion and Youth*. Aldershot, UK: Ashgate.
Connor, Phillip. 2008. "Increase or Decrease? The Impact of the International Migratory Event on Immigrant Religious Participation." *Journal for the Scientific Study of Religion* 47 (2): 243–57.
———. 2009. "Immigrant Religiosity in Canada: Multiple Trajectories." *Journal of International Migration and Integration* 10:159–75.

———. 2014. *Immigrant Faith: Patterns of Immigrant Religion in the United States, Canada and Western Europe.* New York: NYU Press.

Cragun, Ryan T., and Joseph H. Hammer. 2011. "'One Person's Apostate Is Another Person's Convert': What Terminology Tells Us about Pro-Religious Hegemony in the Sociology of Religion." *Humanity and Society* 35:149–75.

Cragun, Ryan T., Joseph H. Hammer, and Jesse M. Smith. 2013. "North America." In *The Oxford Handbook of Atheism*, edited by Stephen Bullivant and Michael Ruse, 601–21. New York: Oxford University Press.

Cragun, Ryan, Barry Kosmin, Ariela Keysar, Joseph Hammer, and Michael Nielsen. 2012. "On the Receiving End: Discrimination toward the Non-Religious in the United States." *Journal of Contemporary Religion* 27 (1): 105–27.

Crockett, Alasdair, and David Voas. 2006. "Generations of Decline: Religious Change in 20th Century Britain." *Journal for the Scientific Study of Religion* 45 (4): 567–84.

CROP. 2006. *Survey on Religious Beliefs* (data set). Data collected by the CROP Inc. research team.

Cross, Katie. 2017. "The Sunday Assembly in Scotland: Vestiges of Religious Memory and Practise in a Secular Congregation." *Practical Theology* 10 (3): 249–62.

Daly, Mike Wood. 2016. "Valuing Toronto's Faith Congregations." Accessed August 17, 2018. www.haloproject.ca.

Davie, Grace. 1994. *Religion in Britain since 1945: Believing without Belonging.* Cambridge, MA: Blackwell.

———. 2000. *Religion in Modern Europe. A Memory Mutates.* Oxford: Oxford University Press.

Day, Abby. 2011. *Believing in Belonging: Belief and Social Identity in the Modern World.* Toronto: Oxford University Press.

Day, Abby, Giselle Vincent, and Christopher R. Cotter, eds. 2013. *Social Identities between the Sacred and the Secular.* New York: Routledge.

Demerath, N. Jay, III. 2000. "The Rise of 'Cultural Religion' in European Christianity: Learning from Poland, Northern Ireland, and Sweden." *Social Compass* 47 (1): 127–39.

Dillon, Michele, and Paul Wink. 2007. *In the Course of a Lifetime: Tracing Religious Belief, Practice, and Change.* Berkeley: University of California Press.

Djupe, Paul A., and J. Tobin Grant. 2001. "Religious Institutions and Political Participation in America." *Journal for the Scientific Study of Religion* 40 (2): 303–14.

Dobbelaere, Karel. 1981. "Secularization: A Multi-Dimensional Concept." *Current Sociology* 29 (2): 1–213.

———. 2002. *Secularization: An Analysis at Three Levels.* New York: Peter Lang.

Drescher, Elizabeth. 2016. *Choosing Our Religion: The Spiritual Lives of America's Nones.* New York: Oxford University Press.

Dunlap, Thomas R. 2004. *Faith in Nature: Environmentalism as Religious Quest.* Seattle: University of Washington Press.

Durkheim, Émile. 2008. *The Elementary Forms of Religious Life.* Translated by Joseph Ward Swain. New York: Dover. Originally published by Allen & Unwin, London, 1915.

Edgell, Penny, Joseph Gerteis, and Douglas Hartmann. 2006. "Atheists as 'Other': Moral Boundaries and Cultural Membership in American Society." *American Sociological Review* 71 (2): 211–34.

Einolf, Christopher J. 2011. "The Link between Religion and Helping Others: The Role of Values, Ideas, and Language." *Sociology of Religion* 72 (4): 435–55.

Environics. 2017. "Canadian Millennials: Social Values Study." Accessed August 29, 2017. www.environicsinstitute.org.

Ferguson, Todd W., and Jeffrey A. Tamburello. 2015. "The Natural Environment as a Spiritual Resource: A Theory of Regional Variation in Religious Adherence." *Sociology of Religion* 76 (3): 295–314.

Fournier, Patrick, Fred Cutler, Stuart Soroka, and Dietlind Stolle (principal investigators). 2017. *2011–2015 Canadian Election Study* (data set). Accessed March 12, 2017. http://ces-eec.arts.ubc.ca.

Friesen, Milton, and Cheryl Clieff. 2014. "Strengthening Vital Signs through Urban Religious Communities." Accessed October 6, 2014. www.cardus.ca.

Frost, Jacqui, and Penny Edgell. 2018. "Rescuing Nones from the Reference Category: Civic Engagement among the Non-Religious in America." *Nonprofit and Voluntary Sector Quarterly* 47 (2): 417–38.

Fuller, Robert. 2001. *Spiritual but Not Religious: Understanding Unchurched America*. New York: Oxford University Press.

Garcia, Alfredo, and Joseph Blankholm. 2016. "The Social Context of Organized Nonbelief: County-Level Predictors of Nonbeliever Organizations in the United States." *Journal for the Scientific Study of Religion* 55 (1): 70–90.

Gee, Ellen M., and Jean E. Veevers. 1989. "Religiously Unaffiliated Canadians: Sex, Age, and Regional Variations." *Social Indicators Research* 21 (6): 611–27.

George, Linda K., Christopher G. Ellison, and David B. Larson. 2002. "Explaining the Relationships between Religious Involvement and Health." *Psychological Inquiry* 13 (3): 190–200.

Germain, Annick, Anne-Lise Polo, and INRS-Urbanisation, culture et société. 2003. *Les pratiques municipales de gestion de la diversité à Montréal*. Quebec: INRS-Urbanisation, culture et société.

Gervais, Will M., Ara Norenzayan, and Azim F. Shariff. 2011. "Do You Believe in Atheists? Distrust Is Central to Anti-Atheist Prejudice." *Journal of Personality and Social Psychology* 101 (6): 1189–1206.

Gibson, Troy. 2008. "Religion and Civic Engagement among America's Youth." *Social Science Journal* 45:504–14.

Giddens, Anthony. 1990. *The Consequences of Modernity*. Cambridge, MA: Polity.

———. 1991. *Modernity and Self Identity: Self and Society in the Late Modern Age*. Cambridge, MA: Polity.

———. 1992. *The Transformation of Intimacy*. Cambridge, MA: Polity.

Goodenough, Ursula. 1998. *The Sacred Depths of Nature*. New York: Oxford University Press.

Goplen, Joanna, and E. Ashby Plant. 2015. "A Religious Worldview: Protecting One's Meaning System through Religious Prejudice." *Personality and Social Psychology Bulletin* 41 (11): 1474–87.

Grant, John Webster. 1998. *The Church in the Canadian Era*. 2nd rev. ed. Vancouver: Regent College Publishing.

Greenberg, Anna. 2000. "The Church and the Revitalization of Politics and the Community." *Political Science Quarterly* 115:377–94.

Grim, Brian J., and Melissa E. Grim. 2016. "The Socio-Economic Contribution of Religion to American Society: An Empirical Analysis." *Interdisciplinary Journal of Research on Religion* 12 (3): 1–31.

Guenther, Katja M., and Kerry Mulligan, with Cameron Papp. 2013. "From the Outside In: Crossing Boundaries to Build Collective Identity in the New Atheist Movement." *Social Problems* 60 (4): 457–75.

Hall, Michael, David Lasby, Steven Ayer, and William David Gibbons. 2009. *Caring Canadians, Involved Canadians: Highlights from the 2007 Canada Survey of Giving, Volunteering and Participation*. Accessed June 28, 2009. www.givingandvolunteering.ca.

Hall, Peter Dobkin. 2005. "Religion, Philanthropy, Service, and Civic Engagement in Twentieth-Century America." In *Gifts of Time and Money: The Role of Charity in America's Communities*, edited by Arthur C. Brooks, 159–83. New York: Rowman & Littlefield.

Hammer, Joseph H., Ryan T. Cragun, Karen Hwang, and Jesse M. Smith. 2012. "Forms, Frequency, and Correlates of Perceived Anti-Atheist Discrimination." *Secularism and Nonreligion* 1:43–67.

Harper, Marcel. 2007. "The Stereotyping of Nonreligious People by Religious Students: Contents and Subtypes." *Journal for the Scientific Study of Religion* 46 (4): 539–52.

Harris, Kathleen. 2018. "Trinity Western Loses Fight for Christian Law School as Court Rules Limits on Religious Freedom 'Reasonable.'" Accessed June 15, 2018. www.cbc.ca.

Haskell, David M. 2010. *Through a Lens Darkly: How the News Media Perceive and Portray Evangelicals*. Toronto: Clements.

Hay, D. Alastair. 2014. "An Investigation into the Swiftness and Intensity of Recent Secularization in Canada: Was Berger Right?" *Sociology of Religion* 75 (1): 136–62.

Hayes, Alan L. 2004. *Anglicans in Canada: Controversies and Identity in Historical Perspective*. Chicago: University of Illinois Press.

Hayes, Bernadette C. 2000. "Religious Independents within Western Industrialized Nations: A Socio-Demographic Profile." *Sociology of Religion* 61 (2): 191–207.

Heelas, Paul, and Linda Woodhead. 2005. *The Spiritual Revolution: Why Religion Is Giving Way to Spirituality*. Oxford, UK: Blackwell.

Herberg, Will. 1960. *Protestant-Catholic-Jew*. Garden City, NJ: Anchor.

Hervieu-Léger, Danielle. 1999. *Le pèlerin et le converti: La religion en mouvement*. Paris: Flammarion.

Hood, Ralph, Jr. 2003. "The Relationship between Religion and Spirituality." In *Defining Religion: Investigating the Boundaries between the Sacred and Secular*, edited by Arthur Greil and David Bromley, 241–64. Kidlington, UK: Elsevier Science.

Hout, Michael. 2017. "Religious Ambivalence, Liminality, and the Increase of No Religious Preference in the United States, 2006–2014." *Journal for the Scientific Study of Religion* 56 (1): 52–63.

Hout, Michael, and Claude S. Fischer. 2002. "Why More Americans Have No Religious Preference: Politics and Generations." *American Sociological Review* 67:165–90.

Houtman, Dick, and Stef Aupers. 2007. "The Spiritual Turn and the Decline of Tradition: The Spread of Post-Christian Spirituality in 14 Western Countries, 1981–2000." *Journal for the Scientific Study of Religion* 46 (3): 305–20.

Hunsberger, Bruce, and Bob Altemeyer. 2006. *Atheists: A Groundbreaking Study of America's Nonbelievers*. Amherst, NY: Prometheus.

Igartua, Jos E. 2011. *The Other Quiet Revolution: National Identities in English Canada, 1945–71*. Vancouver: University of British Columbia Press.

Inglis, Tom. 2007. "Catholic Identity in Contemporary Ireland: Belief and Belonging to Tradition." *Journal of Contemporary Religion* 22 (2): 205–20.

Jamieson, Alan. 2002. *A Churchless Faith: Faith Journeys beyond the Churches*. London: Society for Promoting Christian Knowledge.

Janzen, Rich, Mark Chapman, and James Watson. 2012. "Integrating Immigrants into the Life of Canadian Urban Christian Congregations: Findings from a National Survey." *Review of Religious Research* 53 (4): 441–70.

Jelen, Ted G., and Clyde Wilcox. 2003. "Causes and Consequences of Public Attitudes toward Abortion: A Review and Research Agenda." *Political Research Quarterly* 56 (4): 489–500.

Johnston, Joseph B. 2013. "Religion and Volunteering over the Adult Life Course." *Journal for the Scientific Study of Religion* 52:733–52.

Jones-Correa, Michael A., and David L. Leal. 2001. "Political Participation: Does Religion Matter?" *Political Research Quarterly* 54 (4): 751–70.

Kaufmann, Eric, Anne Goujon, and Vegard Skirbekk. 2012. "The End of Secularization in Europe? A Socio-Demographic Perspective." *Sociology of Religion* 73 (1): 69–91.

Killen, Patricia O'Connell, and Mark Silk, eds. 2004. *Religion and Public Life in the Pacific Northwest: The None Zone*. Religion by Region Series. Walnut Creek, CA: AltaMira.

Kinnaman, David, and Aly Hawkins. 2011. *You Lost Me: Why Young Christians Are Leaving Church—and Rethinking Faith*. Grand Rapids, MI: Baker Books.

Knott, Kim, Elizabeth Poole, and Teemu Taira. 2013. *Media Portrayals of Religion and the Secular Sacred: Representation and Change*. Burlington, VT: Ashgate.

Kosmin, Barry, and Ariela Keysar. 2008. "American Nones: The Profile of the No Religion Population." Accessed February 17, 2010. http://commons.trincoll.edu.

Lacombe, Sylvie. 2002. *La rencontre de deux peuples élus. Comparaison des ambitions nationale et impériale au Canada entre 1896 et 1920*. Quebec: Les Presses de l'Université Laval.

Lam, Pui-Yan. 2002. "As the Flocks Gather: How Religion Affects Voluntary Association Participation." *Journal for the Scientific Study of Religion* 41:405–22.

———. 2006. "Religion and Civic Culture: A Cross-National Study of Voluntary Association Membership." *Journal for the Scientific Study of Religion* 45:177–93.

Lamoureux Scholes, Laurie. 2003. *The Social Authority of Religion in Canada: A Study of Contemporary Death Rituals*. Master's thesis, McGill University.

Lasby, David, and Cathy Barr. 2018. "30 Years of Giving in Canada: The Giving Behaviour of Canadians: Who Gives, How, and Why?" Accessed July 19, 2018. www.imaginecanada.ca.

Lazarsfeld, Paul F., and Robert K. Merton. 1954. "Friendship as a Social Process: A Substantive and Methodological Analysis." In *Freedom and Control in Modern Society*, edited by M. Berger, T. Abel, and C. H. Page. New York: Octogon Books.

LeDrew, Stephen. 2013. "Discovering Atheism: Heterogeneity in Trajectories to Atheist Identity and Activism." *Sociology of Religion* 74 (4): 431–53.

———. 2015. *The Evolution of Atheism: The Politics of a Modern Movement*. New York: Oxford University Press.

Lee, Lois. 2015. *Recognizing the Non-Religious: Reimagining the Secular*. New York: Oxford University Press.

Lee, Sharon, Feng Hou, Barry Edmonston, and Zheng Wu. 2017. "Religious Intermarriage in Canada, 1981–2011." *Journal for the Scientific Study of Religion* 56 (3): 667–77.

———. 2018. "Group Size and Secular Endogamy among the Religiously Unaffiliated in Canada." *Social Science Research* 74:196–209.

Leege, David C., and Lyman A. Kellstedt. 1993. *Rediscovering the Religious Factor in American Politics*. Armonk, NY: M. E. Sharpe.

Lefebvre, Solange. 2005. *La religion dans la sphère publique*. Montreal, QC: Presses de l'Université de Montréal.

Lemieux, Raymond, and Jean-Paul Montminy. 2000. *Le catholicisme québécois*. Quebec: Les Éditions de l'IQRC, Collection Diagnostic.

Leon McDaniel, Eric, Irfan Nooruddin, and Allyson Faith Shortle. 2011. "Divine Boundaries: How Religion Shapes Citizens' Attitudes toward Immigrants." *American Politics Research* 39 (1): 205–33.

Lewis, James R., Sean E. Currie, and Michael P. Oman-Reagan. 2016. "The Religion of the Educated Classes Revisited: New Religions, the Nonreligious, and Education Levels." *Journal for the Scientific Study of Religion* 55 (1): 91–104.

Lewis, Valerie A., Carol Ann MacGregor, and Robert D. Putnam. 2013. "Religion, Networks, and Neighborliness: The Impact of Religious Social Networks on Civic Engagement." *Social Science Research* 42 (2): 331–46.

Lim, Chaeyoon, and Carol Ann MacGregor. 2012. "Religion and Volunteering in Context: Disentangling the Contextual Effects of Religion on Voluntary Behavior." *American Sociological Review* 20:1–33.

Lim, Chaeyoon, Carol Ann MacGregor, and Robert Putnam. 2010. "Secular and Liminal: Discovering Heterogeneity among Religious Nones." *Journal for the Scientific Study of Religion* 49 (4): 596–618.

Linneman, Thomas, and Margaret Clendenen. 2010. "Sexuality and the Sacred." In *Atheism and Secularity*, vol. 1, edited by Phil Zuckerman, 89–111. Santa Barbara, CA: Praeger.

Liogier, Raphaël. 2010. "La distinction sociocognitive et normative entre bonne et mauvaise religion." In *Pluralisme religieux et citoyenneté*, edited by Micheline Milot, Philippe Portier et Jean-Paul Willaime, 99–122. Rennes, France: Presses Universitaires de Rennes.

Lipka, Michael. 2015. "A Closer Look at America's Rapidly Growing Religious 'Nones.'" Accessed May 16, 2017. www.pewresearch.org.

Lipset, Seymour M. 1991. *Continental Divide: The Values and Institutions of the United States and Canada*. New York: Routledge, Chapman and Hall.

Longhurst, John. 2018. "The Role of Religion in Civil Society." Accessed July 19, 2018. http://onfaithcanada.blogspot.com.

Luria, Gil, Ram A. Cnaan, and Amnon Boehm. 2017. "Religious Attendance and Volunteering: Testing National Culture as a Boundary Condition." *Journal for the Scientific Study of Religion* 56 (3): 577–99.

Madge, Nicola, Peter J. Hemming, and Kevin Stenson. 2014. *Youth on Religion: The Development, Negotiation and Impact of Faith and Non-Faith Identity*. New York: Routledge.

Manning, Christel. 2013. "Unaffiliated Parents and the Religious Training of Their Children." *Sociology of Religion* 74 (2): 149–75.

———. 2015. *Losing Our Religion: How Unaffiliated Parents Are Raising Their Children*. New York: New York University Press.

Marks, Lynne. 2007. "'Leaving God Behind When They Crossed the Rocky Mountains': Exploring Unbelief in Turn of the Century British Columbia." In *Household Counts: Canadian Households and Families in 1901*, edited by Peter A. Baskerville and Eric William Sager, 371–404. Toronto: University of Toronto Press.

———. 2017. *Infidels and the Damn Churches: Irreligion and Religion in Settler British Columbia*. Vancouver: University of British Columbia Press.

Marler, Penny L., and C. Kirk Hadaway. 2002. "Being Religious or Being Spiritual in America: A Zero-Sum Proposition?" *Journal for the Scientific Study of Religion* 41 (2): 289–300.

Martin, David. 1978. *A General Theory of Secularization*. New York: Harper & Row.

———. 2005. *On Secularization: Towards a Revised General Theory*. Burlington, VT: Ashgate.

McGrath, Alister. 2002. *The Reenchantment of Nature: The Denial of Religion and the Ecological Crisis*. New York: Doubleday.

McPherson, Miller, Lynn Smith-Lovin, and James M. Cook. 2001. "Birds of a Feather: Homophily in Social Networks." *Annual Review of Sociology* 27:415–44.

Mehta, Hemant. 2018. "Pastor: Without Evangelicals, We'd Be Living in a 'Godless, Immoral' Nightmare." Accessed July 24, 2018. www.patheos.com.

Mencken, F. Carson, and Brittany Fitz. 2013. "Image of God and Community Volunteering among Religious Adherents in the United States." *Review of Religious Research* 55 (3): 491–508.

Merino, Stephen M. 2012. "Irreligious Socialization? The Adult Religious Preferences of Individuals Raised with No Religion." *Secularism and Nonreligion* 1:1–16.

———. 2013. "Religious Social Networks and Volunteering: Examining Recruitment via Close Ties." *Review of Religious Research* 55:509–27.

Meunier, E.-Martin, and Sarah Wilkins-Laflamme. 2011. "Sécularisation, catholicisme et transformation du régime de religiosité au Québec. Étude comparative avec le catholicisme au Canada (1968–2007)." *Recherches sociographiques* 52 (3): 683–729.

Miller, Donald. 1997. *Reinventing American Protestantism: Christianity in the New Millennium*. Berkeley: University of California Press.

Milot, Micheline, Philippe Portier, and Jean-Paul Willaime, eds. 2010. *Pluralisme religieux et citoyenneté*. Rennes, France: Presses Universitaires de Rennes.

Monsma, Stephen V. 2007. "Religion and Philanthropic Giving and Volunteering: Building Blocks for Civic Responsibility." *Interdisciplinary Journal of Research on Religion* 3:1–28.

National Opinion Research Center. 2017. *General Social Survey 1972–2016* (data set). Accessed April 2, 2017. http://gss.norc.org/Get-The-Data.

Nemeth, Roger J., and Donald Al Luidens. 2003. "The Religious Basis of Charitable Giving in America: A Social Capital Perspective." In *Religion as Social Capital: Producing the Common Good*, edited by Corwin Smidt, 107–20. Waco, TX: Baylor University Press.

Nicolet, Sarah, and Anke Tresch. 2009. "Changing Religiosity, Changing Politics? The Influence of 'Belonging' and 'Believing' on Political Attitudes in Switzerland." *Politics and Religion* 2:76–99.

Niose, David. 2012. *Nonbeliever Nation: The Rise of Secular Americans*. New York: Palgrave Macmillan.

Noll, Mark. 1992. *A History of Christianity in the United States and Canada*. Grand Rapids, MI: William B. Eerdmans.

———. 2006. "What Happened to Christian Canada?" *American Society of Church History* 75 (2): 245–73.

Norris, Pippa, and Ronald Inglehart. 2011. *Sacred and Secular: Religion and Politics Worldwide*. 2nd ed. New York: Cambridge University Press.

O'Connell, Nicholas. 2003. *On Sacred Ground: The Spirit of Place in Pacific Northwest Literature*. Seattle: University of Washington Press.

Olson, Daniel. 1989. "Church Friendships: Boon or Barrier to Church Growth?" *Journal for the Scientific Study of Religion* 28:432–37.

———. 1993. "Fellowship Ties and the Transmission of Religious Identity." In *Beyond Establishment: Protestant Identity in a Post-Protestant Age*, edited by Jackson Carroll and Wade Clark Roof, 32–53. Louisville, KY: Westminster.

Olson, Daniel V. A., and Paul Perl. 2011. "A Friend in Creed: Does the Religious Composition of Geographic Areas Affect the Religious Composition of a Person's Close Friends?" *Journal for the Scientific Study of Religion* 50 (3): 483–502.

Olson, Laura R., Wendy Cadge, and James T. Harrison. 2006. "Religion and Public Opinion about Same-Sex Marriage." *Social Science Quarterly* 87 (2): 340–60.

Olson, Paul J., and David Beckworth. 2011. "Religious Change and Stability: Seasonality in Church Attendance from the 1940s to the 2000s." *Journal for the Scientific Study of Religion* 50 (2): 388–96.

O'Neill, Brenda. 2001. "A Simple Difference of Opinion? Religious Beliefs and Gender Gaps in Public Opinion in Canada." *Canadian Journal of Political Science* 34:275–98.

Pacific Northwest Social Survey. 2017. Data collected by Sarah Wilkins-Laflamme, Paul Bramadat, and team. Victoria, Canada. https://uwspace.uwaterloo.ca/handle/10012/13406.

Parboteeah, K. Praveen, John B. Cullen, and Lrong Lim. 2004. "Formal Volunteering: A Cross-National Test." *Journal of World Business* 39 (4): 431–41.

Partners for Sacred Places. 2016. "The Economic Halo Effect of Historic Sacred Places." Accessed August 17, 2018. www.sacredplaces.org.

Pasquale, Frank L. 2007. "The 'Non-Religious' in the American Northwest." In *Secularism and Secularity: Contemporary International Perspectives*, edited by Barry A. Kosmin and Ariela Kaysar, 41–58. Hartford, CT: Institute for the Study of Secularism in Society and Culture.

———. 2010. "An Assessment of the Role of Early Parental Loss in the Adoption of Atheism or Irreligion." *Archives for the Psychology of Religion* 32:375–96.

Paxton, Pamela, Nicholas E. Reith, and Jennifer L. Glanville. 2014. "Volunteering and the Dimensions of Religiosity: A Cross-National Analysis." *Review of Religious Research* 56 (4): 597–625.

Peel District School Board. 2017. "Peel District School Board: Religious Accommodation." Accessed May 26, 2018. www.peelschools.org.

Perks, Thomas, and Michael Haan. 2010. "Youth Religious Involvement and Adult Community Participation: Do Levels of Youth Religious Involvement Matter?" *Nonprofit and Voluntary Sector Quarterly* 40 (1): 107–29.

Perry, James L., Jeffrey L. Brudney, David Coursey, and Laura Littlepage. 2008. "What Drives Morally Committed Citizens? A Study of the Antecedents of Public Service Motivation." *Public Administration Review* 68 (3): 445–58.

Pew Research Center. 2014a. *Religious Landscape Study* (data set). Accessed July 2, 2017. www.pewforum.org.

———. 2014b. "How Americans Feel about Religious Groups." Accessed March 21, 2018. www.pewforum.org.

———. 2015. "America's Changing Religious Landscape." Accessed May 16, 2017. www.pewforum.org.

———. 2016. "Why America's Nones Left Religion Behind." Accessed January 24, 2019. www.pewresearch.org.

———. 2017. American Trends Panel, Wave 24 (data set). Accessed March 12, 2018. www.pewresearch.org.

Phillips, Macon. 2009. "President Barack Obama's Inaugural Address." Accessed May 28, 2018. https://obamawhitehouse.archives.gov.

Project Canada Survey. 2005. Data collected by Reginald W. Bibby. Lethbridge, Alberta.

Putnam, Robert. 2000. *Bowling Alone: The Collapse and Revival of American Community*. New York: Simon & Schuster.
Putnam, Robert, and David Campbell. 2010. *American Grace: How Religion Divides and Unites Us*. New York: Simon & Schuster.
Ramji, Rubina. 2013. "A Variable but Convergent Islam: Muslim Women." In *Growing Up Canadian: Muslims, Hindus, Buddhists*, edited by Peter Beyer and Rubina Ramji, 112–44. Montreal, QC: McGill-Queen's University Press.
Raymond, Christopher. 2011. "The Continued Salience of Religious Voting in the United States, Germany, and Great Britain." *Electoral Studies* 30:125–35.
Rayside, David, Jerald Sabin, and Paul E. J. Thomas. 2017. *Religion and Canadian Party Politics*. Vancouver: University of British Columbia Press.
Reimer, Sam. 2003. *Evangelicals and the Continental Divide: The Evangelical Subculture in Canada and the United States*. Montreal, QC: McGill-Queen's University Press.
Reimer, Sam, and Rick Hiemstra. 2018. "The Gains/Losses of Canadian Religious Groups from Immigration: Immigration Flows, Attendance and Switching." *Studies in Religion* 47 (3): 327–44.
Reimer, Sam, and Michael Wilkinson. 2015. *A Culture of Faith: Evangelical Congregations in Canada*. Montreal, QC: McGill-Queen's University Press.
Ribberink, Egbert, Peter Achterberg, and Dick Houtman. 2017. "Secular Tolerance? Anti-Muslim Sentiment in Western Europe." *Journal for the Scientific Study of Religion* 56:259–76.
Robbins, William G., ed. 2001. *The Great Northwest: The Search for Regional Identity*. Corvallis: Oregon State University Press.
Rocher, François. 2014. "Québec's Secularism Regime Under (High) Tension." In *Revealing Democracy: Secularism and Religion in Liberal Democratic States*, edited by Chantal Maillé, Greg Marc Nielsen, and Daniel Salée, 199–56. Brussels: Peter Lang AG, Internationaler Verlag der Wissenschaften.
Roof, Wade Clark. 1999. *Spiritual Marketplace: Baby Boomers and the Remaking of American Religion*. Princeton, NJ: Princeton University Press.
Roozen, David A. 1980. "Church Dropouts: Changing Patterns of Disengagement and Re-Entry." *Review of Religious Research* 21 (4): 427–50.
Rousseau, Louis. 2012. *Québec après Bouchard-Taylor: les identités religieuses de l'immigration*. Quebec: Presses de l'Université du Québec.
Ruiter, Stijn, and Nan Dirk de Graaf. 2006. "National Context, Religiosity, and Volunteering: Results from 53 Countries." *American Sociological Review* 71:191–210.
Sahgal, Neha. 2018. "10 Key Findings about Religion in Western Europe." Pew Research Centre, Fact Tank. www.pewresearch.org.
Saroglou, Vassilis, Vanessa Delpierre, and Rebecca Dernelle. 2004. "Values and Religiosity: A Meta-Analysis of Studies Using Schwartz's Model." *Personality and Individual Differences* 37 (4): 721–34.
Scheepers, Peer, Merove Gijsberts, and Evelyn Hello. 2002. "Religiosity and Prejudice against Ethnic Minorities in Europe: Cross-National Tests on a Controversial Relationship." *Review of Religious Research* 43 (3): 242–65.

Scheufele, Dietram A., Matthew C. Nisbet, and Dominique Brossard. 2003. "Pathways to Political Participation? Religion, Communication Contexts, and Mass Media." *International Journal of Public Opinion Research* 15 (3): 300–324.

Schmidt, Leigh Eric. 2016. *Village Atheists: How America's Unbelievers Made Their Way in a Godly Nation*. Princeton, NJ: Princeton University Press.

Schwadel, Philip. 2010. "Period and Cohort Effects on Religious Nonaffiliation and Religious Disaffiliation: A Research Note." *Journal for the Scientific Study of Religion* 49 (2): 311–9.

Schwartz, Shalom H., and Sipke Huismans. 1995. "Value Priorities and Religiosity in Four Western Religions." *Social Psychology Quarterly* 58:88–107.

Sherkat, Darren E. 2014. *Changing Faith: The Dynamics and Consequences of Americans' Shifting Identities*. New York: New York University Press.

Sherkat, Darren E., Melissa Powell Williams, Gregory Maddox, and Kylan Mattiasde Vries. 2011. "Religion, Politics, and Support for Same-Sex Marriage in the United States, 1988–2008." *Social Science Research* 40 (1): 167–80.

Shibley, Mark A. 2011. "Sacred Nature: Earth-Based Spirituality as Popular Religion in the Pacific Northwest." *Journal for the Study of Religion, Nature and Culture* 5 (2): 164–85.

Skirbekk, Vegard, Éric Caron Malenfant, Stuart Basten, and Marcin Stonawski. 2012. "The Religious Composition of the Chinese Diaspora, Focusing on Canada." *Journal for the Scientific Study of Religion* 5 (1): 173–83.

Smidt, Corwin, ed. 2003. *Religion as Social Capital: Producing the Common Good*. Waco, TX: Baylor University Press.

Smidt, Corwin E., Kevin den Dulk, Bryan Froehle, James Penning, Stephen Monsma, and Douglas Koopman. 2010. *The Disappearing God Gap? Religion in the 2008 Presidential Election*. Oxford: Oxford University Press.

Smidt, Corwin E., Lyman A. Kellstedt, and James L. Guth. 2009. "The Role of Religion in American Politics: Explanatory Theories and Associated Analytical and Measurement Issues." In *Oxford Handbook on Religion and American Politics*, edited by Corwin Smidt, Lyman A. Kellstedt, and James L. Guth, 3–42. Oxford: Oxford University Press.

Smith, Christian, 1998. *American Evangelicalism: Embattled and Thriving*. Chicago: University of Chicago Press.

Smith, Christian, with Patricia Snell. 2009. *Souls in Transition: The Religious and Spiritual Lives of Emerging Adults*. New York: Oxford University Press.

Smith, Gregory A., and Jessica Martinez. 2016. "How the Faithful Voted: A Preliminary 2016 Analysis." Accessed June 14, 2018. www.pewresearch.org.

Smith, Jeffrey A., Miller McPherson, and Lynn Smith-Lovin. 2014. "Social Distance in the United States: Sex, Race, Religion, Age, and Education Homophily among Confidants, 1985 to 2004." *American Sociological Review* 79 (3): 432–56.

Smith, Jesse M. 2011. "Becoming an Atheist in America: Constructing Identity and Meaning from the Rejection of Theism." *Sociology of Religion* 72 (2): 215–37.

———. 2013. "Creating a Godless Community: The Collective Identity Work of Contemporary American Atheists." *Journal for the Scientific Study of Religion* 52 (1): 80–99.

———. 2017. "The Secular as Object of Belief and Belonging? The Case of the Sunday Assembly." *Qualitative Sociology* 40 (1): 83–109.
Son, Joonmo, and John Wilson. 2011. "Generativity and Volunteering." *Sociological Forum* 26 (3): 644–67.
Speed, David, Thomas J. Coleman III, and Joseph Langston. 2018. "What Do you Mean 'What Does It All Mean?' Atheism, Nonreligion, and Life Meaning." *Sage Open* 8 (1): 1–13.
Stackhouse, John Gordon. 1998. *Canadian Evangelicalism in the Twentieth Century: An Introduction to Its Character*. Vancouver, BC: Regent College Publishing.
Stark, Rodney, and William Sims Bainbridge. 1985. *The Future of Religion: Secularization, Revival, and Cult Formation*. Berkeley: University of California Press.
Stark, Rodney, and Roger Finke. 1992. *The Churching of America, 1776–1990: Winners and Losers in Our Religious Economy*. New Brunswick, NJ: Rutgers University Press.
———. 2000. *Acts of Faith: Explaining the Human Side of Religion*. Los Angeles: University of California Press.
Stark, Rodney, Eva Hamburg, and Alan Miller. 2004. "Exploring Spirituality and Unchurched Religion in America, Sweden, and Japan." *Journal of Contemporary Religion* 20 (1): 3–23.
Statistics Canada. 2015a. *1971, 1981, 1991 and 2001 Census of Population [Canada] Public Use Microdata Files (PUMF): Individual Files (Province Level)*. Data sets.
———. 2015b. *2011 National Household Survey [Canada] Public Use Microdata File (PUMF): Individual File*. Data set.
———. 2016. *Cycles 1–28 (1985–2014), General Social Survey [Canada] Public Use Microdata Files (PUMF): Individual Files*. Data sets.
Storm, Ingrid. 2009. "Halfway to Heaven: Four Types of Fuzzy Fidelity in Europe." *Journal for the Scientific Study of Religion* 48 (4): 702–18.
———. 2014. "Civic Engagement in Britain: The Role of Religion and Inclusive Values." *European Sociological Review* 31:14–29.
Sumerau, J. E., and Ryan T. Cragun. 2016. "'I Think Some People Need Religion': The Social Construction of Nonreligious Moral Identities." *Sociology of Religion* 77 (4): 386–407.
Taylor, Charles. 2007. *A Secular Age*. Cambridge, MA: Belknap Press of Harvard University Press.
Thiessen, Joel. 2015. *The Meaning of Sunday: The Practice of Belief in a Secular Age*. Montreal, QC: McGill-Queen's University Press.
———. 2016. "Kids, You Make the Choice: Religious and Secular Socialization among Marginal Affiliates and Nonreligious Individuals." *Secularism and Nonreligion* 5 (1): 1–16.
Thiessen, Joel, and Sarah Wilkins-Laflamme. 2017. "Becoming a Religious None: Irreligious Socialization and Disaffiliation." *Journal for the Scientific Study of Religion* 56 (1): 64–82.
Thomas, William I., and Dorothy S. Thomas. 1928. *The Child in America: Behavior Problems and Programs*. New York: Knopf.

Todd, Douglas. 2008. *Cascadia: The Elusive Utopia; Exploring the Spirit of the Pacific Northwest*. Vancouver: Ronsdale Press.
Uecker, Jeremy E., Damon Mayrl, and Samuel Stroope. 2016. "Family Formation and Returning to Institutional Religion in Young Adulthood." *Journal for the Scientific Study of Religion* 55 (2): 384–406.
Uslaner, Eric M. 2002. "Religion and Civic Engagement in Canada and the United States." *Journal for the Scientific Study of Religion* 41 (2):239–54.
van der Brug, Wouter, Sara B. Hobolt, and Claes H. de Vreese. 2009. "Religion and Party Choice in Europe." *West European Politics* 32:1266–83.
van Tubergen, Frank. 2006. "Religious Affiliation and Attendance among Immigrants in Eight Western Countries: Individual and Contextual Effects." *Journal for the Scientific Study of Religion* 45 (1):1–22.
———. 2007. "Religious Affiliation and Participation among Immigrants in a Secular Society: A Study of Immigrants in the Netherlands." *Journal of Ethnic and Migration Studies* 33 (5):747–65.
van Tubergen, Frank, and Jorunn I. Sindradottir. 2011. "The Religiosity of Immigrants in Europe: A Cross-National Study." *Journal for the Scientific Study of Religion* 50 (2):272–88.
Vargas, Nicholas. 2012. "Retrospective Accounts of Religious Disaffiliation in the United States: Stressors, Skepticism, and Political Factors." *Sociology of Religion* 73 (2):200–223.
Verba, Sidney, Kay Lehman Schlozman, and Henry E. Brady. 1995. *Voice and Equality: Civic Voluntarism in American Politics*. Cambridge, MA: Harvard University Press.
Vernon, Glenn M. 1968. "The Religious 'Nones': A Neglected Category." Presented at the Society for the Scientific Study of Religion. Montreal, CA.
Voas, David. 2006. "Religious Decline in Scotland: New Evidence on Timing and Spatial Patterns." *Journal for the Scientific Study of Religion* 45 (1):107–18.
———. 2007. "Surveys of Behavior, Beliefs and Affiliation: Micro-Quantitative." In *The SAGE Handbook of the Sociology of Religion*, edited by James A. Beckford and Jan Demerath, 144–66. London: Sage.
———. 2009. "The Rise and Fall of Fuzzy Fidelity in Europe." *European Sociological Review* 25 (2):155–68.
Voas, David, and Mark Chaves. 2016. "Is the United States a Counterexample to the Secularization Thesis?" *American Journal of Sociology* 121 (5):1517–56.
Voas, David, and Alasdair Crockett. 2005. "Religion in Britain: Neither Believing nor Belonging." *Sociology* 39 (1):11–28.
Voas, David, and Abby Day. 2010. "Recognizing Secular Christians: Toward an Unexcluded Middle in the Study of Religion." Association of Religion Data Archives. Accessed March 23, 2011. www.thearda.com.
Voisine, Nive, Jean Hamelin, and Nicole Gagnon. 1984. *Histoire du catholicisme québécois. Le XXe siècle. Tome I: 1898–1940*. Montreal, QC: Boréal Express.
Wald, Kenneth D., and Clyde Wilcox. 2006. "Getting Religion: Has Political Science Rediscovered the Faith Factor?" *American Political Science Review* 100 (4):523–29.

Walliss, John. 2002. "Loved the Wedding, Invite Me to the Marriage: The Secularization of Weddings in Contemporary Britain." *Sociological Research Online* 7 (4): www.socresonline.org.uk.

Watts, Galen. 2018. "On the Politics of Self-Spirituality: A Canadian Case Study." *Studies in Religion* 47 (3):345–72.

Wilkins-Laflamme, Sarah. 2014. "Towards Religious Polarization? Time Effects on Religious Commitment in US, UK and Canadian Regions." *Sociology of Religion* 75 (2):284–308.

———. 2015. "How Unreligious Are the Religious 'Nones'? Religious Dynamics of the Unaffiliated in Canada." *Canadian Journal of Sociology* 40 (4):477–500.

———. 2016a. "The Remaining Core: A Fresh Look at Religiosity Trends in Great Britain." *British Journal of Sociology* 67 (4):632–54.

———. 2016b. "Secularization and the Wider Gap in Values and Personal Religiosity between the Religious and Non-Religious." *Journal for the Scientific Study of Religion* 55 (4):717–36.

———. 2016c. "The Changing Religious Cleavage in Canadians' Voting Behaviour." *Canadian Journal of Political Science* 49 (3):499–518.

———. 2017. "Religious-Secular Polarization Compared: The Cases of Quebec and British Columbia." *Studies in Religion* 46 (2):166–85. doi:0008429817695662.

———. 2018. "Islamophobia in Canada: Measuring the Realities of Negative Attitudes towards Muslims and Religious Discrimination." *Canadian Review of Sociology* 55 (1):86–110.

Wilkinson, Michael. 2018. "The Transformation of Religion and the Self in the Age of Authenticity." *Pneuma* 40 (1–2):91–108.

Williamson, David A., and George Yancey. 2013. *There Is No God: Atheists in America*. Lanham, MD: Rowman & Littlefield.

Wilson, John, and Thomas Janoski. 1995. "The Contribution of Religion to Volunteer Work." *Sociology of Religion* 56:137–52.

Woodhead, Linda. 2016. "The Rise of 'No Religion' in Britain: The Emergence of a New Cultural Majority." *Journal of the British Academy* 4:245–61.

Wright, Bradley R. E., Dina Giovanelli, Emily G. Dolan, and Mark Evan Edwards. 2011. "Explaining Deconversion from Christianity." *Journal of Religion and Society* 13:1–17.

Wuthnow, Robert. 2004. *Saving America? Faith-Based Services and the Future of Civil Society*. Princeton, NJ: Princeton University Press.

———. 2007. *After the Baby Boomers: How Twenty- and Thirty-Somethings Are Shaping the Future of American Religion*. Princeton, NJ: Princeton University Press.

Wuthnow, Robert, and Kevin Christiano. 1979. "The Effects of Residential Migration on Church Attendance in the United States." In *The Religious Dimension: New Directions in Quantitative Research*, edited by Robert Wuthnow, 257–76. New York: Academic Press.

Wymer, Walter W., Jr. 1997. "A Religious Motivation to Volunteer? Exploring the Linkage between Volunteering and Religious Values." *Journal of Nonprofit and Public Sector Marketing* 5 (3):3–17.

Zimmerman, Kevin J., Jesse M. Smith, Kevin Simonson, and Benjamin W. Myers. 2015. "Familial Relationship Outcomes of Coming Out as an Atheist." *Secularism and Nonreligion* 4 (4):1–13.

Zinnbauer, Brian, Kenneth Pargament, and Allie Scott. 1999. "The Emerging Meanings of Religiousness and Spirituality: Problems and Prospects." *Journal of Personality* 67 (6):879–919.

Zuckerman, Phil. 2008. *Society without God: What the Least Religious Nations Can Tell Us about Contentment*. New York: New York University Press.

———. 2012. *Faith No More: Why People Reject Religion*. New York: Oxford University Press.

Zuckerman, Phil, Luke W. Galen, and Frank L. Pasquale. 2016. *The Nonreligious: Understanding Secular People and Societies*. New York: Oxford University Press.

INDEX

abortion, 94–95; believing, behavior, and, 101; in Canada, *98*, 100–101, 166–67; Catholicism on, 101–2; regional variations on, 100, 115; religious nones interviewed on, 98–99, 101–2, 104; religious nones surveyed on, 96, *96*, *98*, 100–101, 117; in US, 96, *96*, 99–101

afterlife, belief in, 61, *62*, *63*

age, 183; age pyramids, 45–46, *46*; atheists, perception of, and, 147, 149, *149*; BWB and, 90; in Canada, religious none, 45–46, *46*; decline stages and, 90; demographics of, 15, *16*, 45–46, *46*; of disaffiliation, 30, 46; generational shifts and, 90–91; nonbelief varying by, *90*, 90–91; as proportional factor, 45–46, *46*; reaffiliation and, 51; subtypes, variation in, by, 89, *90*, 90–91; in US, religious none, 45–46, *46*; volunteering and, 135

agnostics: discrimination against, 150; as subtype, 78

Alberta, Canada, 33, 107, 124

American Grace (Putnam and Campbell, D.), 142

Ammerman, Nancy: on abortion, homosexuality, 99, 102; on environment, 108–9; *Sacred Stories, Spiritual Tribes*, 20–21, 99; on spirituality, 20–21, 84–85; on substantial seculars, 191; on volunteer work, 131

Anglicans, 34, 144

apostasy, 11–12; deep, 35; gradual, 33; in US, Zuckerman studying, 33, 35–37

Asian immigrants, 42–43, 47, *48*, 227n1

assisted dying, 165–66

atheists: age and perception of, 147, 149, *149*; in Canada, perception of, 11, 147–49, 164, 169, 181; discrimination against, 150–51; Evangelicals and, 11, 147–48, 168, 181, 187; on exclusive religions, 169; label of, 76–77; new, 77, 80; organizations of, 76; polarization and, 164, 169, 186–87; religious and, symbolic boundaries between, 145–46, 148–49; on science, 74–75; as subtype, religious none, 78; in United Kingdom, bus campaign of, 164–65; in US, perception of, 146–49, *149*, 164, 169, 181

attendance, 27

Australia, religious nones in, 188

authenticity, age of, 176

autonomy, child, 38–39

Baker, Joseph, 78, 161–62.

Beaman, Lori, 165–69, 192

behavior, religious, 3; abortion and, 101; BWB and, 67–69, *69*, 70–71, 91; in Canada, religious nones and, 68–69, *69*, 70–71, 91; nonbelievers and, 72; same-sex marriage and, 103–4; in sociology, 190–91; spectrum of, subtypes on, 78–79, *79*; US religious nones and, 68, *69*

belief: abortion and, 101; in afterlife, 61, *62*, *63*; in Canada, rates of, 61–62, *63*; in God, 27, 59, 61, *62*, 72, 87; same-sex marriage and, 103–4; in sociology, 190–91; spectrum of, subtypes on, 78–79, *79*; in US, rates of, *62*. *See also* none, as religious term

249

believers, inactive. *See* inactive believers
believers, involved. *See* involved believers
believing without belonging (BWB), 78; age and, 90; behavior, religious, and, 67–69, *69*, 70–71, 91; beliefs less important for, 65–66, *66*; in Canada, 61–63, *63*, 64–65, 67, *67*, 71–72; decline stages and, 71; in God, 59, 61, 62; prevalence of, 71–72; in US, 60–61, 62, 65, *66*, 67, 71–72
Bellah, Robert, 175
belonging: in sociology, 190–91; spiritual behavior and religious, 67–69, *69*, 70
Berger, Peter, 17–19
Bibby, Reginald, 61, 68, 75
birth rates, 5, *55*, 181, 183. *See also* fertility rates
black Evangelicals, US, 126
Blankholm, Joseph, 80–81
Britain. *See* United Kingdom
British Columbia: Asian immigrants in, 42–43; nonreligious in, 76–77; religious nones higher in, 13, *14*, 14–15, 42–44, 154; religious none subtypes in, 86, *87*; Trinity Western University case in, 167; Victoria, religious nones in, 42–43
Brossard, Dominique, 121
Bruce, Steve, 17–18, 185, 188
Buddhists, 29, 153–54, 158–59, 227n1
Bullivant, Stephen, 28
BWB. *See* believing without belonging

Campbell, Colin, 143–45
Campbell, David, 11, 33, 117, 142
Canada: Alberta, 33, 107, 124; Anglicans in, 34, 144; assisted dying in, 165–66; on atheists, perception in, 11, 147–49, 164, 169, 181; belief in God in, 61, 72; belief rates in, 61–62, *63*; birth and fertility rates in, 50, 183; British Columbia, 13, *14*, 14–15, 42–44, 76–77, 86, *87*, 154, 167; British identity and, 144–45; Catholicism in, 27–28, 144–45, 154–55, 165, 189; as Christian nation, 144–45, 192; Conservative Party, 120–21; conservative religious subculture absent in, 9–10; diversity and pluralism of, 145, 165–69; elections in, 120–21; Evangelicalism in, 11, 124, 147–48, 155–56; government in, philanthropy and, 138–39; GSS of, affiliation question in, 56; individualization, religious, and, 21; intermarriage, religious, rising in, 34–35; liberal multiculturalism of, 9–10, 115, 145, 148, 178–79, 187; Liberal Party, 120–21; NDP, 120–21; Ontario, 107, 165; Pacific Northwest of, US compared with, 44; religion, place of, in, 9; secularization trends in, explaining, 19; welfare state in, 189–90
Canada, French. *See* French Canadians
Canada, religious nones in, 228n1; abortion and, 98, 100–101, 166–67; age and, 45–46, *46*; BWB, 61–63, *63*, 64–65, 67, *67*, 71–72; charitable giving and, *130*, 133–34, 136–38, 186; demographics of, US compared with, 15, *16*, 17; on environment, 96, *99*, 108–9; on Evangelicals, 11, 153, 155–56; on government aid, 96, *99*, 110; growth of, 1, 5, 7–8, *8*, *9*, 13–14, *14*, 15, 54–57, 144–45, 171, 178–79; in GSS, plateauing, 56–57; immigrants and, 42–43, 47, *48*, 49–50; on immigration, 96, *99*, 111–12; inactive believers, 86, *87*; inactive nonbelievers, 86, *87*; involved believers, 86, *87*; involved seculars, 79–80, 86, *87*; irreligious socialization rates and, 39–40, *40*; on left/right spectrum, 112–13, *113*, 114; morality of, 76; nonaffiliated, religious backgrounds of, 29; nonbelievers in, 72, 86, *87*; nonreligious, 73, 76–77; nonverts, 27, 30, *30*; parental affiliation and, 12, 30, *30*; polarization and, 22–23, 165–67, 177, 186–87; political

engagement, active, and, 121–22, *122*, *123*, 123–24; reaffiliation, likelihood of, and, 51–52; regional variations of, 4–6, 13–14, *14*, 15, 147; religious behavior of, 68–69, *69*, 70–71, 91; on religious groups, 153–54; same-sex marriage and, 96, *98*, 103–5; SBNR, 84–86, *87*; subtypes of, 86, *87*; from US, 47, 50; US religious nones compared with, 2, 4–5, 7–8, *8*, 15, *16*, 17, 44, 174, 178–82; volunteering and, 126–29, *129*, 130–31, 137–38, 186; on women, in workforce, 96, *98*, 106–7
Canadian Election Studies (CES), 95–96, 227n1
Casanova, José, 23
Catholicism: on abortion, 101–2; in Canada, 27–28, 144–45, 154–55, 165, 189; charismatic movement in, 185; criticisms of, 27, 154–55; cultural, 189; as exclusive religion, 154–55, 160; French Canadian, 27–28, 144–45, 154, 189; Ontario Catholic school case of, 165
CES. *See* Canadian Election Studies
charitable giving, 119; in Canada, *130*, 133–34, 136–38, 186; civil society, future of, and, 135–36; future of, religious nones and, 185–86; individualism hypothesis and, 134; for marginal affiliates, lowest, 135; religiosity and higher, 125–27, *130*, *131*, 133–35, 139, 185; religious, declining, 136; by religious nones, 127, *130*, *131*, 133–35, 137, 139, 185–86; in US, *128*, 133–34, 136–39, 186
Chaves, Mark, 18
Chinese immigrants, 47; in British Columbia, 42–43; religious identification and, 227n1
Christian nation: Canada as, 144–45, 192; US as, 143, 148, 192
Christian Right. *See* Religious Right
Church of England, 189
Cimino, Richard, 80, 83

civic engagement, 119, 139, 185
civil society, future of, 135–39, 185
civil society summit, Canada, 137
Clarke, Brian, 18
coexistence, affiliated and unaffiliated, 25
coming out, 9
confidence, of religious nones, 1, 27, 64, 187
Conservative Party, Canadian, 120–21
conservative religious subculture. *See* Religious Right
conversion, 53–54
cradle nones: irreligious socialization of, 28–29, 37–40, *40*; SBNR, 85–86
Cragun, Ryan, 60, 150–51, 158
Cross, Katie, 81–82
cultural legitimacy, struggle over, 23, 142, 164, 177
cycle hypothesis, 184–85

Daly, Mike Wood, 137
data sources, on religious nones, 5–6
Davie, Grace, 59, 71
Dawkins, Richard, 77
decline, stages of, 57, 87–88, 171, 179; age and, 90; Berger and Martin on, 17–19; BWB and, 71; disaffiliation and, 28–29; future of, 182, 188; individualization and, 19–21, 23, 36, 188; pluralism in, 18–19; polarization and, 22–23, 117–18, 173, 177–78; religion, replacements for, in, 20; scientific worldview in, 18; secularization and, 17–18, 178
deep apostasy, 35
deep equality, 142, 167–69, 192
Democrats, US, 120
demographics, of religious nones, 3–4; affiliated and unaffiliated, similarities in, *16*, 17; age, 15, *16*, 45–46, *46*; Canadian and US, compared, 15, *16*, 17; countervailing trends in, 45; immigration, religious, 47, *48*, 49; traditional family structures, 15, *16*, 17; trends in, 5, 24

deprivatization thesis, 23
de-traditionalization, 174–76, 185, 188
disaffiliation, 55; in adolescence, young adulthood, 30, 46; age of, 30, 46; decline stages and, 28–29; as gradual, 30, 33; irreligious socialization and, 32; mild and transformative, 31; nonvert, 28–30, 30, 31–37; parental affiliation and, 29–30, 30, 34–35; polarization and, 56; reasons for, 27–29, 179; slowing, possibility of, 56; social context of, 41, 42, 57
discrimination: against atheists, 150–51; against religious nones, 150–54
diversity: Canadian, pluralism and, 145, 165–69; deep equality and, 142, 167–69, 192
Dobbs, Lou, 92
Drescher, Elizabeth, 77, 85; on disaffiliation, 31; on Golden Rule, 75–76, 94; homosexuality and, 104; on volunteering, 131
Durkheim, Émile, 21, 58

East Asian immigrants, 42–43, 47, 227n1
Edgell, Penny, 126, 135, 137–38, 145–46
elections, national, 120–21
emigration, religious none, 49–50, 55
Enlightenment era, 18
environment, 95; Canadian religious nones on, 96, 99, 108–9; interviews on, 98; regional variations on, 108, 115; religious nones on, surveys of, 96, 97, 99, 107–8, 115, 117; US religious nones on, 96, 96, 108–9
equality, deep, 142, 167–69, 192
Europe, religious nones in, 188, 190
euthanasia, 165–66
Evangelicals, 22; on abortion, 102; atheists and, 11, 147–48, 168, 181, 187; black, US, volunteering among, 126; in Canada, 11, 124, 147–48, 155–56; Canadian religious nones on, 11, 153, 155–56; as

exclusive religion, 1, 155–56, 160, 162; involved seculars and, 80–81; polarization and, 141–42, 177, 186–87; religious nones on, 1, 11, 149, 153, 155–56, 160, 162; Religious Right and, religious nones reacting to, 10–11, 33, 117, 179; Republican Party and, 10; secularist organizations and prevalence of, 80–81; US, Canadians on, 10–11, 155–56; US, criticism of, 10–11, 155–56, 179; in US, role of, 9, 118, 143, 184, 187
exclusive religions: atheists on, 169; Catholicism, 154–55, 160; Evangelicalism, 1, 155–56, 160, 162; Islam, 156, 158, 160, 163, 169; media and perception of, 163; Muslims and, 156, 158, 160, 163, 169; nonverts opposing, 37; religious nones on, 37, 154–58, 160, 162, 164, 169
expressive individualism, 174–77, 185
extraterrestrials, belief in, 61–62, 63

family: irreligious socialization and, 162–63; reaffiliation and, 51–52; traditional structures of, 15, 16, 17
fertility rates, 45, 50, 56
Fischer, Claude, 11, 33
French Canadians: Catholicism of, 27–28, 144–45, 154, 189; religious nones lower among, 14, 14–15, 189. See also Quebec
Frost, Jacqui, 126, 135, 137–38
future, of religious nones, 25, 174, 181; cycle hypothesis and, 184–85; decline stages and, 182, 188; immigration and, 187–88; inactive nonbelievers, growth of, in, 172; liminal nones and, 182–83; macro-demographic trends influencing, 5; marginal affiliates and, 182, 184; national context and, 188–90, 193; non-Christian religions and, 192–93; polarization in, 173, 184, 186–87, 190–91, 193–94; reaffiliation and, 182–83; regional variations and, 179–80, 187; sociology and, 193–95;

substantial secularity in, 191–92; volunteering, charitable giving in, 185–86

Gaither Vocal Band, 3, 70
Galen, Luke W., 39, 50, 138
Garcia, Alfredo, 80–81
General Social Survey (GSS): Canadian, affiliation question in, 56; Canadian, religious nones plateauing in, 56–57; US, affiliation question in, 227n4
Gerteis, Joseph, 145–46
globalization, 174, 177, 188
God, belief in, 27; in BWB, 59, 61, 62; in Canada, 61, 72; in US, 61, 62, 72, 87
Golden Rule, 75–76, 94
government, philanthropy and, 138–39
government aid, religious nones on, 95; interviews on, 98, 110; surveys of, 96, 97, 99, 109–10, 115, 117
Graaf, Nan Dirk de, 126
Grim, Brian, 137
Grim, Melissa, 137
growth rates, of religious nones: Canadian, 7–8, 8; Canadian, stalled, 55–57; regional, Canadian, 13–14, 14, 15; regional, US, 13, 13–15; US, 7–8, 8
GSS. *See* General Social Survey

halo effect, 137
Hammer, Joseph, 60, 150
Hartmann, Douglas, 145–46
Hay, Alastair, 19
Herberg, Will, 143
homophily, 114–15, 161, 168
homosexuality, 99; coming out, 9; among religious nones, 104; science and, 104–5
Hout, Michael, 11, 33
Hwang, Karen, 150–51

identity labels, nonreligious, 76–77
immigration, 55; affiliation, higher, and, 47, 50; Asian immigrants, 42–43, 47, 48, 227n1; in Canada, 42–43, 47, 48, 49–50; to Canada, by US religious nones, 47, 50; Canadian religious nones on, 96, 99, 111–12; Chinese immigrants, 42–43, 47, 227n1; demographics of religious, 47, 48, 49; future religious nones and, 187–88; in Pacific Northwest, 42–43; religious nones, rates of, and, 47, 48, 49–50, 183, 187–88; religious nones on, 95–97, 97, 99, 111–12, 115; religious nones on, regional variations in, 111–12, 115; second-generation immigrants, Canadian, 49; in US, negative attitudes on, 111; US religious nones and, 47, 48, 49–50, 96, 97, 111; by world region, 47, 48, 49
inactive believers, 24, 78, 172; age and, 90, 91; in Canada, 86, 87; morality of, 93, 93; sociopolitical attitudes of, 96, 97; in US, 86, 87, 89, 89, 90
inactive nonbelievers, 24, 180; agnostics as, 78; in Canada, 86, 87; secularization, growth of, and, 172; in US, 86, 87, 88–89, 89
inclusive religions: Buddhism as, religious nones on, 154, 158–59; religious nones on, 154, 158–60
individualism, expressive, 174–77, 185
individualization, 41; charitable giving and, 134; decline stages and, 19–21, 23, 36, 188; in late modern society, 174–77, 185, 188; pluralism and, 21; polarization and, 23; spiritualization and, 20–21, 172, 176
Inglehart, Ronald, 18
intellectual disagreements, 27, 32–35
intermarriage, religious, 34–35
intolerance, 142
involved believers, 24; on believing and behavior spectrums, 79, 79; in Canada, 86, 87; morality of, 93, 93–94; sociopolitical attitudes of, 96, 101; in US, 86, 87, 89, 89, 90

involved nonbelievers, 88–89, *89*
involved seculars, 24; on believing and behavior spectrums, 78, *79*; in Canada, 79–80, 86, *87*; communities of, 75–76, 78–83, 137; Evangelicals and, 80–81; online discourse and, 83; Sunday Assembly, 75–76, 78, 81–83, 137; in US, 86, *87*
involvement, desire for, 51–52
irreligious socialization, 4–5, 172, 179; autonomy, child and, 38–39; in Canada, rates of, 39–40, *40*; of cradle nones, 28–29, 37–40, *40*; disaffiliation and, 32; friends, families and, 162–63; generational differences in, 40; growing, 12; parents and, 37–39, *40*, 71–72, 163; population size, religious none and, 54–55, *55*; social context of, 41, *42*, 57; in US, rates of, 39–40, *40*
Islam. *See* Muslims

Japanese immigrants, 42–43, 47
Jeffress, Robert, 92, 139
Jehovah's Witnesses, 156–57, 160
Judeo-Christian societies, 2, 143

late modern society, 178; de-traditionalization in, 174–76, 185, 188; expressive individualism in, 174–77, 185; globalization in, 174, 177, 188; polarization in, 174; secularization in, 174–75; spiritualization in, 174, 176
Lazarsfeld, Paul, 115, 161
Lee, Lois, 60, 163, 191
left/right spectrum. *See* sociopolitical issues, religious nones on
liberalization, 21, 23
liberal multiculturalism, Canadian. *See* multiculturalism, Canadian
Liberal Party, Canadian, 120–21
life transition, 36–37
liminal nones, 52–53, 59, 182–83
Longhurst, John, 137
Losing Our Religion (Manning), 163

Macdonald, Stuart, 18
Madsen, Richard, 175
Manning, Christel, 163
marginal affiliates: on atheists, 149, *149*; charitable giving, volunteering of, 135; future religious nones and, 182, 184
Martin, David, 17–19
material security, 18
meaning, for religious nones, 5, 72–75, 77
Merton, Robert, 115, 161
mild disaffiliation, 31
Millennials, volunteering by, 135
mixed-marriage parents, 34–35
morality, 139; convergence on, 94; Golden Rule, 75–76, 94; of inactive believers, 93, *93*; of involved believers, *93*, 93–94; of nonbelievers, *93*, 93–94; religious none, guiding sources of, 92–93, *93*; SBNR, *93*, *93*; science informing, *93*, 94; secular, 75–76
Mormons, 156, 159–60, 163
multiculturalism, Canadian: as Canadian national identity, 9–10, 115, 145, 148, 178–79, 187; religious nones, sociopolitical attitudes of, and, 115; US compared with, 9–10, 115, 178–79
Muslims, 146–48, *149*; Buddhists, perception of, compared with, 159; European, 190; as exclusive, religious nones on, 156, 158, 160, 163, 169

NDP. *See* New Democratic Party, Canadian
negative stereotypes, of religious nones, 92, 145
new atheism, 77, 80
New Democratic Party, Canadian (NDP), 120–21
New Zealand, religious nones in, 188
Nisbet, Matthew C., 121
nonbelievers, 227n2; by age, variation in, *90*, 90–91; inactive, 24, 78, 86, *87*, 88–89, *89*, 172, 180; involved, 88–89, *89*; morality of, *93*, 93–94; regional

variations in US, 87–88, *88*, 91; religious behavior and, 72; sociopolitical attitudes of, *96*, *97*, 101; in US, rates of, 87–88, *88*, 89, *89*, *90*, 91
none, as religious term, 60
nonreligious: in British Columbia, 76–77; in Canada, 73, 76–77; identity labels and, 76–77; meaning and purpose for, 72–75, 77; research on, 72; scientific worldview among, 74–75; secular humanism and morality among, 75–76; secularist organizations of, 75–76, 78–83, 137, 194; by state, US, *88*; in US, 73–74, 76–77, *88*
nonverts: in Canada, 27, 30, *30*; choice, parents giving, and, 31–32, 34; disaffiliation and, 28–30, *30*, 31–37; exclusivity opposed by, 37; intellectual disagreements driving, 27, 32–35; life transition driving, 36–37; Religious Right provoking, 33; on science, 33; social influences on, 35–36; in US, 29–30, *30*, 33

Obama, Barack, 164–65
Ontario, Canada, 107, 165
organized religion, decline of, 5, 43, 142

Pacific Northwest: Asian immigrants in, 42–43; British Columbia, 13, *14*, 14–15, 42–44, 76–77, 86, *87*, 154, 167; Canadian and US, compared, 44; decline, religious, earlier in, 43–44; organized religion, fractured, in, 43; religious nones highest in, 42–44, 188; religious none subtypes in, 86, *87*; spirituality, reverential naturalist, in, 44; US, 42–44, 86, *87*, 161–62, 188
parents: affiliation of, disaffiliation and, 29–30, *30*, 34–35; affiliation of, religious nones and, 12, 29–30, *30*, 34–35; autonomy privileged by, 38–39; choice given by, nonverts and, 31–32, 34; choice given by, religious nones and, 31–32, 34, 71–72; irreligious socialization and, 37–39, *40*, 71–72, 163; mixed-marriage, 34–35
Pasquale, Frank L., 39, 50, 138
pastoral care, 82–83
philanthropy. *See* charitable giving
pluralism, 190; Canadian, diversity and, 145, 165–69; decline stages and, 18–19; individualization and, 21
polarization, 180; atheists and, 164, 169, 186–87; in Canada, 22–23, 165–67, 177, 186–87; cultural legitimacy, struggle over, and, 23, 142, 164, 177; decline stages and, 22–23, 117–18, 173, 177–78; deep equality and, 142, 167–69; deprivatization thesis on, 23; disaffiliation and, 56; Evangelicals and, 141–42, 177, 186–87; framework of, 21–23, 142; future of, 173, 184, 186–87, 190–91, 193–94; individualization and, 23; in late modern society, 174; religious, perceived marginalization of, and, 166–67; sociopolitical issues and, 116–18, 181; US and, 23, 169, 177, 186–87
political issues, religious nones on. *See* sociopolitical issues, religious nones on
politics, engagement in: active, 121–22, *122*, *123*, 123–24; elections, national, 120–21; online, *122*, 122–23, *123*, 139
population size, religious, factors influencing, 54–55, *55*
Protestantism: mainline, 29, 136; in Pacific Northwest, 43
Putnam, Robert, 11, 33, 117, 142

Quebec: Catholicism of, 144–45, 154, 189; Quiet Revolution in, 145, 154, 189; religious nones in, on religion, 154; religious nones lower in, *14*, 14–15, 189

reaffiliation, *55*, 56; age and, 51; conversion, 53–54; family and, 51–52; future of, 182–83; likelihood of, 51–52; liminal nones and, 52–53, 183 regional variations, 172–73, 177; on abortion, 100, 115; in Canada, 4–6, 13–14, *14*, 15, 147; on environment, 108, 115; future religious nones and, 179–80, 187; on government aid, 109–10, 115; in growth rates, Canadian, 13–14, *14*, 15; in growth rates, US, *13*, 13–15; in immigration, attitudes toward, 111–12, 115; left political orientation and, 115–16; in nonbelievers, US, 87–88, *88*, 91; Pacific Northwest, 13, *14*, 14–15, 42–44, 76–77, 86, *87*, 154, 161–62, 167; in political participation, 124; in religious groups, perceptions of, 154, 161–62; on same-sex marriage, 103, 115; stability in, 14–15; subtypes and, 180; in US, 4–6, *13*, 13–15, 44, 87–88, *88*, 91; on women, in workforce, 106–7

Reimer, Sam, 105
religion, defining, 58–59
religion, place of, 9, 143–44, 148
religious groups, religious nones on, 157–59; in Canada, 153–54; Evangelicals, 11, *149*, 153, 155–56, 160, 162; factors influencing, 160–64; regional variations in, 154, 161–62
religious nones. *See specific topics*
religious population size, factors influencing, 54–55, *55*
Religious Right, 23, 185; in Canada, absence of, 9–10; reaction to, religious nones and, 10–11, 33, 117, 179
religious studies: frameworks of, religious nones in, 17–23, 174; SBNR label in, 84
Republicans, US, 10, 120, 149
Resilient Gods (Bibby), 61
reverential naturalism, 44
revivals, religious, 185
Ruiter, Stijn, 126

sacred-profane distinction, 21
Sacred Stories, Spiritual Tribes (Ammerman), 20–21, 99

same-sex marriage, 94–95; believing, behavior and, 103–4; in Canada, 96, *98*, 103–5; interviews on, 98–99, 104–6; regional variations in, 103, 115; surveys on, 96, *96*, *98*, 103–4; in US, 96, *96*, 103–4. *See also* homosexuality
SBNR. *See* spiritual but not religious
Scheufele, Dietram A., 121
science, 41; atheists on, 74–75; in decline stages, as worldview, 18; homosexuality and, 104–5; morality informed by, 93, 94; among nonreligious, worldview of, 74–75; nonverts on, 33
second-generation immigrants, 49
secular humanism, 75–76
secularist organizations, 194; Evangelicals, prevalence of, and, 80–81; Sunday Assembly, 75–76, 81–83, 137
secularization: in Canada, explaining, 19; decline stages and, 17–18, 178; de-traditionalization and, 174–76; inactive nonbelievers, growth of, and, 172; in late modern society, 174–75
seculars, substantial, 191–92
September 11, 2001 attacks, 184–85
Sikhs, 125
Skirbekk, Vegard, 227n1
Smidt, Corwin, 120
Smith, Buster, 78, 161–62
Smith, Christian, 80
Smith, Christopher, 80, 83
Smith, Jesse, 150–51
social acceptance, of religious nones, 8–9, 19, 186–87
socialization. *See* irreligious socialization
sociology: belief, behavior, and belonging in, 190–91; Durkheimian, 21, 58; future religious nones and, 193–95; religious nones as term in, 59; SBNR label in, 84
sociopolitical issues, religious nones on, 141; civic engagement and, 119; homophily and, 114–15; inactive believers, 96, *97*; in interviews, 98–99, 101–2, 104,

109, 117; involved believers, 96, 101; as left-leaning, in voting, 120–21; as left-leaning, social environment and, 114–18, 181; left-leaning tendency of, 94–95, 96, 97, 97–98, 98, 99, 102, 104, 109–10, 112–13, *113*, 119, 173, 180; nonbelievers, 96, 97, 101; polarization and, 116–18, 181; regional variations and, 115–16; with religious, widening gap in, 116; SBNR, 96, 97, 116; by subtype, variation in, 95, 96, 96–97, *97*, 101, 108, 112, 116. *See also* morality

spiritual behavior, belonging and, 67–69, *69*, 70

spiritual but not religious (SBNR), 24, 59; age and, *90*, *91*; on believing and behavior spectrums, 78–79, *79*; in Canada, 84–86, *87*; cradle nones as, 85–86; expressive individualism epitomized by, 176; as label, 84–86, 116; left-leaning attitudes most likely for, 96, 97, 116; morality of, 93, *93*; in US, 85–86, *87*, 89, *89*, *90*

spirituality, 24, 59; Ammerman on, 20–21, 84–85; in Pacific Northwest, reverential naturalism, 44

spiritualization: individualization and, 20–21, 172, 176; in late modern society, 174, 176

state church, 188–89

Steele, Cory, 165–66

stereotypes, of religious nones, 92, 145

subcultural identity theory, 80–81

substantial seculars, 191–92

subtypes, religious nones, 60, 77, 177; by age, variation in, 89, *90*, 90–91; atheists, agnostics as, 78; on believing and behavior spectrums, 78–79, *79*; estimates and trends of, 86–87, *87*, 88–89, *89*, *90*; in Pacific Northwest, 86, *87*; regional variations and, 180; on sociopolitical issues, variation by, 95, 96, 96–97, *97*, 101, 108, 112, 116; values linked to, 24–25

Sullivan, William M., 175

Sumerau, J. E., 158

Sunday Assembly: involved seculars in, 75–76, 78, 81–83, 137; volunteer, charitable activities of, 82–83, 137

Swidler, Ann, 175

Taylor, Charles, 72, 176

Thomas, Dorothy S., 169

Thomas, William I., 169

Tipton, Steven M., 175

Toward a Sociology of Irreligion (Campbell, C.), 143–44

transformative disaffiliation, 31

Trinity Western University, British Columbia, 167

Trudeau, Justin, 121, 190

Trump, Donald, 10, 120, 190

United Church of Canada, 109, 144

United Kingdom, 21; atheist bus campaign in, 164–65; Canadian identity and, 144–45

United States (US): atheists, perception of, 146–49, *149*, 164, 169, 181; belief in God in, 61, *62*, 72, *87*; belief rates in, *62*; birth and fertility rates in, 50, 183; black Evangelicals in, 126; Canadian liberal multiculturalism compared with, 9–10, 115, 178–79; as Christian nation, 143, 148, 192; Democrats, 120; elections in, 120; Evangelicalism in, criticism of, 10–11, 155–56, 179; Evangelicalism in, role of, 9, 118, 143, 184, 187; government in, philanthropy and, 138–39; GSS of, affiliation question in, 227n4; individualization, religious, and, 21; Pacific Northwest, 42–44, 86, *87*, 161–62, 188; place of religion in, 9, 143–44, 148; Religious Right in, 9, 10–11, 23, 33, 117, 179; Republicans, 10, 120, 149

United States, religious nones in: abortion and, 96, *96*, 99–101; age and, 45–46, *46*; apostasy and, 33, 35–37; BWB, 60–61, 62, 65, *66*, 67, 71–72; to Canada, emigration by, 47, 50; Canadian religious nones compared with, 2, 4–5, 7–8, *8*, 15, *16*, 17, 44, 174, 178–82; charitable giving and, *128*, 133–34, 136–39, 186; coming out and, 9; demographics of, Canadian compared with, 15, *16*, 17; disaffiliation of, parental affiliation and, 29–30, *30*; on environment, 96, *96*, 108–9; on government aid, 96, *97*, 109–10; growth of, 1, 5, 7–8, *8*, 9, *13*, 13–15, 54–55, 57, 88, 144–45, 171, 178–79; immigrants and, 47, *48*, 49–50; on immigration, 96, *97*, 111; inactive believers, 86, *87*, 89, *89*, *90*; inactive nonbelievers, 86, *87*, 88–89, *89*; involved believers, 86, *87*, 89, *89*, *90*; involved seculars, 79–80; irreligious socialization rates and, 39–40, *40*; on left/right spectrum, 112–13, *113*, 114; liminal nones, 52–53; morality of, 75–76; nonaffiliated, 29; nonbelievers, 72, 87–88, *88*, 89, *89*, *90*, 91, 227n2; nonreligious, 73–74, 76–77, *88*; nonverts, 29–30, *30*, 33; parental affiliation and, 12, 29–30, *30*; polarization and, 23, 169, 177, 186–87; political engagement, active, and, 121–22, *122*, 123–24; regional variations and, 4–6, *13*, 13–15, 87–88, *88*, 91; religious behavior of, 68, *69*; same-sex marriage and, 96, *96*, 103–4; SBNR and, 85–86, *87*, 89, *89*, *90*; volunteering and, 126–27, *127*, 137–38, 186; West Coast, 13, *13*, 15; on women, in workforce, 96, *96*, 106–7

US. *See* United States

Victoria, British Columbia, 42–43
Voas, David, 18
volunteering: age and, 135; in Canada, 126–29, *129*, 130–31, 137–38, 186; civil society and, 136; interviews on, 131–33; for marginal affiliates, lowest, 135; religiosity and higher, 124–27, *127*, *128*, 128–29, *129*, 130–32, 135, 139, 185; by religious nones, 82–83, 111, 119–20, 126–27, *127*, *128*, 128–29, *129*, 130–33, 135, 137–39, 185–86; religious nones and future of, 185–86; in US, 126–27, *127*, 137–38, 186

welfare state, 189–90
West Coast, US, 13, *13*, 15
Wilkinson, Michael, 105
women, workforce participation by, 95; Canadian religious nones on, 96, *98*, 106–7; religious nones on, regional variations in, 106–7; religious nones on, surveys of, 96, *96*, *98*, 106–7, 117; US religious nones on, 96, *96*, 106–7
Woodhead, Linda, 21, 23

Zuckerman, Phil: on autonomy, secular emphasizing, 39; on fertility rates, religious nones and, 50; homosexuality and, 104; on mild disaffiliation, 31; US apostates studied by, 33, 35–37; on volunteering, 138

ABOUT THE AUTHORS

JOEL THIESSEN is Professor of Sociology at Ambrose University in Calgary, Alberta, Canada. His books include *The Meaning of Sunday: The Practice of Belief in a Secular Age*, *The Millennial Mosaic: How Pluralism and Choice Are Shaping Canadian Youth and the Future of Canada* (with Reginald W. Bibby and Monetta Bailey), and *The Sociology of Religion: A Canadian Perspective* (with Lorne L. Dawson). His research interests include religious nones, congregations, and Millennials. For more, see www.joelthiessen.ca.

SARAH WILKINS-LAFLAMME is Assistant Professor in the Department of Sociology and Legal Studies at the University of Waterloo. She completed her DPhil (PhD equivalent) in sociology at the University of Oxford. Her research interests include quantitative methods, sociology of religion, immigration and ethnicity, and political sociology.

www.ingramcontent.com/pod-product-compliance
Lightning Source LLC
Chambersburg PA
CBHW020402080526
44584CB00014B/1131